The Organizational Revolution

The Organizational Revolution

A Study in the
Ethics of Economic Organization

by Kenneth E. Boulding

with a Commentary by
REINHOLD NIEBUHR

GREENWOOD PRESS, PUBLISHERS
WESTPORT, CONNECTICUT

Library of Congress Cataloging in Publication Data

Boulding, Kenneth Ewart, 1910–
   The organizational revolution.

   Reprint. Originally published: New York : Harper,
c1953.
   Includes index.
   1. Organizational change.   2. Trade and professional
associations.   3. Business enterprises.   4. Communist
state.   5. Welfare state.   6. Social ethics.   I. Title.
HD58.8.B67 1984   330'.06   84-15695
ISBN 0-313-24371-9 (lib. bdg.)

This volume has been prepared under the direction of a study group authorized by the Federal Council of the Churches in 1949. The National Council of the Churches, into which the Federal Council has been merged, points out that the volume is not a statement or pronouncement of the National Council. Each author is solely responsible for what appears under his name.

Reprinted with the permission of Harper & Row, Publishers

Reprinted in 1984 by Greenwood Press
A division of Congressional Information Service, Inc.,
88 Post Road West, Westport, Connecticut 06881

Printed in the United States of America

10 9 8 7 6 5 4 3 2 1

Contents

Foreword

by CHARLES P. TAFT

*Chairman of the Department of the Church and Economic
Life and of Its Study Committee*

This volume forms part of a larger study of *Christian Ethics and
Economic Life* which was begun by the Department of the Church
and Economic Life of the Federal Council of the Churches of Christ
in America in 1949. At the beginning of 1951 the Federal Council
was merged with other interdenominational agencies to form the
National Council of the Churches of Christ in the United States of
America, made up of twenty-nine Protestant and Orthodox church
bodies within the United States.

In recent years, religious leaders have recognized that the ethical
problems of economic life are becoming increasingly urgent. The
ethics of everyday decisions and practices in economic life, private
and public, as we earn our livings, are matters also of wide public
concern. We need to go behind the observed individual acts and
group pressures for a deeper understanding of the motives underlying what people do in order to eat, of how the system fits together,
and of how close our preconceived ideas are to reality.

Change is a dominant characteristic of our national life and
perhaps nowhere so much so as in its economic aspects. During
the past half century our ways of life and work have undergone a
vast alteration. This change has been accomplished without violence
and without great apparent upset, but the tempo of its pace is truly
revolutionary. Certainly if people whose span of life was in the nineteenth century could see what we see in everyday life, they would
hardly accept any word but revolution for the process that has
brought it about.

This accelerated change, for all thoughtful people, demands an
understanding of the effects of this revolution upon ethics and
human values. How shall we deal with the dynamism in our
economic life as it affects every segment of national existence, in
order to preserve and extend freedom and justice, concern for the

dignity of the individual, respect for the rights of minorities, sensitivity to the public welfare, and free discussion and peaceful persuasion? We cannot rely upon business statistics to measure these intangibles. Judgments of even the best qualified individuals about actual or impending changes, affected as they are by individual temperament, vested interests, or political partisanship, are equally inadequate if considered separately. The fullest use of all our resources for information and discussion is required for sound progress toward solution of our complex problems.

There is no vital threat to our inherited and cherished values either in the status quo or in change as such. We cannot take ethics into the stratosphere and separate it from practical economic concerns. What is needed is a better understanding both of economic facts and also of those ethical values which have special significance in the meaning and direction which they give to economic activity.

Our world finds many who adopt a fanatic cynicism or a false philosophy in opposition to the very foundations upon which Western society is based. What earlier generations took for granted, such as the value and integrity of the individual, the character of government as a tool only for service of the people, the capacity of human life for essential decency and justice—these are now challenged with emotional zeal in the name of conflicting assumptions claimed also to be moral. Here lies the real crisis of the second half of the present century. We must meet this challenge of evil, insofar as it is evil, and clarify in relation to our own institutions the basic ethical affirmations which we support.

The Federal Council of Churches conducted for many years an educational program on the ethical issues involved in economic life. Many denominational bodies have likewise been active in this field. It has become clear, however, that we need a more careful and realistic investigation of economic life and its relation to spiritual and moral values. We need to make use of the capacities of social scientists and theologians, in close association with lay persons drawn from many occupations.

Accordingly, as a beginning of such an investigation, a three-year research study was commenced in 1949 under a grant from the Rockefeller Foundation. The Foundation has not exercised any supervisory control over the studies and does not assume responsibility for any of the findings. The results of the study are to be presented in six volumes: *Goals of Economic Life, The American Economy and the Lives of People, Social Responsibilities of the Businessman, The Organizational Revolution, American Income and Its Use,* and *Ethics and Economic Life.*

Sincere gratitude is due to the author for his devotion and creativity in the writing of this volume. He is also one of the authors of the volume *Goals of Economic Life,* which is part of this series.

Others have made valuable contributions to the total study effort of which this volume is an important part. The Reverend Cameron P. Hall, Executive Director of the Department, has given the project his unfailing and effective administrative support. Professor Howard R. Bowen, Economic Consultant to the Study, made an invaluable contribution in the formulation of the project and aided also in criticism of the manuscripts. The Reverend A. Dudley Ward, Director of Studies, has carried out his responsibilities as organizer and coordinator, and in the process of evaluation, with imagination and efficiency. A Study Committee of the Department, including both lay and clerical members and representing a variety of occupations, has reviewed the program of the study at various stages. Mr. Charles H. Seaver, Secretary of the Department and a member of the Study Committee, has carefully edited the manuscripts and has been available consistently for counsel. As in the other volumes of this series, the authors have been free to write as they wished and to accept or reject suggestions or criticisms. In the final analysis the book is the responsibility of the authors.

The National Council of Churches has taken no official position and assumed no responsibility regarding the content of any of the volumes. In no sense, therefore, can or should any statement in this series be regarded as an official declaration of the National Council of Churches or of any of its units.

Preface

The subject of this work is a striking movement in modern life which I have described as the "organizational revolution." It consists in a great rise in the number, size, and power of organizations of many diverse kinds, and especially of economic organizations. The rise of the labor movement, the farm organization movement, the great corporation, the trust and the cartel, even the enormous rise in the activity of the national state itself, are all part of a general movement in history, a movement which has suffered a remarkable acceleration of pace in the past seventy or eighty years. The main object of the study is to inquire into the impact of this movement on the standards by which we judge economic policy and personal conduct. It is part of a larger inquiry into the ethics of economic life, which has been briefly outlined in the Foreword to this volume.

Part I of the study consists of an analysis of the forces which have led to the growth of economic organizations; an analysis of some of the consequences of this movement, for economic, political, and personal life; and a discussion of the kind of ethical problems which the movement has created. Part II consists of a number of brief "case studies" to illustrate the principles developed in Part I. These are illustrative rather than exhaustive. The labor movement, farm organizations, business organizations, all come under review. Because I believe that it is necessary to bring out the essential similarity between political states and other organizations, I have also written two chapters on how the organizational revolution has affected national states, in their economic aspects. The final chapter of Part II summarizes the conclusions. Part III is devoted to Professor Niebuhr's critical chapter and others' comments, with my replies.

Every study of this kind must have a theoretical background. The rest of this introduction is concerned with that part of social and ethical theory which the author regards as appropriate background material for the rest of the study. The reader who is in a hurry to get to the meat of the argument itself may be advised to proceed straight to Chapter 1.

1. ETHICS AND SOCIAL SCIENCE

The first question which must be raised is that of the meaning of "ethics" in an inquiry of this kind. It is not the purpose of the study to examine the more philosophical aspects of ethical theory. Rather it is confined to what might be called "practical" ethics, which is the study of the *criteria* which are employed in "rating" phenomena on some scale of goodness or badness. The basic question is by what standards do we appraise institutions, policies, or even people; what constitutes "betterment" or "worsening"?

At this point a question may arise in the minds of some readers as to whether ethics, even in this restricted sense, is a proper subject for objective inquiry and research—I avoid the word "scientific" on the ground that it is too much charged with emotional content. What, especially, is the function of a writer in such a field? He may perhaps have two legitimate functions.

Still at the level of description and explanation of the social universe around him—i.e., still operating in the role of a social scientist—he can regard the ethical ideas and judgments of the society which he is studying as part of the system which he is studying. Indeed, the student of society must include the ethical beliefs, formulations, and practices as part of his data; they form an essential part of the universe with which he is dealing, and cannot be neglected. Ideas of good and evil, of what is right and wrong, of what constitutes a "good union man" or a "fair employer," a "good citizen" or a "scoundrel," are as much variables of the social universe as the price of cheese, the vote in an election, or the birth rate.

The writer, however, also may have a role as a "moralist" himself—not merely as the describer of the moral ideas and ideals of others, but as the creator and propagator of his own ideas and ideals, seeking not merely to describe but to change. The role of the moralist in society is an important one: he corresponds to the "innovator" in the realm of techniques. Sometimes his innovations succeed, sometimes they do not, but without him there would be no development in the moral standards and practices of men.

1. *Obstacles to Objectivity*

It is impossible to avoid being a moralist to some degree. Even if a writer adopts the role of scientific objectivity, this in itself constitutes a moral judgment; such objectivity stands higher on the scale of "goodness" than any possible alternative. This itself is a view which has held favor only in certain limited cultures; one might almost say that it is almost nonexistent except in certain aspects of Atlantic civilization in the past two or three hundred years. It is a view which is heresy in Russia, and which seems likely to become heresy in America. Objectivity has no friends in a garrison state, or in any spiritually totalitarian regime.

Many of the most influential writers in social science—Adam Smith, Marx, Freud—have been "moralists" in the sense that their works are permeated with a strong emotional coloring derived from a well-established scale of moral values. They know what they like and especially what they don't like, and have no hesitation in giving their work a persuasive tone. Nor is this accidental. Things which are significant in social science are so because they are highly affected with ethical connotations; the "dull" is that which doesn't matter, in the sense that it lacks moral importance. A writer, therefore, who is writing about important problems in society is writing about things which are of necessity highly charged with moral tone, i.e., which stand either high or low, but not in a middle position, on scales of "goodness." If the writer is himself part of his culture—and if he were not he would be quite incapable of writing—he must himself be affected by the moral ratings of the phenomenon with which he deals.

What, then, "should" be the position of the social scientist as a moralist? The question itself is, of course, one which requires a moralist to answer, however it is answered—which means in a sense that we must answer the question before it can be answered. This particular dilemma can be resolved only by the writer's stating his own view—as a moralist—in the hope that his moralizing will command acceptance.

It will be generally accepted, I think, that a moralist should also be a social scientist. His moral judgments should be based firmly on a sound knowledge of the structure and dimensions of society, and of the causal relations which are at work determining the movement of its innumerable interrelated variables. A great deal of the work of men with profound moral insight has been vitiated because they did not understand some of the *necessities* of society or the true causal factors at work within society. This is generally apt to be true of "reformers." While Marx, the Prohibitionists, Henry George, the late Archbishop of Canterbury, and Woodrow Wilson might object to each other strenuously as bedfellows, in this regard they are at least in the same boat. Indeed, it is at least in doubt whether reformers and revolutionists who have had strong and persuasive ethical systems have not done more harm than good. It is even less in doubt that the great changes in human life and society are brought about not by reform and violent revolution, but by the "silent revolutions" in techniques, in customs, in morals, in manners, in ways of doing things of all kinds, which have spread by the almost imperceptible processes of imitation.

On the other side it must also be said that social science, while it has made immense strides even in the past generation, still is far from being a certain guide to the complexities of social relationships; and that today, as in the past, there is room for the rash reformer whose moral insight carries him beyond the doubts—or even the present certainties—of the social scientists and who does something which the social scientist does not think possible. It is good for economists, especially, to remember that it was the Christians, by and large, who abolished slavery and who drove for the British Factory Acts. This was frequently over the opposition of the economists of the day, whose science was too narrow and who themselves lived in too small a world to catch the import of the great social movements which were in the making.

While it will be pretty generally accepted that the moralist should at the same time understand the society on which he passes judgment, it is not so generally accepted that the social scientist should also be a moralist, and should employ his technical proficiencies in the service of "improvement." The best case for this proposition is that the social scientist will be a moralist in any case and that he will be a better one, and also a less dangerous one, if he admits it and spells out as clearly as he can his ethical system. A moral system is dangerous when it is hidden—when it serves merely to give emotional color to writing without ever revealing explicitly the system of values or standards of judgment from which the emotional coloring is derived. Innuendo, though it may be the most powerful propaganda weapon of the moralist, is not conducive to the clarification of ethical confusions. In this study, therefore, I shall write unashamedly in part as a moralist. I will, however, endeavor to make the moral system as explicit as possible.

2. The Possible and the Good

One can put the matter in another way. The great object of social science, as of all science, is to find out what is *possible*. The "laws" of science are in fact possibility functions, limiting the relationships among things within certain boundaries. Thus if we have a law relating to the volume, pressure, and temperature of a gas, this states in effect that there are only certain volumes, pressures, and temperatures which can possibly coexist as long as the law holds. Similarly, if we have a law relating the quantity of money, the velocity of circulation, the price level, and the volume of transactions, there are only certain values of these quantities which can coexist.

Ethics, however, is the study of what, among the things that are possible, is "better" or "worse"—or, of course, neutral. Ethics, that is to say, postulates the existence of a quantity called "goodness" which is potentially related to all the other variables of the universe through a "goodness function," which expresses a judgment of whether one state of affairs is better or worse than another. Over a wide range of variables—for instance, in astronomy—the variables of the universe are neutral in regard to goodness. Thus most of us who do not believe in astrology do not now regard one position of the planets as "better" than another. As we move toward those things which more obviously affect the welfare of man, however, we tend to ascribe more and more goodness or badness to them. Thus we may feel, not without some reason, that certain pressures and temperatures and mixtures of gases in which we can survive are better than others in which we cannot. Similarly, the science of nutrition unhesitatingly recommends certain constituents of diet as good and others as bad. It is a short step from this to the economist's recommendation of certain policies as good and others as bad, or the psychologist's recommendation of certain habits of living as good and others as bad.

All these recommendations, however, can be broken down into

two links. The first is a statement of relationship—that is, of possibility or impossibility—that if, for instance, we breathe ammonia we will die in so many minutes, or if we do not eat certain vitamins we will suffer from pellagra, or if we persistently increase the quantity of money faster than a certain rate we will have a general rise of prices. The second is an appraisal of results, according to some criterion of goodness: that, for instance, death, pellagra, and inflation are bad. The first link is what properly belongs to science, the second to ethics.

It is a basic tenet of any ethical religion that there is some "real" standard of goodness which is independent of human whims and fancies, just as it is a basic faith of science that there is some objective universe of related objects which is itself independent of the errors of observation of fallible human observers. This objective standard of goodness is the "will of God." It does not necessarily correspond with any individual's judgments, or even with human welfare in a narrow sense, though it is also a basic tenet of religion that objective truth in this field can be sought for and found to a degree.

The present study does not pretend to probe to these absolutes. Its main concern is with the first link on the chain of ethical judgment; that is, with the possible relationships of social facts. We shall be mainly concerned with the exploration of those aspects of the social possibility function which relate to the growth of economic organizations, not with the establishment of any peak of goodness on it. Nevertheless such a task, lowly as it is, is a vital contribution to the ethical judgment itself, for the impossible is not relevant to the problem of ethical choice. The main business of social science in regard to ethics is to teach us what moons we should not cry for.

2. ORGANISMS AND ORGANIZATIONS

Even to begin to do this, however, we must have some theory. We cannot get far in the study of organizations or of anything else unless we have some kind of theoretical "model" as a guide to perceiving what is essential in the midst of the immense mass of subordinate detail. It is important, therefore, to ask right at the outset whether there are any features of form or structure which most organizations have in common.

We shall find that there are such features; that, in fact, it is possible to construct a general model of an organization which embodies in somewhat abstract form the essential features of all organizations. We shall find, also, that many of the features of social organizations are also found in biological organisms. It is not necessary to waste time discussing the question whether a social organization "is" an organism, for in important respects the many properties of social organizations differ from those of biological organisms. Nevertheless, there are enough similarities so that we are justified in regarding both biological organisms, like bacteria, mice, and men, and social organizations, like labor unions, churches, and states, as part of an inclusive group of "creatures" which might be called "behavior units" or "behavior systems."[1]

1. General Similarities

Both biological organisms and social organizations have a certain degree of unity and can be *described*; both of them exhibit behavior, in the sense that they respond in fairly definite ways to changes in their external or internal environments. We shall find also that they both have a certain machinery of existence, without which they perish, and that both probably exhibit a "life cycle"—are born, grow, mature, and die—though this is not so clear in the case of social organizations. Where social organizations differ most sharply from biological organisms is in their reproductive processes and in the processes of consciousness. Only biological organisms are centers of consciousness; and, though in common speech we endow social organizations with personality, as when we think of "Uncle Sam" or "John Bull," these personifications are merely figures of speech and do not correspond to superconscious realities. The relation of individual citizens to their country is a very different relationship from that of cells to a human body.

Both organizations and organisms can be described in terms which are suggestive of the accountant's concepts of the balance sheet and the income account. In describing an organization or an organism as it exists at a moment of time, we make a listing, or

[1] Reavis Cox and Wroe Alderson, editors, *Theory in Marketing*, Homewood, Illinois, Richard D. Irwin, Inc., 1949.

perhaps a map, of the *parts*. Such a listing may be called a "position statement," if one may borrow a phrase from the accountants and use it in a somewhat wider sense. A chemical formula of a compound, a map in anatomy or in geography, the balance sheet of a firm, the organization chart of an organization, even the credal statement of a church, are all examples of position statements at various levels of abstraction. They all represent the analysis of a whole into parts which are not further analyzed and which for the purposes of the problem in hand are regarded as homogeneous. These parts I shall call "components." Thus, the atoms H and O are components of the chemical formula H_2O; the organs, veins, arteries, etc. of an anatomical chart or the provinces, cities, railroads, etc. of a map are components of the body or of the region; the assets and liabilities are components of the balance sheet of a firm; the organizational categories and lines of communication and authority are components of an organization chart; and the various articles are components of a credal statement.[2]

Living matter, and living organizations, contain many unstable components which left to themselves would soon decay. Moth and rust are the gods of the physical universe, which seems to be running down (or out) in a vast cosmic spectacle of perpetual decay. Life is a strange process of shoring up the unstable temples of the organism by a complex and perpetual process of "throughput." It is this which corresponds to the income account of the accountant. It always involves *exchange*, which is a transformation of one component into another, more useful to the organism, by a mutual transfer of components between different organisms, or between an organism and the inorganic world. It always involves *production*, which is the internal transformation of one component or set of components into another set. It may involve theft, in which something is taken from outside the organism without any *quid pro quo*.

[2] It should be observed that negative components are possible, especially in social organizations, though they are not found much at the biological or chemical level. From this point of view the balance sheet of a firm would be clearer if the contractual liabilities were taken over to the assets side as "negative assets," so that the net worth appeared as equal to the sum of all assets, both positive and negative; then the balance sheet would correspond more closely in appearance to what in fact it is—a breakdown of the net worth into its components.

2. The Process of Exchange

Exchange is a concept so fundamental to the understanding of both organism and organization that it is worth examining closely. From the point of view of a single individual it represents a loss of some quantity of one component and a gain, as a result, of some quantity of another. Thus the animal body gains oxygen and loses carbon dioxide as a result of breathing; the atmosphere loses oxygen and gains carbon dioxide as a result of the same process. If the process goes on in a closed room for long the body cannot continue breathing, as the air comes to have too high a proportion of carbon dioxide and too little oxygen to sustain life, and the animal dies. Fortunately plants perform a similar exchange with the atmosphere in an opposite direction, taking in carbon dioxide and giving out oxygen. In this regard, therefore, animals and plants form a community which can continue indefinitely without change in the composition of the atmosphere if they are properly balanced. The atmosphere in this case represents a kind of go-between or "market": a reservoir which permits each party to the exchange to continue for a while without the other, but which depends for the stability of its own composition on the completion of the exchange. There are, of course, many such systems of exchange and many such communities in the biological sphere, some of them of great complexity.

In economic life the "market" performs something of the same function that the atmosphere does in the case of simple metabolic processes. When an individual "sells" he gets rid of some commodity which he holds, and acquires money. When he "buys" he gets rid of money, and acquires the commodity bought. Clearly neither buying nor selling can go on for long unless there are other compensating changes; an individual who did nothing but buy would soon run out of money, and an individual who did nothing but sell would soon run out of commodity. An individual or an organization is able to keep up buying and selling only if it *produces*; i.e., if its activity results in something which can be sold. Then money can be seen truly as a "medium of exchange." The organization produces something (which may, of course, be labor, or may be a commodity resulting from labor, or may be the services of capital which it owns). What it produces it sells, thus obtaining money;

with the money thus obtained it buys things from other organizations, things which are necessary to sustain life and comfort and to enable it to continue producing. The ultimate metabolic process involved here is the exchange of the things which the organization produces and sells for the things which it buys.

One organization, however, is not going to be able to produce and sell A in exchange for B unless some other organization is producing B in exchange for A. This means that continued processes of exchange require continued processes of specialized production. To return to the biological case, animals can be considered as "producers" and "sellers" of carbon dioxide and "buyers" of oxygen. They can continue to produce in this fashion only if somewhere else in the system there are producers and sellers of oxygen and purchasers of carbon dioxide. In the biosphere the sellers of oxygen and the buyers of carbon dioxide are generally the same organisms. This does not have to be the case, and in social systems we generally find that multilateral trade is the rule: organization X sells A and buys B; organization Y sells B and buys C; organization Z sells C and buys A.

3. INFLUENCE OF THE ENVIRONMENT

It should now be clear that if the forces leading to the survival of any particular organization are to be discovered, the organization must be considered in its relation to its whole environment. A totality of human organizations, like a totality of biological organisms, constitutes an *ecosystem*—this being defined as a self-contained and self-perpetuating system of interacting populations of various kinds.

Perhaps the simplest example of a biological ecosystem is a balanced aquarium, or a pond, in which the various populations of fish, snails, water plants, algae, bacteria, and so on are enabled to sustain themselves indefinitely in the absence of any change in the general physical environment such as changes in temperature or sediment. These populations exist in complex competitive and complementary relationships one with another; the whole effect, however, is one of ultimate cooperation. Strangely enough, even the predators and parasites are forced into this fundamentally cooperative over-all pattern, so long as the system is in genuine equilibrium; if predators are too successful in killing their prey they will exterminate themselves by exterminating their food supply.

Society likewise is a great pond, with populations of families, grocery stores, gas stations, automobiles, countries, churches, lodges, universities, and innumerable other species of social organization. If we are to understand the laws which govern the growth and survival of any class of organization, we must understand where it fits into the social ecosystem; i.e., what its relations are with all the other species of organization. Especially we must study its metabolic processes: what it takes from its environment, what it gives to its environment, and how what it gives is transformed in the environment into what it takes. If it takes from the environment without giving (theft), we must study how it is enabled to do this, and how the environment restores what is taken from it.

The environment of any single organization or group of organizations consists partly of the physical and biological world and partly of other organizations. The social ecosystem, that is to say, is not complete in itself, nor is the biological ecosystem. If Kansas grows wheat today instead of prairie grass, and if milk cows thrive where once roamed the buffalo, the explanation lies largely in the social ecosystem. The whole of creation, that is, forms one vast ecosystem. Nevertheless, for purposes of analysis it is frequently convenient to consider a part of the whole as if it were a whole in itself and to take, for instance, the biological factors as given when studying the social system. In such analysis, however, the unity of the whole must not be lost sight of; a social system which thrives on the exploitation of exhaustible resources does not have a long expectation of life, at least as geologists reckon time.

1. Types of Ecological Change

No system, whether biological or social, in fact settles down to an ecological equilibrium for long, for the underlying conditions are constantly liable to change. These changes may consist of invasions of new species from outside, with consequent readjustment to new positions of equilibrium—perhaps with some of the old species much reduced, or even extinct. The colonization of the Americas by Europeans is an excellent example of such an invasion, the consequences of which are by no means worked out yet. The changes may consist also in the formation of new species by mutation or innovation. This has the same kind of effect as an invasion. If there is a new position of equilibrium containing the new species, the system will move toward it in a series of adjustments.

It frequently happens, of course, that both invasion and mutation are unsuccessful, so that the new species does not succeed in finding a place in a new equilibrium and becomes extinct, leaving the old equilibrium much as before. A constant process of mutation seems to take place in nature, however, and we know that innovation is constantly taking place in society; new machines, new products, new organizations, new techniques, new ideas, are constantly making their appearance. Some of them establish permanent positions in the structure of society; others disappear almost at once; others may flourish for a time but do not have any true equilibrium position, and eventually disappear.

Besides the introduction of new species there are also changes of an irreversible nature in the underlying conditions of equilibrium which determine the relative "strengths" of the different species. Thus the reeds and water grasses at the edge of a pond take up matter from the air, and so gradually in the succession of generations raise the level of the pond bottom to the point where they can no longer exist, and the dryer grasses and bushes take their place. The pond by the very operation of the life in it gradually fills up; the successive rings of life types move in toward the center until finally the pond disappears altogether. Similarly, in the retreat of glacial ice we see a succession of ecosystems occupying the slopes, each creating the conditions through its own life for its own extinction and replacement by another.

This is the process known as "ecological succession." It is going on all the time in society. The organizations, institutions, ideas, and techniques of one period permit the rise of new organizations, institutions, ideas, and techniques which eventually may displace the former set almost completely, and which in turn permit the rise of a still further succession. We thus see human history as structurally a continuation of the immense drama of evolution. Countries, businesses, unions, co-ops, churches, are the successors, in the immense process of ecological change, of the humble amoeba, the lichen, and the dinosaurs. Moreover, the organizations of men at any one time form part of the whole ecosystem. One cannot establish even a bridge club in Podunk without affecting to some degree the flora and fauna of perhaps the entire globe. Ecological succession takes place because of certain cumulative changes. In society we may note three great cumulative changes which tend to govern the succession of institutions and ideas. One is the accumulation of capital when the circumstances of society are such that production exceeds consumption. Another is similar: the increase in population when circumstances permit births to exceed deaths. The third is most fundamental of all: the increase and diffusion of knowledge. Humans can hardly live without learning something, and once a society can afford to have specialized teachers and researchers, and has easy means of communication, knowledge builds on knowledge like the coral and is diffused by a process almost akin to cell division. Teaching is the most astonishingly productive of the arts; the teacher who imparts knowledge to others loses none of his own but generally even gains knowledge himself in the act of imparting it.

The accumulation of capital, of population, and of knowledge represents a sort of deposit in society, a deposit which may be fertile of new life but which can also choke and stifle new life. It is well known that population can grow to the point where the difficulty of providing for the teeming multitudes inhibits all economic or social progress. This is the famous "dismal theorem" of Malthus: that, if nothing checks the growth of population except starvation and misery, then the population will grow until it is miserable and starves. The growth of capital also may lead eventually to a stagnation of creative activity, because the very plenty that is around stifles the demand for further production. This phenomenon is noticeable in the arts, where when an art form reaches its highest peak it dies, because it is incapable of further creative development, only of imitation. There is a certain threat also even in the growth of knowledge, for knowledge begets power, and power can be used for destruction. The notion that knowledge might grow to the point where it would become incompatible with the maintenance of human life on earth does not seem so fantastic today as it would have seemed even ten years ago.

These considerations may seem to be leading us somewhat far from the main subject of the monograph; if we are to discuss the ethics of organization, however, it is vital that organizations be placed in the setting of an interpretation of history. The ecological interpretation is, of course, only an interpretation of the mechanics of history; it leaves questions of origins and teleology quite unanswered. Nevertheless, judgments in regard to the ultimate ends of history must operate within the framework of the ecological machinery. This is particularly true of questions of policy, i.e., of deliberate attempts to influence the course of history in desired directions. Just as agriculture is an attempt, and a highly successful attempt, to distort the "natural" ecosystem in favor of man, so that wheat grows in place of grass and orchards in place of brambles, so social policy is a kind of "social agriculture" aimed at a deliberate distortion of the social ecosystem also in favor of man.

We shall not presume in this volume to go too far into the problem of *what* is in favor of man—a question which is much more difficult to answer in the case of statesmanship than it is in the case of farming. What we can say, however, is that some notion of the mechanics of the ecosystem is as necessary in statesmanship as it is in farming, and that much reforming energy has been wasted because of a failure to appreciate the complex interactions of the numerous populations of which society is composed. By concentrating on the expulsion of a single evil, especially, we frequently bring in worse evils to fill the gap in the ecosystem which the first evil occupied. The failure of Prohibition is a case in point.

2. Silent Revolutions

Two important insights which are derived mainly from the study of biological systems, but which have important applications to the social system, should be mentioned. One is the possibility of "ecological revolution" taking place as a result of small changes in the underlying conditions. A classic example in biology is the equilibrium between prairie and forest in the Midwest before the advent of agriculture. There seems to have been a certain critical point of temperature and humidity on one side of which the forest established itself, with trees, forest plants, birds, insects, even bacteria, and on the other side of which prairie established itself with an almost entirely different set of species of all kinds. At about the critical level slight changes in the underlying conditions would eventually bring an almost complete change in the flora and fauna. Ecological revolutions happen also in social life. They are not to be confused with those storms on the surface of history generally called "revolutions" which raise a deal of dust and cause a lot of trouble, but which generally end up with the same old things called by a new set of names. The ecological revolutions in society are the silent revolutions, often taking centuries to accomplish their course. They are the revolutions in ideas, in ideals, in techniques, which carry a society from one way of life to another.

Those quantities which are responsible for revolutions, whether large or small, in whole ecosystems may be called "critical variables." A critical variable—or perhaps a set of such variables—will have a certain value or set of values ("boundary values") on one side of which one ecosystem will establish itself and on the other side of which another will be formed. The coexistence of different ecosystems can be explained by quite slight changes in the critical variables as we move around the geographical or social landscape. Thus in the Midwest certain slight differences in temperature and humidity set the geographical boundary between prairie and forest. In society likewise many widely differing social and ideological ecosystems coexist in the same region: the lush forest of Roman Catholicism and the open prairie of Boston Unitarianism, for instance, existing side by side in different "microclimates" or social strata of the same society.

The actual differences in the critical variables which give rise to such different systems may be quite small, but the end results may differ enormously. This effect is particularly noticeable when cumulative changes occur. Thus geologists estimate that a small decline in the average temperature of the earth would bring on another ice age, because a little more snow, staying a little longer, would reflect back more of the sun's heat and so make the climate a little colder, leading to more snow and a still colder climate, and so on. These slow cumulative changes are of great importance in social life: a slight improvement in underlying conditions of a society may give rise to a vast cumulative change for the better as improvement constantly itself facilitates further improvement. Vicious as well as benevolent spirals of cumulative kind are also not unknown in history.

The second insight which emerges from the study of biosystems, and which has profound implications for social ecosystems, is the idea of catastrophe as a stimulant to the evolutionary process and as an instrument for preventing systems from settling down to an indefinitely prolonged equilibrium at the climax of the process of succession. All systems, both biological and social, tend to settle down into a stationary state if they are left to work out their own implications for a long enough period of time—a state in which the life processes simply result in the perpetuation of the existing populations in number and composition. The cumulative processes which result in ecological succession operate, of course, to disturb any number of short-run equilibrium positions; but even these forces work themselves out in the long run, in what is called the "climactic" ecosystem. The evolutionary process seems to have been punctuated by a series of catastrophes (such as the ice ages) which have upset a previously established climatic equilibrium and have therefore released new energies for change. At a less cosmic level we find that if pine forests are to survive in the Southern United States they must be cut down approximately in every generation; otherwise oaks and hickories grow up in the shade of the pines and eventually displace them. In the shadeless cutover forest, however, the oak and hickory seedlings do not survive and the young pines flourish.

The main problem which concerns us here is the place of ethical ideas and value standards in the whole ecological process of history. To what extent are these "critical" variables determining the rest of the structure of society; to what extent are they determined by, say, technical changes? If they are critical variables, do they follow certain laws of development of their own, on which the history of the other variables of society therefore hangs, or is their development inextricably mixed in with that of society as a whole? These are important questions—to which, however, no definitive answer can be given. What can be asserted with some confidence is that no single, unitary interpretation of history is satisfactory. It cannot be denied that techniques of economic life have a large impact on the whole social ecosystem, profoundly affecting the institutions and ideas of society. It is no doubt true, for instance, that the invention of the rudder in the ninth or tenth centuries led directly to Europe's discovery of America, with all that implies; that the invention of the horse collar had a great deal to do with the ultimate abolition of slavery; and that the invention of the steam engine had a great deal to do with the rise of the labor movement.

But it is equally true that moral and religious ideas have had an immense impact on economic life and on the development of techniques. The basic idea of the steam engine, for instance, was undoubtedly known to the Greeks, and gunpowder was invented by the Chinese a thousand years ago; but the moral, religious, and cultural setting was not one in which use could be made of these discoveries either for production or for destruction. The influence of the Protestant ethic on the development of capitalism has been explored at length by Weber, Sombart, Fanfani, and Tawney, among others; and, though the assessment of the exact contribution of Protestantism to economic change is difficult, there can be no doubt that the technical revolution has proceeded more slowly in the family-centered and more tradition-minded Catholic cultures than in the more individualistic and iconoclastic Protestant cultures.

Once the sacred ark of tradition is broken in one sphere of life it becomes easier to break it in others. Such a break, however, may come in the world of ideas in a way which is relatively independent of what is happening in the world of materials and techniques, or it may come in the world of techniques in a way which is relatively independent of the world of ideas. What must be emphasized is that ideas, ideals, beliefs, theories, commodities, machines, organizations, and men are all part of a single pattern, all acting and reacting on each other as system gives way to system in the manifold and protracted conversations of history.

4. Internal Determinants of Behavior

Having taken this brief glance at the evolutionary setting, it will be profitable now to return to the problem of the individual organism or organization and to consider what principles of its internal structure determine its behavior, its growth, and its survival. Recent work, both in the biological and in the social sciences, has thrown some new light on this problem.

1. Mechanical Controls

At relatively simple and routine levels of behavior the idea of a "control mechanism" is fruitful in the interpretation of apparently complex patterns of behavior. Every organism or organization has certain variables to which it is sensitive, and a certain range of tolerance for each of these variables. The behavior of the organism, then, can be described in large part in terms of a machinery to keep these sensitive variables within the range of tolerance—if one of them rises above the upper limit of toleration, various forces will be brought into play to reduce it; if it falls below the lower limit of toleration, forces—perhaps similar, perhaps different—will be brought into play to increase it. The machinery for effecting the stabilization of a variable within the limits of toleration is what is meant by a "control mechanism"; it is sometimes known as a "feedback," for reasons which will become apparent below.

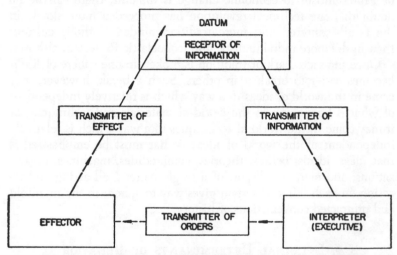

Reprinted from the *Papers of the Michigan Academy of Science, Arts, and Letters,* Vol. XXXVII, p. 278.

In physiology this process of stabilization is known as "homeostasis," and the term may well be applied more widely, for control mechanisms are found in every organism and organization, and even at the purely mechanical level. About the simplest control mechanism is that of the thermostat, familiar in many households. The sensitive variable is the temperature of the air in the neighborhood of its thermometer. If the temperature falls below the level set, the thermostat sends a message to the furnace control which is translated into an "order" to turn on the furnace; turning on the furnace results in heat coming through the pipes or ducts and warms up the air around the thermometer; then as soon as the temperature reaches the set level, another message is sent to the furnace, which turns off the heat.

All control mechanisms follow the same basic pattern, shown in the accompanying chart. There is always a *receptor* of information (the thermometer) which transmits information by a transmitter (the wire to the furnace control) to an "executive" or interpreter (the furnace control), which transforms the information into "orders" to an "effector" (the furnace), which in turn carries out the orders by means of transmitters of effect (the pipes) back to the original sensitive variable (the temperature). In a simple mechanism all that is required of the receptor is an ability to distinguish the qualitative *divergence* of the stabilized variable from the established norm.

2. Conscious Controls

Even at the lowest levels of life, however, something more than a mechanical control mechanism is observable. There is a learning process apparent even in the case of bacteria. That is, there are regular changes in the control mechanism itself, following "favorable" or "unfavorable" experiences with it. If, for instance, we set the thermostat at 65°, and find that uncomfortable, we may adjust the setting of the thermostat itself and stabilize the environment at a somewhat higher temperature. Something like that happens automatically in the body in the case of fever.

In conscious organisms, and therefore in organizations, as these are governed by conscious organisms, expectations also form an important part of the determinants of behavior. Behavior governed by conscious expectations is what we mean by "planning"—that is, it is not determined by current information about current events but is directed by expectations of the future derived from projections of past experience. One of the most difficult problems in the study of organizations is the study of the dynamics of their behavior, and this is intimately bound up with the derivation of expectations. In a planned behavior we need to know two things in order to predict the course of behavior: we must know the laws according to which past experience gives rise to present expectations, and we must know how present expectations affect present and future behavior.

The theory of control mechanisms of the thermostat type is well adapted to the explanation of *routine* behavior. Any organization will have certain variables to which it is sensitive. For each of these variables there is likely to be some degree of tolerance; i.e., a certain range of values within which the organization will not feel moved to action. If the variable goes beyond either the upper or the lower boundary of this range of tolerance, however, routine behavior of some kind is induced in order to correct the situation. Thus a firm may keep its eye on its liquidity position, as measured perhaps by certain asset ratios such as the ratio of its current assets to its current liabilities. If the liquidity measure rises above a certain point, the firm will seek to become less liquid, by expanding its operations. If the liquidity measure falls below a certain point the firm will seek to become more liquid, perhaps by contracting its operations and laying off some men, or perhaps by increasing its selling effort.

There are a great many sensitive variables of this kind which must be considered in the behavior of any organization. Thus firms are sensitive to their profit position, to their share of the market, to their public reputation, and so on. Trade unions are sensitive to dissatisfaction among their members, congressmen to dissatisfaction among their constituents. City officials are sensitive to crime rates, to letters of protest. Almost everybody is sensitive to comparative statistics. It is often not the absolute value of a variable which is significant, but the difference between your value and that of some other comparable person or organization. Trade unions are very sensitive to wage differentials; state governments are sensitive to comparative positions in public health, in education, in the care of the mentally ill. This sensitivity to differences between one organization and another is an important factor in explaining the whole dynamics of society, and explains why a change which occurs anywhere in society tends to propagate itself through the whole society. Fashion governs not merely ladies' hats, but union contracts, state legislation, pricing policy, lodge rituals, barbershop-quartet societies, and innumerable other aspects of organizational life and behavior.

3. *The Individual in the Organization*

Mechanical and biological models have great value in describing the mechanical and organic aspects of organizations. They do not, however, carry us all the way, for an organization differs from either a machine or an organism in that its constituent parts (men) are conscious beings with wills of their own. Organizations, therefore, have to deal with the problem of *consent*—a concept which is not found particularly at the mechanical or organic levels. The cooperation of men in an organization is voluntary in the sense in which the cooperation of parts in a machine, or of cells in a body, is not. An organization cannot survive, therefore, unless its constituent persons are willing to serve its ends. This willingness can, of course, be achieved in a number of different ways. It may be achieved by an identification of the purpose of the individual himself with that of the organization. This is generally the strongest motive in the case of those most directly responsible for the life of the organization as directors or executives, but the motive penetrates far down into the rank and file in the case of churches, unions, countries, and even sometimes in the case of businesses.

The willingness to serve an organization may be obtained also by more strictly economic means; i.e., by giving rewards to an individual sufficient to induce him to devote his time and energies to a particular organization rather than to other uses. In a sense identification of purpose is one of the rewards which association with an organization brings to an individual, so that both the above methods of inducing willingness to serve may be regarded as "economic."

A man works for a corporation or for a union or a church for essentially the same general reason, that it is "worth his while." In one case the reward may consist almost wholly of money wages, with little sense of participation in the purposes of the organization. In another case the reward may consist mainly in a sense of participation in the large purposes of the organization and may include little or no monetary income. The last method by which individuals may be made "willing" to serve an organization is coercion; i.e., fear of the consequences of not serving it rather than the attraction of the rewards of serving it. The cooperation of the slave and of the conscript is of this order, though it should be observed that pure coercion is rare and practically impossible.

There must always be some small element of identification with the purposes of the organization if *effective* cooperation of an individual is to be obtained. Even the slave and the conscript must in some sense be willing to be enslaved or conscripted, and there is some threshold of unwillingness below which no amount of coercive power can force individuals to contribute.

One of the important insights of social science is its emphasis on the almost universal nature of the informal group. It is not man's nature to be solitary. In all spheres of life and activity there is a tendency for people to collect together into groups of some kind, some of which may be highly temporary, others more permanent. No particular "purpose" is necessary for the formation of such groups; mere propinquity will attract individuals into groups through a kind of social gravitation. One of the secrets of successful organization is the ability of the organization to pull with, rather than against, the informal groups that form within it. In this way the organization may acquire a momentum which is in some degree independent of its specific purposes, or even its ability to attract people into serving those purposes. The "buddy" may be more important than the "cause" in inducing people to function in armies, in businesses, even in churches.

4. The Function of Hierarchy

Another characteristic of organizations which is not found to any great extent in the biological organism is *hierarchy*. By this I mean a regular system of subordination and rank within the organization: generals, major generals, colonels, majors, etc., in the army; pope, cardinal, archbishop, bishop, dean, etc., in the church; president, vice-president, general manager, supervisor, foreman, etc., in the business—examples could be multiplied. The universality of hierarchy in organizations of any size above the very smallest and most informal indicates that it arises out of some deep necessity. This necessity seems to lie mainly in the nature of a communications system.

We have seen that in the simplest machinery, as well as in the most complex organization, the function of the executive is to receive information along one set of channels of communication and to transform this information into "orders" which are sent out along other channels. The powers of the human individual, however, to receive information, to assess its relevance to the role which he is playing, and to interpret the information in the form of orders are very limited. It would be utterly impossible, for instance, for the president of even a small corporation to receive and assimilate all the information which is being received daily by the "receptors" of the business; it would be equally impossible for him to issue orders to all the "effectors" of the business. The hierarchy, therefore, acts as a sieve for information and as an analyzer of orders, preventing unnecessary information from reaching the top, transforming at each level some information into some orders, and expanding the general orders which come down from the higher levels into particular orders at the levels of execution.

The necessity for hierarchy in the structure of organization has created a severe moral dilemma which is by no means yet resolved. On the one hand we have the pull toward the organizational necessities of hierarchy, toward an aristocratic, highly stratified society of status. On the other hand there is a profound pull toward the moral ideal of equality—a pull which is especially strong in societies which have been affected by Christianity, with its emphasis on the equality of all men before God and on the universality of love. The tension created by this dilemma has, I suspect, been a creative one in the history of Western civilization. Both political democracy on the one hand and the market economy on the other can be regarded as partial solutions to this problem. Political democracy attempts to solve the problem by making the hierarchical structure circular—by subordinating the executives at the top to the political will of the masses at the bottom. The market economy tackles the problem by permitting the organization to be at once specialized and *small*, and unites large numbers of small organizations in an impersonal monetary nexus.

Neither of these solutions is wholly satisfactory. The forms of political democracy are no guarantee that a state will be able to satisfy its people by an adequate performance of its functions, as the history of Germany so deplorably illustrates. It is not enough to allow the last hen in the pecking order to peck the first. There must be, as well as the forms of democracy, a spirit of mutual respect and an ability to communicate all up and down the hierarchical line. The market-economy solution likewise has grave weaknesses in practice, as we shall develop in more detail later. It is subject to serious instabilities, and it does not prevent the growth of organizations which are large in themselves, even though they may be small relative to the total market. It is impossible to pretend that organizations like General Motors, Standard Oil, or du Pont are cosy little family businesses; they are large enough to exhibit within themselves almost all the internal problems which face a socialist state. This is a problem to which we will return.

PART I

Nature, Causes, and Effects

1

The Nature of the Organizational Revolution

The past fifty or a hundred years have seen a remarkable growth in the number, size, and power of organizations of many kinds, ranging through all areas of life. The extent of this change in the character and atmosphere of society can be visualized if we contrast the situation of 1952 with, say, that of 1852. In 1852 labor unions were practically nonexistent. There were practically no employers' associations or trade associations. There were practically no professional associations. There were no farm organizations of any importance. There was no American Legion. National governments absorbed—by present standards—an almost infinitesimal part of the total national product. There was no Department of Agriculture, no Department of Labor, in Washington. Outside the Masons there were practically no fraternal organizations. There were few corporations and few large businesses. Organizations outside government itself were largely confined to the churches, a few local philanthropic societies, and the political parties. There were, of course, many sporadic attempts at large-scale organizations, in almost all fields, in the first half of the nineteenth century. None of these attempts, however, resulted in the establishment of stable, continuing organizations such as we see today.

Contrast this situation with that of 1952. In place of the sparse fauna of organizations of 1852 we now have what seems like a vast jungle. In the United States 15,000,000 workers are organized into labor unions. At least half the farmers are organized into three large farm organizations. Great corporations dominate many fields of industry. Every trade and every industry, almost without exception, has one or more trade associations. Every profession is organized with its professional associations. There are innumerable organizations representing special-interest groups, from Audubon societies to Zoroastrians. The national state in all countries is immensely more powerful, and reaches much farther down into the lives and pockets of the individual, than a hundred years earlier. Government departments have multiplied and expanded into huge bureaucracies. Veterans' organizations cover millions of ex-soldiers, and wield immense political power. Lodges and fraternal orders have multiplied. Not only are there many more organizations, and many more kinds of organizations, than a century previous, but the organizations themselves are larger, better organized, more closely knit, more efficient in the arts of attracting members and funds and in pursuing their multitudinous ends.

Even this brief sketch makes it clear that at least one aspect of the many-sided revolution through which we have been passing is the "organizational revolution." Yet this revolution has received little study, and is not something of which we are particularly conscious. It has crept upon us silently. It is something which we accept as "natural" almost without thinking. And yet the whole movement raises problems with which we are ill equipped to deal. In our political and economic thinking, and in our ethical thinking as well, we are still often a hundred years behind the times—still thinking in terms of a society in which organizations are rather small and weak, and in which the family is the dominant institution.

1. The Various Origins and Impacts

We are perhaps especially unaware of the great changes which have taken place in economic life as a result of the growth of organizations. It is not easy to distinguish clearly between an "economic organization" and a "noneconomic organization." All organizations have economic aspects and must live in an economic environment. Even religious and charitable organizations, for instance, must be part of the network of monetary payments, and if they are to survive they must be able to make ends meet. An organization is hardly worth the name unless it has a budget. Nevertheless there are some organizations whose main purpose is the economic advancement or protection of their members; this is what I propose to mean by an "economic organization." Thus a labor union is clearly an "economic organization" in a sense that a lodge or a church is not, even though the union performs some of the functions of a lodge or church, and belonging to a lodge or church may not be wholly unconnected with a desire for economic advancement.

Similarly the farm organizations, trade associations, business associations, and of course businesses themselves, especially when they grow beyond the stage of the single proprietorship, all must be regarded as economic associations, even though they all have important noneconomic functions. Many professional associations, such as the American Medical Association, also have economic functions as one of their major interests. When we get to lodges and veterans' organizations the economic functions become hazier, though they still exist.

It is clear that no sharp line divides the economic from the noneconomic organization, or even the economic from the noneconomic aspect of a single organization. Nevertheless it is possible to discuss the impact of organization on economic life, and it is evident that this impact is a large one. Indeed, most of the organizations which have grown up during the past century and which were not important before—labor unions, cartels, employers' associations, farm associations, and so on—are "economic" organizations, and we should expect perhaps the main impact of the "organizational revolution" to be on economic life, even though its impact on political life and even on mental health may be significant.

There are, therefore, important problems which need to be investigated concerning the effects of the organizational revolution on the more technical aspects of economic life. What, for instance, has been, or is likely to be, the effect on the distribution of income or of economic power within the society? What is the impact on the price system, i.e., on the structure of relative prices? What is the impact on economic progress and on trends in productivity? What is its impact on the monetary system—does it, for instance, give an inflationary bias to the economy? What changes has it made in the course of the business cycle? Has it intensified or mitigated the movements of depression and prosperity which are so characteristic of the Western economy? All these questions, and many like them, fall within the scope of this inquiry; and, as the author is by profession an economist, it is in dealing with questions of this type that he feels most competent.

Nevertheless, the scope of the inquiry is broader than the economic aspect. It is impossible to study organizations long without realizing that many considerations of a sociological and psychological nature must be taken into account in explaining both their causes and their consequences. The economist who remains closely confined to the limits of his own abstractions in dealing with problems of this nature will inevitably be leaving out much that is essential to their understanding. In spite of the fact, therefore, that the conclusions of an economist in these fields must be less securely founded than those he comes to in his own field, some discussion is necessary of the deeper forces which have led to the growth of organizations, and of the effects of this growth on the deeper levels of human behavior.

To what extent, for instance, have organizations arisen as a result of spontaneous demands on the part of their members, and to what extent are they the result of the development of "skills of organization" on the part of professional organizers? What are the *emotional* needs which organizations have satisfied—or have not satisfied? What psychological tensions are created by the existence of organizations, and especially of competing organizations? How do we resolve the conflicts of loyalties which arise in the development of organizations? To what extent do organizations develop a "life of their own"—i.e., a pattern of behavior which is almost independent of the wishes or needs of their members? How does the hostility or friendliness of its environment affect the nature of an organization? These questions also, and again many like them, fall clearly within the scope of this inquiry, even though it may not be so easy to answer them.

The political aspects of the problem also must be borne in mind, even though they properly require a separate study to do them justice. The behavior and growth of organizations are often determined by their success in solving their internal political problems. It is unfortunate that political scientists have devoted so much attention to the state, which is only one political organization among many. The internal political problems of labor unions, farm organizations, cooperatives, corporations, churches, and so on are of great importance in explaining the behavior and the interactions of these organizations.

The effects of the growth of private organizations on the policies of the national state are also of great importance—for instance, the effects of the rise of pressure groups on the democratic process.

Furthermore, the state itself is an organization, and many of the broad forces which have contributed to the rising power of organizations have contributed also to the rising power of national states. The problem of the competition of states in war and diplomacy must also be regarded as essentially part of a larger problem of the competition of organizations. Enough of the divinity which used to hedge a king still clings to the flag to make us unwilling to treat the state as simply one of the species of fauna in the social jungle, and there is a naïveté in our approach to the state which prevents us from assessing its true place in society. If, however, we are to be realistic, we must regard the state as an organization—a peculiar one, it is true, but not essentially different in its structure and problems, as an organization, from, say, churches or labor unions. Moreover, practically all the problems which face individuals in their relationships with private organizations face them also in their relationship with the state.

2. The Ethical Aspects

The social science of organizations is the foundation upon which any study of them must be laid. Nevertheless the central interest of this study is not the science but the ethics of organization. We must inquire, therefore: "What, for the purposes of this study at least, are we going to include in the ethical problems?"

Ethical inquiry may be directed at two levels—philosophical and practical. With the first, concerning the ultimates and absolutes of goodness and obligation, we shall not concern ourselves in this study, except insofar as it may prove absolutely necessary. Our focus of interest will be ethics in its practical aspect; it is this which lies most closely adjacent to social science. This does not mean, of course, that we identify ethics with recommendations for policy; we are interested, however, in the kind of ethical judgments which are prerequisite for policy decisions, and which must be added to the merely factual, causal, or hypothetical propositions of social science before any policy recommendations can be made. It is with these additional prerequisites for policy judgments, rather than with these judgments themselves, that we shall be concerned.

What we are looking for, therefore, are *criteria of judgment*, suitable to be applied to organizations and organizational systems, according to which the various potentialities in this field can be rated on a scale of "goodness." It is this rating on a scale of goodness which constitutes the principal problem of ethics for the purposes of this study.

The act of rating anything, whether a person, an act, an institution, or an organization, on some scale of goodness (or badness) is, of course, liable to be associated with emotion. Nevertheless I shall not regard the emotive tone of a statement or a proposition as the essential ethical (as opposed to its scientific) quality. It is true, of course, that when Adam Smith refers to "the wretched spirit of monopoly" he is making an ethical judgment, and this judgment is charged with more emotion than a statement such as "Monopoly results in a rise of the market price above the natural price." It is not, however, the emotion itself which constitutes the essence of the ethical judgment; it is not that "scientific" propositions are written in stodgy prose and spoken in a monotone, while ethical statements are those which rouse the blood and are trumpeted by oratory.

All words carry a greater or lesser emotional overtone, and it is impossible to say anything without some emotional connotation springing from the words. There are some people for whom even technical expressions like "marginal utility" are like a red rag to a bull. It is not, therefore, the associated emotion, but it is the idea of a "rating," whether direct or implied, which gives a statement its ethical connotation. If we talk about the "wretched spirit of monopoly" it is implied that there is some other spirit which is less wretched; i.e., we have rated the "spirit of monopoly" low on some scale of spirits! The fact that we rate it low is likely to make us feel strongly about it, and the strength or weakness of the feeling attached to the rating is an important fact in explaining the *effects* of ethical ideas and ratings on the behavior of men and of organizations, but it is the rating rather than the feeling which constitutes the essential ethical problem.

1. *"Personal" Ethics*

Let us return then to the ethical questions which are raised by the "organizational revolution." We must ask first: "Are there important questions relating to standards of judgment of human behavior which are raised by this development?" To this question I answer an unhesitating "Yes." What might be termed the "common morality" of our Western culture has been built up by long testing and accretion in societies where most organizations were small and where most relationships were on a person-to-person basis. If we analyze a classic statement such as the Ten Commandments, for instance, we find that the last six, which deal with questions of morality involving relations with other people, contemplate no organization larger than a family, and no relationships with a wider circle than a neighborhood. Even the first four Commandments, which deal with religious duties, are intensely personal; they involve relationships of an individual with his God, not with any society of divinities. This is, of course, one of the profound impacts of monotheism on the moral life: it sees religion as well as morality as essentially a problem of person-to-person relations. The Commandments are addressed in the second person singular, not the plural; they begin "Thou shalt not," not "Ye shall not." This is true even of the Great Commandment: "Thou shalt love the Lord thy God—and thy neighbor as thyself."

The development of a highly organized society does not, of course, abrogate the Commandments or in any way diminish the inherent importance of the individual moral life. No matter how complex a society, it remains true that most of the moral problems which face an individual deal with person-to-person relationships. The personal virtues of honesty, truthfulness, kindliness, sincerity, sobriety, self-control, and so on are still the sign of a morally mature spirit and are still the virtues which hold the world together, no matter how complicated it may become. The individual is ultimately the only bearer of moral responsibility; even when an individual acts in the name of others, or in the name of an organization, it is still the individual who acts, and who ultimately must bear responsibility for the consequences of his acts.

Nevertheless, acting "in the name of"—i.e., as a representative of others bound together in an organization—presents moral problems and dilemmas additional to those which concern an individual acting solely on his own account, or even on account of those who are personally very close to him. The growth of organizations certainly does not do away with any of the old commandments; it may call for writing of some new ones. Just what some of these moral dilemmas are will become clearer when we have examined some of the forces which give rise to organization and some of the consequences of organization in society. Even at this point, however, we can indicate some of the problems.

2. *The Two-Sidedness of Organizations*

Many of the dilemmas are created by the fact that organization is on the one hand an expression of solidarity within the organized group, and on the other an expression of a lack of solidarity with those outside the organization. Organization, in other words, may tend to accentuate the division between an "in-group" and an "out-group." Almost every organization, therefore, exhibits two faces—a smiling face which it turns toward its members and a frowning face which it turns to the world outside.

Nowhere is this two-sidedness found more than in the national state. One's country, viewed from within, is an object of love and devotion, an organization capable of calling forth some of the noblest virtues of man—courage, unselfishness, self-sacrifice. Its citizens regard it, and quite rightly, as an organization conferring great good and benefit upon them—especially in these days of the "welfare state." It is the instrument through which the concern of each for the good of all is principally expressed, and a disaster to any one section of its population calls forth an immediate demand from the fortunate that the unfortunate be relieved. In many of its aspects, internally, the national state is a genuine expression of that concern for the welfare of others which is the essence of Christian love. Externally, however, it often presents a shockingly different picture. The state which protects and cherishes the children of its citizens ruthlessly bombs the children of its enemies. Viewed from the outside, every state is a potential monster, willing to sacrifice in its own defense every consideration of mercy, love, tenderness, or concern; it is a roaster of babies, a murderer of cities, a waster of the earth, faithless in its promises, lying in its words, deceitful in its pretensions.

To a lesser degree this two-sidedness is characteristic of all organizations. The fraternity which cherishes brotherhood within its walls seems like a home of prejudice and snobbery to those who are excluded. The church which tenderly nourishes the spirits of its members burns the heretics without—with words, if not with fire! The union which builds up a spirit of solidarity among its members, and even breaks down religious and racial barriers among them, under the splendid banner of "each for all and all for each" is apt to present a somewhat different face to the employer, to its rival union, or to the obstinately nonunion man. The corporation which is viewed by its "insiders" as a great empire of enterprise, to the "outsiders"—even its own employees—presents a face of much less friendly character.

Most of the moral dilemmas which face an individual as a result of the growth of organization seem to arise out of their two-sidedness. On the one hand he recognizes those organizations of which he is a potential or actual member as being in some sense an expression of solidarity with and concern for others, and as therefore affected strongly with moral "goodness." On the other hand, he may also be sensitive to the fact that in allying himself with one organization or set of organizations he thereby excludes himself from solidarity and fellowship with those outside.

The dilemma is particularly acute for the Christian. The idea of group solidarity permeates the New Testament. The moral injunctions of the Old Testament tend to be couched in the second person singular—thou shalt not, thou shalt. The teaching of Jesus nearly always seems to be addressed to a group—Blessed are ye; that ye love one another; ye have heard it said. It is true, no doubt, that the "thou" of the Old Testament frequently refers to the collectivity of Israel. But it is in the New Testament that the greatest insight of the Hebrew poets and prophets—that God is not the tribal father of a handful of "children of Israel," but the Lord and Father of all men, indeed of all creation—flowers into the fullest universalism. It is not surprising, therefore, to find that Christian cultures have generally proved favorable to organization, if only because of the immensely high value placed on fellowship. Without some sense of fellowship or community, an organization cannot exist; given that sense of community, it can hardly help existing; once it exists, it can hardly help fostering a sense of fellowship among its members.

Nevertheless the all-inclusiveness of the Christian ideal of fellowship, arising out of the Christian view of God as the Father of *all*, constantly creates a moral dilemma arising out of the two-sided nature of organization outlined above. The Christian cannot rest content with an exclusive fellowship, especially where the exclusion comes from within the fellowship rather than through the will of the "outsider." In a world of mutually exclusive and competing organizations, therefore, the Christian is continually beset by moral dilemmas. On the one hand he is drawn toward identification with organizations and toward giving himself wholeheartedly to their life and activities, as expressions of that fellowship which to him is one of the chief ends of man. On the other hand he is tormented by the fact that the defense of the inner fellowship so often seems to mean the breaking of the wider fellowship; and yet, how do we include the wider fellowship without breaking the inner fellowship?

> He who loves his enemies betrays his friends.
> This surely is not what Jesus intends. . .

writes Blake in *The Everlasting Gospel.* We shall return to this question again.

3. *Other Ethical Dilemmas*

It is not only the divergence between the internal and the external aspects of organizations which gives rise to moral dilemmas. An individual may also be faced with moral problems because of the internal corruption of organizations with which he is vitally concerned. What is the duty of a subordinate executive who finds that his superiors are dishonest? What is the duty of a trade unionist who finds that his union is run by racketeers? What is the duty of a citizen whose town or country is run by corrupt politicians? These are acutely difficult questions to the sensitive individual. If he attempts to answer them by withdrawal from the corrupt organization, does not that leave corruption unchallenged in the seats of power? If he attempts to answer them by plunging into the life of the organization, will he not become himself corrupted?

Here, of course, we face the perpetual dilemma of power—how can goodness take on power without losing its goodness, for power by its nature corrupts the goodness which seeks to use it? This dilemma lies at the back of a good deal of discussion of the ethics of social organization; for if it is true that power corrupts, one of the objects of social organization should be to distribute power widely in society so that nobody has so much that he is corrupted by it!

I am not proposing to write a personal guide through these moral dilemmas. Nevertheless, they lie in the background in all discussions of social policy, and it is in this connection that they are important for this study.

4. The Development of Ethical Criteria

Personal moral dilemmas are, of course, only the raw material of ethical thinking, and there is a basic question of ethical theory which may profitably be considered at this point. This is the question whether the institutions of society are to be judged by the extent to which they contribute to some specified "goal" or goals of history, or are to be judged by their rating on some present scale of moral attributes. This is a fundamental question which is discussed elsewhere in this series of studies, but it is of such importance that brief mention must be made of it here. The view that contribution to some historic goal is the standard by which actions and institutions are to be judged might justly be called the "eschatological" view of morality; it seeks to justify current phenomena by means of some supposed future "ideal" state of things toward which history is bearing us. This is the view essentially which is held by the Communists, and by the many Adventist sects. It is held almost universally in time of war, when society is virtually united in a single aim—to "win the war"—and every activity is judged by the contribution which it makes toward the war effort.

There is no doubt that the simplification of the moral judgment which such a view makes possible resolves many personal dilemmas and leads to a release of human energy. Nevertheless, it is a view which the present writer finds himself obliged to reject, except as a special case of a much more general ethical theory. All the phenomena of human life—actions, personalities, institutions, organizations—can be and are in fact rated on a great many different scales; there is an immense multiplicity of "properties." An organization, for instance, can be rated as large or small, tight or loose, religious or secular, coercive or noncoercive, public or private, economic or noneconomic, democratic or autocratic, and on dozens of other possible scales. Many, if not all, of these scales have a certain degree of ethical polarity; that is to say, an individual will be able to give some sort of answer to the question whether he regards one end (or some segment) of the scale as "better" than the other. Thus we might give an individual a scale which ran "very autocratic, autocratic, mildly autocratic, mildly democratic, democratic, very democratic," and ask him to rate these character-istics as "best, next best," and so on. These answers will not, of course, be the same for all individuals. If individuals from widely differing culture groups are asked such questions, the answers may be widely divergent.

Nevertheless, the divergence among the answers is not so great as to be completely random, and it is by no means absurd to suppose that an empirical "moral function" could be constructed giving at least a statistical approximation, within a definite range of error, to a moral consensus. I am not arguing, of course, that an empirical moral consensus corresponds to any absolute standard of ethical reality. The fact that there is innovation and, we hope, progress in moral ideas means that the empirical consensus will exhibit shifts in the course of history toward, and perhaps away from, some-thing that could be postulated as an absolute standard. The moral judgments which individuals pass, or the moral sentiments which they hold regarding the properties of the phenomena of human life, are, however, an essential part of the total human picture; and as these moral sentiments frequently follow laws of development of their own, they must be regarded in part as causal factors in the weaving of social change.

The social scientist—and perhaps one should add the social philosopher—can make important contributions to the clarification of ethical confusions. These confusions arise because the world of moral evaluation is not a simple one-dimensional scale in which everything can be arrayed on a line with the best things at the top and the worst things at the bottom. Confusions may consist in part of moral inconsistencies on the part of a single individual—who may, for instance, regard A as better than B, B as better than C, and C as better than A. They may also consist of differences in the moral evaluations of different individuals which are not due to any basic disagreement in the underlying scale of values, but to misunderstandings of identities and differences, or a lack of knowl-edge of causes and necessities in the relationships of the many interacting variables of social life.

A great many differences of opinion in ethical matters can be traced not to differences in what we think is good, but to differences in what we think will produce the things which we agree are good. Particularly is this true in matters of social and economic policy where, because of the extreme interdependence of all social variables, actions frequently have results very different from what seem to be the direct consequences. Thus Prohibition creates a problem of bootlegging; an increase in armaments frequently diminishes security from attack; and tariff protection may not ultimately benefit the interests protected. Whatever help social science can give to the understanding of these relationships is also a help to a more coherent set of moral judgments and to the establishment of practical standards which are more nearly in accord with basic moral desires.

2

Causes of the Organizational Revolution

The growth in the size and importance of organizations of almost all kinds in the past few decades constitutes a change in human affairs which has amounted to an "organizational revolution." Before there can even be an attempt at discussing the ethical problems raised by this revolution some answer must be given to the question "Why has it happened?"

No simple or single answer can be given. Nevertheless, the question is not wholly without an answer. It is useful, for instance, to inquire, whenever a new species appears on the scene or an old species expands or contracts, whether the change has taken place on what economists call the "demand side" or on the "supply side." That is to say, is the change a result of the development of new "needs" which the new species satisfies, or is it the result of a change in the ability of the species to satisfy existing needs? According to the ecological point of view presented in the Preface, we have seen that "fitness" to survive really means the ability to "fit," i.e., the ability to occupy some niche in the whole ecological framework. If, then, a new species arises, there must have been either a new "niche" created for it to fit into, or a new ability to fit into existing niches.

Consider, for instance, the case of the rise of new commodities. The immense increase in the output of cigarettes in the past few decades has not been due to any spectacular change in methods of producing cigarettes; it has been mainly the result of certain changes in habits, especially of women. In this case the change has been largely on the side of "demand." As a result of the change in habits and tastes a greatly enlarged "niche" has appeared for cigarettes in the whole social framework, and the quantity of cigarettes and cigarette production has expanded correspondingly to fill the enlarged niche. In the case of television sets, on the other hand, the potential demand was presumably always there. The rise in the number of television sets has been mainly the result of changes on the side of "supply"; i.e., changes in methods of production which have made it possible to produce television sets good enough, and cheap enough, to displace certain other things from an already existing place in the general structure of demand, occupied previously, say, by movies, hobbies, or even social intercourse.

Turning now to the problem of the causes of the growth of organizations, it is clear that again we can ask whether the change has been on the side of demand or of supply. That is to say, has there been a change in the habits and needs of man which has created new niches into which organizations such as the United Mine Workers, the General Motors Corporation, the Farm Bureau, have grown? Or has the change been mainly in the skills of organization itself—a change on the supply side, creating new social forms which have supplanted older forms in the satisfactions of a pre-existing set of needs? There is little doubt that both sets of forces have been in operation. New needs have arisen both as a result of the growth of literacy and self-consciousness, and as a result of the very development of organization itself, for the development of one type of organization frequently creates a need for another organization as an offset. Thus the growth of the large industrial union is not unrelated to the growth of the great corporation. Nevertheless, I shall argue that the most important forces bringing about the rise of large-scale organizations have been in the side of "supply" rather than of "demand," that is, in the skills and technique of organization itself. This proposition is all the more important because it is so often overlooked.

It must not be thought, of course, that the distinction between "demand" and "supply" changes is rigid or even perfectly clear. Species can help to create the niches into which they fit. The increased demand for cigarettes is not wholly spontaneous; a great deal of it has been created by increased skills in advertising on the part of the cigarette companies. Similarly, the demand for labor unions or for farm organizations is not wholly unconnected with increased propaganda skills on the part of these organizations. In spite of a certain fuzziness, however, the distinction is a useful guide to analysis.

1. THE NEEDS THAT ORGANIZATION MAY SATISFY

Let us take up first, then, the meaning of the "demand" for organizations. We do not have to suppose, of course, that all organizations satisfy the same set of human needs. In one sense, indeed, organizations satisfy *all* those human needs that are better satisfied by cooperation of some sort than by individual operations. As Barnard has pointed out so well, even when two men get together to move a stone, something like an organization comes into being. In part, therefore, the growth of organizations must be accounted for by a belief—whether justified or not—that the ordinary ends of human activity are better served by larger than by smaller organizations. The discussion of the optimum size of the organization, however, belongs more properly to the "supply" side of the question, and we will return to it later. On the demand side it should be observed that there are certain needs which are satisfied by organization itself, almost apart from the ostensible purposes of the organization.

Principal among these needs is the need for *status*. The individual has a profound inner need for a "place" in society. In a very real sense an individual person can exist only as part of the larger organization of society, just as an organ or a cell can exist only within the larger organization of the body. This is not to say, of course, that a person "is" an organ in a larger body. The dangers of argument from analogy are real here, and the exact relationship between an individual person and his society is a different kind of relationship from that of an organ to a body. Nevertheless, relationship of some kind there must be. Even Simon Stylites on his pillar must have been part of a larger society which respected hermits and was willing to support them; otherwise he would have perished in a few days or would have been hauled off to a mental institution (or whatever was the ancient substitute).

Organization *formalizes* the status of an individual and hence makes him more secure in it. Individuals have status of some kind, of course, whether they belong to organizations or not. Even the hobo and the drifter have some status, even if it is not a very desirable one. By formalizing an individual's position, however, the status may be both improved and rendered more apparent; *uncertainty* of status is in itself a painful position for an individual to be in. Thus some Negroes make the choice of living in the South, where their status is low but certain and they *know* that they will be badly treated, rather than in the North, where they never know how they are going to be treated.

In the struggle for status, the "job" is of immense importance, especially in American society, where hereditary status is of small importance, where class structures are mobile, and one's status in society is therefore determined to a large extent by the kind of job which one holds. It is not surprising, therefore, that job-centered organizations are of great importance. Both the labor movement and the farm organizations can be regarded as essentially job-centered, even though in the case of the farm organizations it is an occupation rather than a job in the narrow sense of the word that provides the basis for the organization. As we shall see later when we turn to the more detailed study of these organizations, their job-centeredness and their emphasis on status are vitally important in the interpretation of their growth and their behavior.

The rise of the labor movement is closely related to the fact that business enterprises by their very nature cannot provide the worker with adequate status in them. The worker is part of the "market" of the enterprise—economically he is something like a raw material! —and unless he is tied to the enterprise by some sort of peonage he is not a participant in the enterprise in the same sense that management is. That is to say, workers are part of the environment of the enterprise rather than part of the enterprise itself, something like the customers of the enterprise. Their relationship with the enterprise is continually limited by the fact that they can quit at any time and try to get a job in some other enterprise. In this sense the whole system of enterprises forms the environment of the individual worker, but he does not feel himself to be "part" of any of them. This destruction of status as a result of the development of free and active labor markets is probably one of the most important forces underlying the rise of the labor movement.

Similarly, in the case of farm organizations, even though the farmer commands his own enterprise, he likewise feels himself to be at the mercy of a market which he does not control and to which he does not "belong." In addition there is a certain stigma attached to rural people in virtue of their being rural; the connotations which the words "rustic" and "urbane" have in our society are sufficient testimony to the relative status of rural and urban groups. The farm organizations are to an extent the result of a protest—perhaps largely subconscious—against the status of the "hick" and the "rube." They have taken a political form because that was about the only vehicle of protest; the more strictly economic methods of protest which are open to industrial workers are not generally available to farm groups.

If the establishment and improvement of individual status is one of the principal needs which is satisfied by organizations as such, we may profitably raise the question, "To what extent has the growth of organizations been a result of this increased *demand* for status?" There can be little doubt that there has been some increase in this demand, and that this increase is part of the explanation of the rise of organizations.

The demand for status is in part an attribute of self-consciousness. It is likely to increase with a rise in literacy and with a rise in democratic consciousness. In a feudal society the demand for *rising* status may well be latent, perhaps because of the care with which the individual is integrated into the local organization of the manor or the guild. It is in the rise of the market as a dominant instrument in the organization of society, and in the consequent disorganization of the status structure, that we may look for the reasons of a rising demand for status.

Nevertheless, the explanation does not seem to be quantitatively adequate to explain the immense change in the organizational pattern since 1880. In America and in Western Europe the percentage of literacy is not vastly greater today than it was in 1880. People in these countries are no more imbued with democratic or equalitarian ideals than they were in 1880; these ideas were already old by that time, and familiar. It is difficult, therefore, to see any reason why there should have been, after 1880, a large rise in the demand for the kind of values which organization as such can give. Some rise there may have been, with the increasing literacy and self-consciousness of the mass of the people. It is true, of course, that it was in this period that free public education first became virtually universal in the Western countries, and that in some degree this must have led to an increase in self-consciousness and an awareness of lack of status which did not exist before. Free public education does not in any way, however, mark a watershed between a literate and a preliterate society, and it is difficult to believe that the men of 1776 in America, or even of 1649 in England, were unaware of the problem of status. A Bible-reading Protestantism, at least in the English-speaking world, had created a literate society long before the advent of universal public education.

I have emphasized the demand for status not because I regard this as the only, or even the most important, element in the demand for organizations, but because it seems to me most likely to have suffered change. Probably the most important single element in the demand for organizations today as always is for the material benefits which they may bring. I do not see any reason to suppose, however, that there has been much change in human nature in this regard, at least over the past century. In spite of all developments in the psychology of motivation, the economist's crude assumption that people will generally prefer a larger to a smaller dollar value does not seem any less reasonable as a first approximation than it did a hundred years ago. I have not, therefore, stressed this aspect, as it is with change that I have been primarily concerned. Some may argue that there is an increased awareness of the opportunities for gain through organization, and that this factor should be placed on the "demand side." It must be emphasized again, however, that the distinction between demand factors and supply factors is not always clear, and that there are many items in the analysis like the above which might be discussed under both headings.

2. THE "SUPPLY" SIDE

It seems reasonable, therefore, to look for the major part of the explanation of the "organizational revolution" from the side of supply rather than from the side of demand; that is to say, in the improvement of the skills of organization and in the ability of organizations to grow rather than in any *great* increase in the demand for the special needs which organizations as such serve. We need to inquire, therefore, into the factors which govern the growth of organizations, and especially into the factors which limit their size. This latter subject is fortunately the more important, as we probably know more about it than we do about the forces which govern the rates and patterns of growth of organizations. It probably does not matter so much what the exact rate is at which an organization grows if we know something about what makes it stop growing, for it is the things that make it stop growing that ultimately limit its size, and whether it gets to this point in ten or in twenty years is not so important.

1. *The Limiting Factors*

There seem to be two fundamental reasons why things stop growing, which apply to both biological and social organisms. One is that as an organism grows it absorbs more and more of its environment, and eventually it uses up the more favorable parts of its environment, and the environment turns increasingly less favorable.

This is a factor which does not operate much at the level of the biological individual, most of whom operate in environments which are very large in relation to the size of the individual, and hence operate in something resembling the economist's "perfect competition." Even in the biological case, however, the principle of increasingly unfavorable environment operates in the case of the group or population of individuals. Any species as it increases in numbers is apt to reach a point after which further growth makes life harder and harder for the individual member, through exhaustion of the food supply or inadequacy of shelter or some other limitation.

In the case of the social organization, however, the principle of *increasingly unfavorable environment* operates strongly even in the case of the single organization. A new sect, for instance, expands up to a point easily, gathering in all the people who by nature or history are most likely to be attracted toward it; after a point in its growth, however, it meets much more resistance, as it meets not people who are naturally inclined toward its ideas, but people who are organized closely around other doctrines. Similarly a labor union may find it easy to organize those who are in a sympathetic frame of mind; after a point in its growth, however, it reaches out to the less and less convinced, and the task of organization becomes correspondingly harder. A business enterprise opening up a new product finds at first, once it is over the promotional "hump," that the market seems almost unlimited and will take as much as it can produce at almost any price it cares to ask. As it expands production, however, it is certain eventually to run into what economists call "imperfect markets"—a situation in which in order to sell more it must either lower the price or increase the selling cost in order to wean customers away from competing products. Both these methods of increasing sales are costly, and eventually the firm reaches the point where it does not pay to try to expand sales any further against the increasingly unfavorable market environment. Similar imperfections may also exist in buying markets.

The principle of increasingly unfavorable external environment is not, however, the only limiting factor on the growth of organisms. There is also a principle of *increasingly unfavorable internal structure*. As the size of an organization or organism increases, it is impossible to maintain the proportional structure of the organism intact.

In the biological organism the problem arises because a uniform increase in the linear dimensions of an organism increases its surfaces by the square and its volumes by the cube of the linear increase. Thus, doubling the linear dimensions of any object increases all its areas four times and increases all its volumes eight times. Some biological properties (e.g., muscular strength, respiratory capacity, almost any absorptive system whether of food, water, or air) depend mainly on the areas of the tissues involved. Other properties, such as weight, depend mainly on the volumes of the organisms. Consequently, we have the famous proposition that even though a flea can jump over the top of a model of the Capitol scaled down to his size, a flea the size of a man would not be able to jump at all—he would simply break under his own weight. This explains also why the insect has such slender legs, the mouse small legs, the man sturdy legs, the elephant massive legs, and the whale no legs at all. (In order to support his weight the whale would have to have legs larger than his body.) It explains also why insects, which breathe mainly through the skin, cannot develop beyond a size of inches and seem to reach their greatest efficiency at sizes of fractions of an inch; whereas mammals, whose lungs are in effect an immense increase in surface area relative to volume, are able to attain sizes reckoned in feet, or even tens of feet, and seem to operate most efficiently at about the human size. The communications system likewise is an important limiting factor in the case of biological organisms. A one-celled organism cannot be much larger than an amoeba; in order to be bigger, organisms have had to develop specialized communication (nervous) systems and equally specialized nutritional systems, culminating (*pro tem*) in the convoluted brain, bowels, and lungs of man.

When we come to examine social organizations it is evident that the principle of increasingly unfavorable internal structure likewise applies. As an organization increases in size beyond a certain point, it becomes more and more difficult to maintain an adequate system of communication between those people who are directly in contact with the environment of the organization (foremen, salesmen, parish priests, deacons, privates, instructors, local organizers) and those who are in major executive positions. The major executives are of necessity insulated from the direct environment of the organization which they govern by the very nature of their specialization.

The president of a corporation cannot spend much time in the shop; the president of a university finds it difficult to teach even one course; the Pope is effectively insulated from the parish; and the top labor leader or farm leader seldom spends time at the bench or on the farm. An organization which has got too big for its information system may, of course, survive for a time on sheer routine operations. If the information system is inadequate, however, information which is essential for the survival of the organization does not get transmitted to those who are mainly responsible for its policies. Consequently they are not in a position to adapt the policies to changing circumstances, simply because they are not adequately informed as to what these circumstances are.

If the Pope had really known how people felt about the Church at the time of the Reformation, the split might have been avoided. If the framers of national policies knew the consequences of their policies, most wars could be avoided. The largest corporations are not generally the most efficient. The middle-sized countries of an otherwise comparable group seem to do the best job of government. The difficulty of constructing an adequate communications system extends also to the problem of the transmission of executive decisions down the line to the people who actually carry them out. Here again the larger the organization, the longer the lines of communication; and the longer the lines of communication, the more likely are communications to be garbled. The executive of a large organization, therefore, is in double jeopardy. Information coming up the line may be lost or may reach him as misinformation; instructions going down the line may also be lost or may result in misunderstanding.

2. *Technical Changes Extending Limits*

In seeking for causes of the expansion of organizations on the side of technical changes, then, we must look in two directions. We must look first for changes which have pushed back the limitations of the environment; that is, changes which enable an organization to expand farther into its environment without the appearance of increasingly unfavorable environments. Then we must look also for changes which have pushed back the point at which further expansion runs into increasingly unfavorable internal structure— the point of "diminishing returns."

We do not have to look far in the history of the past hundred years to find such changes. We have had in the first place a tremendous revolution in transportation. The railroad network reached approximate completion in the Western countries about 1890. The decade of the 1870s saw the rise of the steamship as the dominant method of ocean travel. Succeeding years have seen the automobile and the airplane make man even more mobile. Similarly the telegraph, the telephone, and the radio have tended toward the abolition of geography in communication as well as in transportation.

The immense reduction in the limitation imposed on man by space is by itself almost enough to account for the growth in the size of organizations. When costs of transport and communication are high, the geographical factor is probably the most important single limitation of the growth of organizations—especially those of a closely knit and integrated character. When transportation is limited to the oxcart, a firm does not have to grow far before it finds itself running into serious limitations of the market as it expands. Even at a small size it can reach all the customers in its immediate neighborhood, and the effort to expand to more remote customers is blocked by the ever-increasing transportation costs. The nationwide firm so characteristic of the present century would have been impossible before the age of the railroad. There are some apparent exceptions to this rule in the presence of large organizations like the Hudson's Bay Company and the East India Company at earlier dates. These cases, however, are all peculiar; they all involve elements of political protection, and they were all relatively free from the competition of other like enterprises. The proposition holds, therefore, that the sheer decline in costs of transportation has served to push back the possible limits of growth.

In a somewhat similar way the improvement in the physical methods of communication has pushed back the point at which organizations run into increasingly unfavorable internal structures. One has only to try to picture the large organization of today, whether it be a corporation, a government, a labor union, or a farm organization, operating without telephones and conducting all its communication through horse-drawn mails to realize the extent to which the telephone has contributed to the growth of organizations. The stereotype of the executive as a man with five telephones on his desk may be a little overdrawn, but it at least attracts attention to the importance of that instrument. One might list also the improvement in the other mechanical aids to the recording, communication, and interpretation of information: the typewriter, the duplicator, the business machine, and finally, of course, the electronic calculator, which may have an impact on the structure of human organization beyond even its own calculation.

3. Expansion Through Structural Changes

It is not only in the mechanical aids, however, that we have seen changes. There have been important changes in the structure of organizations themselves. We have observed in the biological world how a limitation of size can be overcome by the development of new types of structure, like the convoluted lung, bowel, and brain of the mammal. Similarly, in social organizations, when one type of structure reaches its limits of possible expansion, further increase in size can be achieved by new structural forms and new methods of specialization. Thus, as long as the communications system is limited to informal contacts, as in the family, the organization cannot grow beyond the number of people who can maintain informal contacts one with another. The more complex the relationship which is thus maintained, the fewer are the number of people who can be organized. This fact undoubtedly accounts for the stability of the family as a household unit through almost all human history.

It is a form of organization which runs into diminishing returns rapidly as it expands in number, both on the side of the market—for in a society which contains the sexes in about equal numbers, polygamy can be achieved by one man only at the cost of celibacy on the part of others—and also on the side of the internal structure, because of the extreme difficulty in maintaining the kind of communication which effective family living requires among large numbers of people. Similarly the "family business," while it can grow beyond the limits of family size because of the relative simplicity of economic by comparison with family relationships, is strictly limited in its growth by the difficulties of maintaining effective personal contacts between the "boss" and his "big happy family." Increasing size is possible only at the cost of increasing complexity of structure. Organizational inventions, however, which permit the development of more complex structures without at the same time breaking down the efficiency of communication, push back the point at which this complexity becomes a limiting factor on size.

The "invention" of the professional, specialized organizer is probably one of the most important developments in the structure of organization relating to the growth of size. The church, of course, has always employed such professional organizers (missionaries), and it may be that an important element in the growth of Christianity was the "invention" of the missionary. The "walking delegate" or professional organizer in the labor movement and the county agent in farm organizations have played much the same kind of role as the missionary in the church. The salesman performs much the same function for the business enterprise.

"Selling" activity, whether in the form of missions, organization drives, or simple commercial advertising, represents activity devoted directly to an expansion into the environment—i.e., pushing back the point at which the environment becomes harder to expand into. The past seventy or eighty years have seen a marked advance in the skills of salesmanship, not merely in commercial life, but also in the church, in the labor movement, and in almost all the other organizations of social life. Indeed, as David Riesman has pointed out,[1] salesmanship has likewise invaded the individual personality. The characteristically "inner-directed" person of an earlier day, who

[1] David Riesman, *The Lonely Crowd; a Study of the Changing American Character*, New Haven, Connecticut, Yale University Press, 1950.

was content to go on producing the immutable product of his personality without any thought of "selling himself" or of adjusting himself to different environments, has given way to a great extent to the "other-directed" person, who is acutely aware of the problem of "selling himself," who is all things to all men, whose personality depends largely on the group around him, and who devotes so much attention to playing roles that his inner life dries up and he becomes almost pure actor who cannot "be himself" because he doesn't have any "self" to "be."

The kind of product diversification which characterizes the "other-directed" personality is characteristic of all expansion of the individual organization by a selling effort. When the market becomes saturated with one product, whether it be a commodity, a form of religion, an idea, or anything else which an organization has to offer, a natural way of expanding the organization is by developing a new product the market for which is not saturated.

The Church of England is a remarkable example of an organization in the religious sphere which has carried the art of diversification of the product to an extraordinary extent, offering on the one hand in Anglo-Catholicism a form of religion almost identical with that of Roman Catholicism, and on the other ultra-Protestant forms culminating in the Church Army, which is a conscious imitation of the Salvation Army.

Canada is a good example of a country which has maintained its unity by diversifying its product. What Canada means to the French Canadians is a different thing from what it means to the English-speaking Canadians. The fact that they are able to sing together a national anthem in which the French words carry a wholly contrary meaning to the English words is a striking testimony to the value of diversified and separated markets in establishing the unity of a large organization. Diversification, however, carries with it a serious penalty—the loss of internal homogeneity and unity. If the heterogeneity is serious enough there may be a split in the organization, or at least a serious danger of splitting. The American Civil War is a good example of the difficulties into which a large federal union runs when it is too heterogeneous, economically and culturally, especially when it has elements in it which object to the diversification of its product.

One can perceive, then, in the history of almost all organizations, a certain tension between two opposite forces: the desire for "purity" —that is, the desire to keep the organization homogeneous, without any admixture of strange or alien elements—and the desire for growth, which can so often be achieved only at the expense of purity, i.e., by diversification.

The dilemma is not, of course, as simple or as straightforward as the above statement might indicate. The growth of an organization depends on the strength of its own inner life, which in turn depends on its ability to meet the needs of those who compose it and those whom it serves. A return to greater purity, by ridding the organization of internal tensions which have absorbed a great deal of energy and have therefore rendered the organization fairly inactive in the external environment, can sometimes be the signal for a new period of rapid growth. Diversification may defeat itself, if the addition of new products in some sense lowers the quality of the old, or if the markets for the various products are not adequately separated so that a good deal of energy which seems to be devoted to promoting a new product actually results in cutting down the market for the old. Ethical considerations are of great importance here, as the tension between purity and diversification generally has strong ethical connotation; "purity" is frequently regarded as a good in itself and diversification as an adulteration of the "good old ways." The tension frequently manifests itself also as a struggle between the "conservative" elements, who generally favor purity, and the "progressive" elements who are more interested in expansion.

4. The Dynamic Effect of Growth

A feature of the life of organizations which also plays an important role in determining growth, or at least the pressure for growth, is the positive value which is placed in much of Western culture on growth itself. The internal morale of the organization itself may depend to a considerable extent on its ability to maintain a rapid rate of growth; people are attracted to the organization and are willing to serve its ends *because* it is a growing concern. This essentially dynamic character of many organizations may create serious problems when the organization has grown up to what may be its "natural" limit in respect to the place which it occupies in the total system. A dynamic organization is a different *kind* of organization from a static organization (one that is not growing), both in structure and in spirit. Consequently, a cessation of growth, which may be perfectly natural, may create a severe crisis of morale in the organization. This crisis may either undermine the organization altogether and cause it to decline and eventually disappear; or it may cause the directors of the organization to attempt to advance at all costs, often with the result of disaster; or it may cause a radical change in the whole outlook and composition of the organization as it adjusts itself successfully to a static situation. Thus, it is an important part of the folklore of business that a business cannot stand still—it must either be advancing or it will decline.

The dynamic character of a good many political movements has brought disaster both on them and on the world around them. National Socialism, in Germany, for instance, was essentially dynamic in this sense that it could not "stop." The morale of the movement was essentially bound up with "going somewhere" and, when the easy victories were over and it began to run into the iron law of eventually increasing unfavorableness of the environment, it had to press on to ultimate disaster. International communism seems to be a movement of like character. On the other hand, some movements and organizations succeed in adapting themselves to a more or less static condition at the end of the period of rapid growth. Such adaptation, however, is universally obtained at the cost of great transformations in the nature of the organization itself.

Every "movement," whether in religion, in economic life, or in politics, starts as an essentially dynamic organization. When the period of growth is over, it either collapses or it becomes a "sect," cherishing a quiet and sober inner life on the memories of the saints and prophets of more violent and dynamic days. This frequently happens to religious movements; it happens also to labor organizations. It can even happen to political movements, like the Prohibition movement.

5. Other Factors

A further point in the theory of growth—the importance of which, however, is not easy to assess—is the proposition that growth is frequently the result of an attempt to correct disproportionalities. A family that moves into a big, empty house is likely to make some special effort to fill it with furniture or even with children. The existence of an underutilized part of any organization is a constant provocation to expansion. If the components of an organization are not easily divisible into small units, the attempt to correct disproportionality may result in a constant pressure to expand, as the correction of an underemployed component by adding another unit may create a lack of proportion elsewhere. The familiar story of the man who had to take some more meat to finish his mustard and then some more mustard to finish his meat is apt to be repeated in the history of most organizations, and the more complex the structure, the more likely is this factor to be important.

One final word of caution should be added regarding the *measure* of the size of organizations. Mere numbers of members may be a misleading measure of significant size. The nutrition of organizations is human time and energy, and it is the amount of human time and energy which is devoted to an organization, not its membership roll, which is the most significant measure of its importance in the over-all human economy. We can think of the total amount of human time and energy available as a strictly limited, though not an absolutely fixed, quantity. Human energy can be released, for instance, by the demands of emergencies, but normally human time and energy which are devoted to one use must be withdrawn from others. An organization expands in this time-and-energy field, and as it absorbs time and energy into itself it must be either withdrawing time and energy from other organizations (including the family) or it must be withdrawing it from purely individual uses such as sleep and contemplation.

Thus we visualize the growth of organization in this setting: Has it meant simply that instead of being devoted to a large number of small organizations (families, small firms), human energy is now being devoted to a smaller number of larger organizations (labor unions, corporations)? This seems to have happened to some extent. It may also be, however, that some time and energy which formerly were devoted to individual pursuits now are absorbed by organizations of all kinds. There may be a real "cost" of the rise of organization in the decline of purely individual uses of time. In our evaluation of the rise of organization this factor must not be overlooked, and our evaluation will depend somewhat on how we value these individual pursuits. "What is this life, if full of care, We have no time to stand and stare" may be a valid criticism of an overorganized and overbusy age.

Nevertheless, the power of organization to release new sources of energy, and also, especially, to increase the productivity of the time and energy that are applied through them, is probably an even more important element in the total picture. We shall discuss this topic in the next chapter. It should be observed at this point, however, that, because of the increased productivity of time and energy when applied through organizations, the rise of organizations up to a point does not necessarily mean a reduction in time given to individual uses; it may actually so increase the efficiency of those economically necessary uses of time that more time may be available for individual uses. Thus, the rise of organization has also, paradoxically enough, gone hand in hand with an increase in leisure probably unprecedented in human history. Some of this leisure has provided an opportunity for the expansion of the voluntary and free-time organizations—clubs, lodges, and the like. Some of it has also been available for individual pursuits which were not possible in a day when the working day was a grueling twelve hours that left room for little but meals and an exhausted sleep.

3

Economic Effects of the Growth of Organizations

The economic effects of the increase in the number, size, and power of organizations can be discussed under three main headings: the effect on productivity, the effect on the nature and organization of the market, and the effect on the movements of inflation and deflation.

1. EFFECT ON PRODUCTIVITY

The first of these may be dealt with briefly. As one of the main motives leading men to form organizations is the belief that in so doing they can increase their per capita productivity, it would be surprising, indeed, if we did not find an increase in productivity as a frequent result of the formation of organizations. We form organizations, that is to say, because we believe that there are things which can be done in an organized way better than they can be done individually.

There seem to be two reasons why organization should increase productivity. In the first place it increases the size of the "body"; i.e., it creates "giants" who can do things that puny man by himself cannot do. When three men come together to move a big stone they are in effect, for the purposes of this operation, acting as one man with the strength of three; they have created a temporary giant. Permanent organizations are permanent giants—or at least semi-permanent; these giants throw bridges across rivers, pick up men and goods and carry them all over the world with seven-leagued boots, erect skyscrapers, and even achieve knowledge which no single individual could possibly do. The second reason why organization increases productivity is that it permits and encourages

33

specialization. This is the familiar principle of the division of labor classically expounded by Adam Smith—that by concentrating on a single task an individual can become much more productive at that task than he could be if he were a jack-of-all-trades, and that he is likely to become not only manually skilled but also inventive. Thus by concentration at the single task a constant movement for improvement is generated, either by dexterity or by the invention of new tools and instruments.

There is an important distinction, however, between the kind of specialization which is achieved through the existence of a market and the kind of specialization which is achieved through organization. It is possible to envisage a system of specialized occupations in which there is very little organization: in which every man works for himself at his own trade and exchanges the products of his work for the products of the work of others. The specialization in this case is made possible not by the existence of any large over-all organization but by the possibility of exchange—especially, of course, exchange through the intermediary of money. Up to a point a market is a *substitute* for organization, in that it permits a society to develop the advantages of specialization without *conscious* coordination.

A good deal of the debate between socialism and capitalism is in fact a debate over the merits of conscious over against unconscious coordination of specialists. Within organizations the coordination is conscious; in a free market economy the coordination of the activities of the various organizations is unconscious, though none the less real, just as the coordination of species in a biological ecosystem is none the less real for being unconscious.

Expressed in these terms it is clear that one of the main points at issue in the debate is that of the best *size* of the organization. In the centrally planned economy there is in theory only a single firm, and the specialization of its innumerable parts is consciously coordinated by a political process. This single firm must of necessity be large; in a socialist state it becomes brontosaurian in its dimensions, far exceeding in size even the largest corporations of the capitalist world. The best defense of the market economy lies in its ability to coordinate organizations of smaller size—and therefore more efficient—into an "ecosystem" which is not centrally integrated. Even in the capitalist world, however, in many cases the firm has grown to the point where it becomes an essentially collectivist type of enterprise, and where it runs into many of these internal problems of the conscious coordination of large numbers of specialists which prove so intractable for the socialist state. In income produced General Motors is almost as large an organization as Yugoslavia!

It is possible, therefore, for organization to be carried to the point where it diminishes rather than increases productivity because of the "brontosaurus principle"—i.e., the disadvantages of scale. This is likely to happen in societies which have a prejudice against the market as an institution. It may happen even in societies which accept the market, because of some of the other causes of growth in size which we have noted in the previous chapter. There is also another reason why an increase in organization does not always lead to an increase in over-all productivity. Even though it is true that an organization generally arises because people feel that they can produce more efficiently together than apart, the impact on the over-all productivity of society depends on what the organization is designed to produce. Thus the more perfect organization of thieves may increase the efficiency of thieving, but it can hardly be said to improve the over-all performance of a society. There is a tendency for many organizations to become parasitic upon the society that supports them. This is particularly true of organizations which rely on the coercive power (that is, on their ability to injure others) for their defense. An improvement in the efficiency of these organizations can well lead to a general decline in productivity of the society at large.

In the Western world the organizational revolution has gone hand in hand with a rapid rise in the over-all productivity of the society—a rise which was going on before the great growth of organizations, but which does not seem to have been abated by them. It is thus difficult to assess the total impact of the growth of organizations on the rate of increase of productivity (which may be roughly identified with the rate of economic progress). It seems probable that the rise of the large corporate business enterprise has had a favorable influence on the rate of progress through its ability to subsidize organized research. Some of the most rapid rates of increase in productivity have taken place in those industries which are characterized by rather large firms. Nevertheless, the case is by no means clear.

There have also been rapid rises in productivity in agriculture, some of which may perhaps be attributed to the large agricultural implement companies and the state colleges, but much of which has been due to the work of quite small organizations (hybrid corn is a good example). It is likewise difficult to assess the impact of the rise of the labor movement on economic progress. On the debit side is the restrictionism which characterizes certain parts of the labor movement, as expressed in make-work rules, featherbedding, over-strict seniority provisions, closed shops with restricted entry into the union, and so on. On the other hand, the pressure of the labor movement for the extension of free public education has been an important factor in raising the general productivity of the society; also, by discouraging employers from working out their problems in terms of lower money wages unions may have forced them into giving attention to increased productivity. The farm organizations as such have probably had a considerable impact in spreading the knowledge of improved methods among farm groups, even though their main activity has not been centered in that direction.

2. Effect on Structure of the Market

We are on more certain ground when we come to consider the impact of the rise of organization on the structure of the market, that is, on its monopolistic or competitive character. The economist distinguishes a number of different "states of the market" which approximate the conditions found in various parts of the economy. Where the internal forces which limit the size of a firm come into play, even when the firm is small, it will stop growing long before it runs into increasing difficulties in its market environment. For a small firm in a big market, that is to say, there are no obstacles to an increase in sales at the market price; for all practical purposes the firm can sell as much or as little as it wishes in the unlimited market without either taking a lower price or incurring selling cost. This is a condition characteristic of what the economist calls "perfect competition." It is still the situation in which most individual farmers, most small sellers or buyers on the stock exchange or the commodity markets, and a few businesses producing highly standardized products find themselves. It would perhaps be more accurate to call this situation the "unlimited market." At the other extreme lies the situation in which the individual firm is large enough in relation to the total markets for either the things it buys or the things it sells so that it cannot expand its sales without incurring some "cost," either in the shape of increased selling cost or in the shape of a reduction in price. This condition can properly be called the "limited market."

The technical improvements in methods of organization noted in the previous chapter have the effect of pushing back the internal limitations on growth and hence they are likely to result in an increase in size to the point where growth is halted by a limited market. We could reasonably expect, therefore, the growth of organization to result in an increase in limited relative to unlimited markets. It must not be thought, of course, that only large organizations involving hundreds or thousands of people have limited markets. The limitation is relative to the size of the available market. The small-town barber working on his own or employing a handful of men may have just as limited a market as the giant corporation which operates on a nationwide basis. Whether absolute numbers run in tens or tens of thousands, however, the principle still holds that a removal of internal limitations is likely to result in an increase in market limitations.

A form of market limitation which is of great interest and importance, and which also seems likely to grow with the diminution in the internal limitations on size, is that known as "oligopoly." This is the situation in which only a few competitors are producing a homogeneous product; that is, the product of each firm is identical in the mind of the buyer, so that he is swayed only by consideration of price. In this situation an individual firm lowering its prices will find that its market is practically unlimited as long as other firms do not change their prices; but that if other firms (as they almost certainly will) change their prices to match any change in the original firm's price, the original firm will find its market as sharply limited as before. We thus find that oligopoly is characterized by "cutthroat" competition, where it is not stabilized by outright collusive agreement or by some sort of tacit "gentlemen's agreement." Action to expand sales on the part of any one firm in an oligopolistic situation, whether by a cut in its price below that of its competitors or by an increase in sales effort, is not likely to be passed unnoticed by the other firms, who will find their sales cut noticeably by the aggressive tactics of the first. The other firms are likely to reply in kind, in which case there may be some general expansion in the total sales of all the firms involved; but the expansion in the sales of the initiator of the "aggression" will be much less than it was initially before the retaliation took place.

The principles of the theory of oligopoly, though they have been worked out mainly in the field of pricing theory, are in fact fairly general and apply to most cases where a *few* organizations are competing in a limited environment. Such a condition is characterized by "intense" competition, in the sense that the one organization can expand only at the expense of others and any attempt on the part of one to expand is observed by others and usually calls forth some kind of retaliatory action. If, on the other hand, there is a large number of organizations operating in a fairly homogeneous environment, the expansion of one, even though it may in fact be at the expense of all the others, may affect any one of the other organizations only slightly, so that they do not feel particularly injured or insecure.

It is clear that the growth of organizations increases the danger of oligopoly in almost all fields. Probably the most serious aspect of this problem is the growth of the national state to the point where to all intents and purposes there are only two centers of independent political power left in the world. The extreme instability and insecurity of this situation, compared even with that of the nineteenth century, when there were at least six or seven independent centers of political power and hence the competition of arms was at least moderately diffuse, are all too apparent.

The growth of organizational size naturally raises the question of monopoly. We have seen that the diminution of internal limitations of growth is likely to lead to the increase in imperfect markets, which are one of the signs of monopoly. Nevertheless, it is not so easy to answer the question whether the growth of organization has created a monopoly "problem." The most significant feature of a monopolistic organization is an absence of substitutes for its product. An organization in such a position may be able to exploit its customers by limiting its output and so being in a position to raise its price above that which would give it what might be considered a "normal" return. The impact of monopoly, then, is two-fold: it distorts the structure of production, in that less of the monopolized product and more of other products are produced than might be thought desirable; and it also distorts the structure of income, in that the monopolist is enabled to exact a greater income from society in return for its product than is strictly necessary.

Unfortunately, once we leave the delightful simplicities of static equilibrium neither the concept nor the appraisal of monopoly retains its clarity, as the remarkable intellectual confusion which surrounds the antitrust laws demonstrates. It seems probable that some degree of *immobility* of resources is necessary in society if technical progress is to be made; otherwise the profits of innovation will be immediately eroded away by a rush of imitators, and the incentives to innovation will be much reduced. The patent law is in fact an attempt to introduce into society an element of immobility of resources (i.e., of monopoly) which would not otherwise exist, presumably in the interest of protecting the innovator. Whether the present arrangements are in fact the best possible is a point which I shall not argue here.

It cannot be denied, however, that there is a real problem in society of attaining the "optimum" degree of monopoly in it which will give an adequate incentive to innovation. We cannot, therefore, adopt any simple criterion and say that anything which increases the degree of monopoly is by that very fact evil. Nor can we turn around and say that there is no problem. In many holes and corners of the economy genuinely monopolistic exploitation exists. Unless this exploitation is supported by the coercive power of the state, however, it is apt to be unstable. A purely private monopoly which is making abnormally high gains is a standing invitation to the rest of the world to find substitutes for its product, and in a dynamic economy it is likely that substitutes will soon be found.

To take but a single example—Formosa has a virtual monopoly of natural camphor, a substance with many important industrial uses in the chemical and film industries. Not unnaturally, the Japanese when in control of Formosa monopolized the export of natural camphor and for some years were able to make substantial monopolistic gains as a result. The high price of natural camphor, however, stimulated chemists to find a synthetic process, which they eventually did, thus completely undermining the original monopoly. Most commodities in the complex society of today have many near-substitutes which act as an important check on some apparent monopolies. Thus aluminum, which until the recent antitrust decision was almost all produced in the United States by a single producer, nevertheless had close substitutes in almost all its fields of use. It is doubtful whether the Aluminum Company of America ever had much effective monopoly power, unless perhaps in its early stages; as it expanded the use of aluminum into a large number of uses by successive reductions in price, the competition of wood, steel, copper, plastics, and so on became increasingly important.

Furthermore, the threat of potential competition is an important factor in preventing monopolists from exploiting to the full the immediate possibilities of monopoly gain. It can almost be said that the general principle of monopoly pricing is not to set the price at that which will maximize present net returns, but at the level which is just below what will tempt a potential competitor to enter the field. Indeed, as the alternative to monopoly is never perfect competition but some form of oligopoly, a situation which we have seen is disagreeable and unstable to the participants, monopolists may be moderate in their price policy, preferring a low price and a low return to the constant fear of turning a relatively stable monopolistic situation into an unstable oligopolistic one. We thus find the odd situation of antitrust proceedings attempting to raise the price of a commodity in order to permit less efficient competitors to enter the field.

Turning now to the results of organization in the labor market we find much the same story. There is no doubt that in some places and at some times labor unions have exercised monopoly power either for the benefit of their members or, in the case of the racketeering unions, their officers. Taking the labor movement as a whole, however, the degree of monopoly power which it has exhibited over its history, and which it exhibits today, is not large. A labor union can achieve monopoly power only if it can control the number of people seeking employment in its particular occupation and can control also the more immediate substitutes for its form of labor. It may attempt to do this by restriction of entry into the occupation, either through onerous apprenticeship rules or through various restrictions on entry into the union by high membership fees, by racial, religious, national, or sex discrimination in its qualifications for admission, or by direct refusal to accept members beyond a certain quota. Such restrictions, however, have never been of much quantitative importance in the American economy and have furthermore been declining. The courageous (and often costly) insistence within the C.I.O. on racial equality, for instance, has been followed by a progressive elimination of racial restrictions even in the more conservative craft unions.

Restriction of entry into the union, however, will not give monopoly power unless the union has control of the available jobs in its particular trade. As a matter of fact, if the control of jobs is complete enough the union does not have to worry about restriction of membership—it can rely on the employer to do that. In the extreme case of the closed shop, therefore, it cannot be denied that the union has a degree of monopoly power and that it can extract from society, via the employer (or, if the employer himself has previously been exploiting a monopoly situation in his product, from the employer himself), a wage which represents a monopoly gain. Such cases, however, are rare. They are made difficult to maintain, first, by the enormous spread of the geographical market, which subjects firms to nonunion competition from other areas and which sometimes gives them an opportunity to skip to less heavily unionized areas (printing and boots and shoes are good examples). In the second place, again the dynamic nature of our society makes it difficult to establish craft monopolies, for they are always being undermined by new products and new industrial processes. In this as in other fields the exercise of monopoly power may act as a strong incentive to technical change designed to provide substitutes for the monopolized product. Thus the strong unionization in the coal industry may well have stimulated the growth of oil and natural gas substitutes, though these effects are uncertain and difficult to trace.

In the field of agricultural organization there are few cases of the attainment or exercise of monopoly power, mainly because of the geographically diffuse character of most agricultural production. There are some examples of attempts to exercise monopoly power in milk production through the formation of cooperatives; these, however, have proved to be quite unstable. Probably the most successful agricultural monopoly has been that of the lemon growers, where by reason of the limited area suitable for cultivation of the crop and the specialized and nonsubstitutable nature of the product the growers have been able, through the agency of their cooperative, to exercise an appreciable degree of monopoly power. In the whole agricultural picture, however, the use of organization to obtain private monopoly has been unsuccessful, for much the same reasons that make monopoly everywhere difficult to sustain in a dynamic society.

The political effects of the farm movement are another story again. Unlike the labor movement, the farm movement has directed most of its energies not to the private control of its markets but to their public regulation. We shall examine the consequences of agricultural legislation in a later chapter; it will suffice to remind the reader here that its main objective has been the establishment of "parity" prices for agricultural products through a program of export dumping, restriction of output, government purchase of surplus products, and discriminatory pricing. Apart from the direct subsidy aspects, agricultural policy in itself has not had a great impact on agricultural prices, which have been affected much more by the general inflationary movement of the past twenty years than by any policy specifically directed at them. Nevertheless the existence of a strong agricultural pressure group poses problems of some magnitude for the future of the economy.

3. Effect on Distribution of Income

The question of the impact of the growth of economic organizations on the distribution of income is fairly closely related to the problem of their monopoly power, and, just as the evidence is inconclusive in regard to monopoly, so it is inconclusive in regard to their effects on the distribution of income. This conclusion may come as a surprise to some readers, for much of the literature on the subject, especially that put out by economic organizations themselves, suggests that they have had an important impact on the distribution of income, say toward wages or toward farmers. All the available evidence, however, both in the form of the over-all figures of the economy and in the form of special studies, indicates that the effect both of labor organizations and of farm organizations on the general distribution of income has been small.

The proportion of national income going to labor, for instance, according to the figures published by the Department of Commerce (see Appendix), shows little trend since the figures were first published in 1929. It rises during the great depression, as a result of the disappearance of profit from the national income, and has been falling for the most part since 1932, in spite of the fivefold increase in the number of trade unionists. Special studies of union and non-union wages (Appendix) also show little evidence of any striking impact of unionism on the trend of real wages. Unionized wages tend to stay up in depression when nonunion wages fall, but in a period of inflation the nonunion wages rise much faster than the union wages and generally catch up with their long-term trend. Comparisons of union with nonunion wages are not enough to give a definitive answer to the question of the impact of unions on wages, for it can always be argued that nonunion wages rise for fear of union-wage competition or to stave off unions. Whatever the direction of the effect, however, there is no evidence whatever that the effect is large.

The proportion of national income going to farmers likewise has not shown any striking changes—the rise in farm income has come mainly from the rise in the total national income.

The main changes in the distribution of income come from two sources—taxation and inflation. Both of these are only indirectly related to the rise of organizational power, though the relationship may be by no means negligible.

There is undoubtedly some relationship between the rise of progressive income and inheritance taxation and the rise of the labor movement. It is probably more accurate, however, to regard them both as aspects of a more deep-lying social phenomenon than to assume much direct causal connection. For instance, it was not on labor votes alone that the progressive tax system was adopted.

Similarly, there is some connection between the inflationary movement of our time and the rise of organizations. Inflation and deflation have probably been the most potent factors affecting the distribution of income between broad classes of receivers. Thus we have already noted that the deflation of 1929-32 materially increased the proportion of national income going to wages and to interest and practically wiped out profit. The inflationary movement since 1932 has had a pronounced impact on income from interest, reducing it from 13 per cent of the national income to about 3 per cent. This has happened both because interest is a fixed sum in dollars and does not share in the rise in dollar values of the national income, and also because the shift to other forms of income has facilitated a substantial repayment of debt. Most of what has been taken away from the bondholder seems to have gone into profits rather than into wages; we have witnessed a rather drastic redistribution of income among capitalists, but not much redistribution as between capitalists and labor groups.

Neither the deflation nor the inflation has been the result of direct pressures on the part of the organized economic groups. The deflation of 1929-32 was part of the complex cyclical movement of the economy combined with a pronounced breakdown of the banking system. The inflationary movement from 1932 to the present (1952) has been largely a matter of the methods of war finance. Roughly speaking, if the war had been financed more by taxes and less by borrowing, especially borrowing from the banks, there would have been less inflation.

Nevertheless, one of the most interesting and important questions relating to the economic effects of the rise of economic organization is whether it introduces a long-run inflationary bias into the economy. The rise of organization has not had any large effect either on long-run monopoly power or on long-run trends in distribution. Where it has had a most profound effect is on the *flexibility of prices.* To some extent this is an inevitable result of the development of more imperfect and limited markets. An organization faced with an approximately perfect or unlimited market for its product will always find that lowering the price of its product will have a large effect on its sales. The more imperfect the market, the less will be the effect of a fall (or a rise) in the price of the product on sales. Consequently any price-quoting organization, faced with a decline in sales, is less likely to follow the policy of price reduction if its market is more limited. The alternative to price reduction in such a case is either expansion in selling cost or a cutback in output of the product, both of which are apt to be socially wasteful. The fact that the alternative to price reduction is frequently output reduction is what makes price inflexibility such a serious matter for the economy, for it means that under these circumstances a general deflation takes the form of a reduction in output, real income, and employment rather than a reduction of the general price-wage level.

4. Some Principles of Employment Theory

The point is of such fundamental importance, especially when it comes to assessing the value of organization, that it may be profitable to digress at this point to acquaint the reader who is not familiar with the modern theory of employment with some of its basic principles.[2]

First, for the purpose of this exposition, we will regard "output" and "employment" as virtually equivalent. That is to say, we are assuming the average output per man-hour to be constant, so that any increase in employment results in a proportional increase in output. Over short periods this assumption is not too far from the truth. The next step is to perceive a simple but basic identity: the identity between total output in any period and the sum of the amounts consumed or accumulated. Of the total production of a given period, anything that has not been consumed (removed from the economy in some way) must be still around in the possession of some persons or organizations within the economy.

The next step is the proposition that the total amount of product actually accumulated (added to stocks) during a period may be more than the holders of this stock of goods wish to take. The stock cannot, in a closed society, be disposed of by selling it; and buying and selling merely circulate an existing stock among various owners. The attempt on the part of the holders of the stock to dispose of it may result in a sharp fall in prices. If wages are flexible (as in agriculture) the fall in prices is almost certain to produce a similar decline in money wages. There is in consequence a rise in the real purchasing power of bondholders, pensioners, and others with incomes fixed in terms of money and a corresponding decline in the real purchasing power of other elements in the society, especially the profit makers. A generally falling price-wage structure always affects profit makers adversely, as profits are made by buying at one time and selling at a higher price later; if all prices have fallen in the interim the chance of selling at a higher price than one bought

[2] The reader who is familiar with this theory may wish to skip the rest of this chapter.

is correspondingly diminished. If the fixed-income people are high dissavers (consume more than they produce), and if the profit receivers are high savers (produce more than they consume), as is frequently the case, this shift in income distribution will increase the consumption from a given income. The result may be, if the changes work out in a compensating manner, that the decline in accumulation is counteracted by an increase in consumption, and no decline in output, and therefore no decline in employment, need follow. This is the essence of the "classical" solution to the problem of underemployment through price-wage flexibility.

There are two weaknesses to this solution. One is the practical one that there is no way of achieving price flexibility short of a drastic revolution in our forms of economic organization; indeed, it is difficult to see any set of institutions which would give us the contemplated degree of price-wage flexibility. The second weakness is that a system of the required degree of flexibility would be unstable in itself. A deflationary movement would be likely to go a long way before it was reversed, and similarly an inflationary movement, because of the effect of both deflation and inflation on expectations of further price movements in the same direction. This is a phenomenon sometimes called the principle of self-justified expectations. If everyone expects prices to fall, everyone will try to get rid of commodities and hold more money, as money will be rising in value, and the result of this attempt is to create the fall in prices which was anticipated. Similarly, an expected rise causes people to try to get rid of money and buy goods; this is sufficient to cause the expected rise. In a flexible price system, therefore, we should expect to find large and rather meaningless fluctuations in the absolute level of prices and wages, because of the inherent instability of the price level itself.

If, on the other hand, prices are inflexible, a situation in which accumulation is proceeding at too rapid a rate for people to "take" gives rise to a decrease in production and a rise in unemployment. Individuals cannot get rid of their individual excessive stocks by cutting prices; they try to get rid of them, therefore, by cutting output. A fall in output, however, is practically the same thing as a decline in income, and this fall in income causes a further fall in consumption. People may still find, then, that they are accumulating goods at too fast a rate, because although production has dropped, consumption has also dropped; so there may be further cutbacks in production, causing yet another decline in consumption. This attempt to narrow the gap between production and consumption, and so cut down the rate of accumulation, may go on until a large proportion of the resources of the society are unemployed.

The influence of price inflexibility can be expressed in yet another way. The money value of the national income is equal to the total output, multiplied by the price level of that output. If the output is, say 100 billion "bushels," and the price level is $2 a bushel, the national money income will be 200 billion dollars. Suppose now that because of various forces in the monetary system the national money income falls to 150 billion dollars. This can be accomplished either by retaining the output at 100 billion bushels with a price level of $1.50 per bushel or by cutting output to 75 billion bushels at the old price of $2, or of course by any other combination of price and output which multiplies out to 150 billion.

What this means, then, is that if the price-wage level is inflexible, a deflationary situation will work itself out not in lowered money prices and money wages but in reduced output and employment. In such a situation, therefore, if we wish to avoid unemployment we cannot afford to have a deflation. If, however, we cannot have a deflation we can never correct an inflation; by that very fact we have introduced a long-run inflationary bias into a full-employment system.

There are other reasons, also, for supposing that an economy which is highly organized will find itself with pressures toward inflation. Psychologically a highly organized economy gets along better in a slightly inflationary situation.

This is particularly apparent in the labor movement; labor leaders are expected to bring home "gains" from every collective bargaining conference. If the general level of money wages and prices is rising, it is easy to do this. The bargainers can come home with the gains which would have happened even without collective bargaining, but their followers are none the wiser. The gain in money wages is something which the union "gets"; the rise in the cost of living which accompanies it is something which "happens," but for which the union does not get the blame. On the other hand, during a period of deflation a cut in money wages is something for which the union (or the employer) gets blamed, while the fall in the cost of living merely "happens"—and is something for which neither union leader nor employer gets any credit. It is little wonder that times of deflation are times of acute industrial unrest, while times of inflation are relatively easy both for the union and for the personnel management. Similarly, farm organizations can take credit for the improvement in the farmers' lot which inflation generally brings and take little blame for the impoverishment which follows from deflation.

It is no wonder that there is little effective opposition to inflation in our society; the people who are really hurt by it—the widows and orphans, the pensioners, and the retired—are unorganized, unpublicized, unheard, and uncared for.

It must not be supposed, of course, that the rise of organizations *necessitates* a long-run inflation. I am merely arguing that it creates a certain predisposition toward inflation which does not exist in a less organized society. On the other hand, the increasing efficiency of the tax system which is a striking feature of our times is also an aspect of the "organizational revolution" and constitutes an important weapon *against* inflation which governments of an earlier day, when pressed by unusual expenditures, did not possess. It is by no means impossible that ways may be found either to prevent long-run inflation or to live with it. It is, however, one of the problems posed by the organizational revolution which has not been given adequate attention.

4

Political and Psychological Effects
of the Organizational Revolution

It has been my main thesis that the organizational revolution of our time has been in the main the result of certain technical changes in the ability to organize: changes both on the physical side in the improvement of transportation and communication, and on the structural side in the forms and skills of organization itself. These changes have resulted in a lessening of the *internal* resistances to the growth of organizations, and therefore organizations have grown until the *external* resistances have become more important. The political theorist might feel, with some justification, that this whole revolution is essentially a political one, insofar as "politics" is the art of living together in organizations and of using organizations to accomplish the purposes of mankind. It has certainly resulted in a great "politicizing" of human life.

One can almost describe the history of the present era as a continuous encroachment of politics on economics. We mean here by "politics" the conscious organization and planning through the instruments of authority and subordination, private and public; by "economics" the unconscious and automatic coordination of human activity through the market and the price-profit mechanism. The politicizing of human life is seen most dramatically in the increasing power of the state, in democratic and in totalitarian regimes alike. We shall be missing some of the most important political aspects of life, however, if we concentrate, as so many political scientists do, on the state alone. The political problem is one which is found in all organizations, whether state, church, firm, union, lodge, or family. In all these organizations we have seen a change in political structure as a result of the organizational revolution. The problems of power and freedom, of order and authority, of defense and survival, apply to them all.

1. The Distribution of Power

Probably the most fundamental political problem is that of power—its distribution, its sources, and its use. The problem of freedom is essentially the same problem. If we wish to make a distinction we might say that the problem of freedom is one of the limitations on power imposed on one individual or organization by the existence of other individuals and organizations, rather than a problem of those limitations on power which are imposed by the laws of physical nature. Thus we might say that a young man who cannot finish his education because of mental inadequacy is hampered by a lack of power; but power in this sense does not constitute a political problem. The young man who cannot finish his education because the state conscripts him, or because other young men with more money than he are able to fill all the places in the colleges, is suffering not merely from lack of power but from lack of freedom.

Lack of power over nature is something which can be tackled by the fairly simple method of improvement in techniques. The problem of freedom as defined here, however, is much more delicate, because it involves the *distribution* of power. It is because in so many fields of human activity my power necessarily involves your impotence that the problem of politics arises—and, indeed, the problem of economics also. The basic problem of scarcity which dominates economics likewise dominates politics; if there were no scarcity, there would be no problem of distribution. It is because there is not enough for all, of either Cadillacs or influence, that the problem of justice arises, a problem which social institutions represent an imperfect attempt to solve.

What, then, has been the influence of the organizational revolution on the concentration of power or on its opposite, the diffusion of freedom? The growth of organization profoundly changes the nature of the problem. I have observed earlier that there are two methods of distributing power. One is through the wide distribution of property in a society in which the market is the main instrument of coordination of human activity. The other is by legal and constitutional limitations on the power of those in positions of authority and by political arrangements for subjecting the actions of governors to the will of the governed. If there are no limitations on power from the side of the market, then the question of political and constitutional limitations (that is, the problem of the internal political structure of organizations) becomes of immense importance.

I can illustrate the point, perhaps, by reference to the difference between the political nature of universities in Britain and in America. In America the internal constitution of the typical university is that of the corporation; it is autocratic and totalitarian. The governing body is a board of trustees; and the trustees appoint the president, the president appoints the deans, the deans appoint the heads of departments, the administration generally appoints the faculty, and the faculty, in spite of an occasional façade of faculty committees (the company union!), has little control over administrative policies or the government of the institution. Nevertheless this is not generally felt as a great hardship, or as a great infringement of individual freedom. One reason is the existence of certain traditional limitations on the conduct of university administrations imposed by the general sentiment for academic freedom (supplemented by occasional needling by the American Association of University Professors). But the main reasons are the existence, at least in prosperous times, of an active labor market in professors and the existence of noticeable competition among deans and presidents for faculty members, especially, of course, for good ones. The type of "checks and balances" which the professor exercises to limit the theoretically arbitrary power of the university administration is not the ability to vote the offending administrators out of office, but the presumptive ability to quit with a nice offer from another institution in his pocket. No system of political checks and balances can make a dean so amenable to a professor's point of view as an agreeable letter in the professor's pocket from some other dean.

In Great Britain, by contrast, the market is much more limited; there are only a few universities and there is a strong tradition against active competition for professors. In such a condition the American system would prove to be almost intolerably restrictive to the liberty of the teacher; it is not surprising to find, therefore, a much more democratic *internal* system of university government. At Oxford and Cambridge, in fact, the characteristic form of university government is a kind of educational cooperative. The faculty (the fellows of the college) themselves constitute the governing body; the universities of Oxford and Cambridge are loose federations of these educational cooperatives (colleges). Democracy in internal government, however, is obtained at a price: the absorption of many members of the faculty in administrative and domestic problems, and also a certain immobility in the labor market and the premature immobilization of gifted young people. A fellowship at an Oxford or Cambridge college has often proved a comfortable fur-lined trap for the bright young man or woman, from which escape becomes increasingly difficult as the years slip by in the agreeable routine of academic life.

It is evident, therefore, that the rise of organizations increases the necessity of internal democracy within organizational structure if liberty is not to be endangered. Economic organizations, whether firms, unions, or farm groups, have grown up by and large in the environment of an active market economy and have not, therefore, felt the pressure of the problem of internal democracy. To some extent the various groups act as checks on each other. Thus the labor movement has grown up to a considerable extent as a result of a failure of the market to provide additional job opportunities, especially in time of depression. Depressions, that is to say, have been largely responsible for creating the emotional pressure of the sense of need; the actual growth of unions takes place for the most part during the more favorable opportunities of the booms. It is the constant fear of a failure of the market that has created a need for some kind of political organization to blunt the edge of the arbitrary power of the "boss." One of the most important aspects of union-management relationships is precisely this: the development of a system of industrial law under the terms of a collective bargaining contract which provides contractual limitations on the right of the boss to hire and fire, to promote or demote, or to provide whatever working conditions he sees fit. Nevertheless, it is by no means a foregone conclusion that the solution to the problem provided by collective conflict is necessarily the most fruitful, though it may frequently be the most obvious.

Another problem which is partly of a political but perhaps even more of a social-psychological nature is that of authority and subordination. The rise of organization inevitably results in an increase in this type of human relationship in economic life as well as in other fields. What this means is that the problem of interpersonal relationships becomes a vital part of the *economic* experience of more and more individuals. The "jolly miller" who could sing "I care for nobody, no, not I, for nobody cares for me" is a relic of an age when a much larger proportion of people earned their living by selling the direct product of their labor to a lot of customers, and who therefore did not have to be particularly beholden to any one of them. The replacement of the relative impersonality of the "market" by an acutely personal relationship to the foreman or the supervisor or whoever is the next man up the totem pole has increased the importance and danger of breakdowns in interpersonal relations. In earlier days a neurotic personality merely had the power of making his wife and family miserable. He now has the power—if he is in a position of authority—to make a whole crew of subordinates (and even superiors) miserable. Unfortunately neurotic personalities who are incapable of having satisfactory relationships with other people are apt to transfer their frustrated personal relationships into "drive," aggressiveness, and ambition. They are, therefore, not unlikely to rise to positions of authority where the quieter and better adjusted persons remain unnoticed by their superiors.

The relation of neuroticism to hierarchy is one that needs careful investigation. We have seen some deplorable examples in recent years (e.g., Hitler) of highly neurotic types who have risen to positions of great authority in a hierarchical structure, to the detriment of practically everybody. If this is a general principle, then the cost of organization is indeed high. It would be surprising, however, if it were a *necessity* of organization. Nevertheless the problem is serious enough so that the evaluation of organizations may depend a great deal on the nature of the process by which individuals rise in them to positions of authority, for the *type* of personality that attains power depends on the nature of the process by which individuals are promoted. Fortunately the ultimate success of organizations also depends on their patterns of promotion and on the type of person who attains leadership in them. Organizations which get into the hands of neurotic or unimaginative personalities do not generally have a long expectation of life. Unfortunately little empirical study has been given to this problem.

2. THE PROBLEM OF DEFENSE

Another interesting problem of a political-psychological nature is that of the relationship between the character of organizations, also of the personalities who lead them, and the nature of the environment which surrounds them. It is particularly noticeable in the labor movement that the character of a labor union seems to be dependent to a considerable extent on the nature of the opposition which it meets and the industry in which it operates. Racketeering employers and racketeering unions generally go together; so do "tough" employers and "tough" unions; so do accommodating employers and accommodating unions. A union which has to fight every inch of its way against violent and unscrupulous opposition tends likewise to become violent and unscrupulous. Employers who face bitter and uncompromising unions also tend to become bitter and uncompromising.

An important question therefore is raised: where are the organizations (or individuals) in society which have some degree of autonomy in this regard; that is, who do not merely reflect their environment, but make a contribution toward it, whether of a positive or of a negative character? It becomes important to understand the sources of autonomy in examining any social process, for a completely "other-directed" society is obviously impossible. We cannot explain the behavior of everybody and every organization by assuming that they are mirrors, reflecting each other; for even in a society of mirrors there must be something for them all to reflect. It is probable that one of the principal sources of autonomy in the behavior of individuals and organizations is moral ideas and ideals. In a mirror society, then, these moral ideas may exert an influence quite out of proportion to the numbers of people who are autonomously motivated by them. It is probable, therefore, that organizations which regard themselves as "moral" organizations are likely to be centers of autonomous behavior. A good illustration of this principle is the impact which the "idealistic" garment workers' unions have had in cleaning up their industry.

The "mirror principle" noted above is closely related to an even more important problem—that of defense. One of the most powerful forces motivating any organization is the desire for survival. Every organization, therefore, and not merely the national state, faces a problem of defense. The growth in the size and power of individual organizations makes this problem much more difficult. Indeed, it is hardly an exaggeration to say that the most important problem facing mankind today is how to prevent the defense of each from becoming the destruction of all. This problem becomes most acute in the case of the national state itself, where we are witnessing a worldwide breakdown in the ability of the national state to defend itself except at a stupendous cost in terms of economic resources, human dignity and freedom, and human kindness. The problem is felt, however, at all levels of organizations as organizations become bigger and fewer. It is of such importance that a brief discussion of some of the principles involved may be in order even at the risk of some digression from the main theme.

In the first place it must be emphasized that the problem of *survival* is not the same as the problem of defense. We have already seen that the ability of a species or of a single organism to survive depends on its ability to "fit" into the larger framework of the ecosystem. It is possible for organisms to survive without any defensive apparatus at all. The vegetable kingdom is dominated by completely defenseless organisms, such as the grasses. A few vegetable species, such as the cacti, operating in an unusually unfavorable environment, have developed specialized organs for passive defense in the shape of spines and tough skins; but over the great range of the vegetable kingdom there is nothing in the structure of the organism itself to prevent its being destroyed by others. Grass makes no effort to prevent itself from being eaten; it survives because of its fecundity and because of the place which it occupies in the whole system.

Working up into the animal kingdom, we find again that many species have virtually no specialized organs of defense, and rely on fecundity or fleetness to insure themselves a place in the system. Nevertheless, defense becomes of more importance in the animal kingdom. It is possible to distinguish between two different kinds of specialized organs of defense, which may be called passive and active instruments respectively. A passive instrument of defense is a specialized arrangement designed to prevent injury by other elements in the environment without particularly injuring the environment. Tough skins, shells, houses, holes, are good examples. One might differentiate further between those passive instruments of defense which are innocuous, i.e., which do not injure the attacker but merely prevent him from injuring the attacked, and those which are noxious (e.g., the porcupine's quills, the skunk's scent) and which operate to injure the attacker if he attacks but do not injure a merely potential attacker. Finally there are the active instruments of defense designed to injure potential attackers even before the attack is made; the teeth and claws of the tiger perhaps fall into this category. It is not always easy to distinguish between the categories of "noxious passive" and "active" instruments of defense, as both require for their effectiveness the development of fear.

The use of fear as an instrument of defense is so important that it is worth careful examination. Fear develops in the evolutionary process along with the development of learning and becomes important as learning develops into consciousness. It is found in a rudimentary form even at the level of the one-celled organism, which apparently learns to avoid unpleasant experiences after a sufficient repetition. It hardly exists at all in the vegetable kingdom—perhaps because vegetation represents a form of life in which the *cell* has developed rather strong passive defenses in the shape of walls and hence has lost the learning and adaptive capacity. The vegetable kingdom in that sense, in spite of the defenselessness of the plant, represents an early example of what seems to be a cardinal principle in the evolutionary process: that success in passive defense is a blind alley, leading to a loss in adaptability and therefore in evolutionary capacity. The vegetable cell is a stiff, proud creature, a little walled city of life, and its very success in walling itself condemns the vegetable kingdom to a relatively lowly rung on the evolutionary ladder. As we move toward more mobile and adaptable forms of life, whether fish, reptile, or mammal, learning capacity and fear grow together. The essence of the learning process is the ability to recognize the nature of situations *before* they arise by means of certain signs and symbols. Learning, that is to say, always involves language in a rudimentary form, and it therefore involves *expectation.*

Fear, in its simplest form, is the expectation of the undesirable resulting from a perception of meaning in symbols which are remembered as previously foreshadowing some actual unfavorable event. The burnt child dreads the fire; the stung flee from the bee. In this form fear is a useful instrument of preservation of both individuals and species from obvious and unnecessary dangers. It is interesting to observe, however, that even at the animal level it frequently takes morbid forms which work toward destruction rather than preservation. The terror which inhibits action or which leads to frantic and unsuitable behavior is not unknown in the animal kingdom, even if stories about the ability of a snake to freeze a rabbit with his eye have to be taken cautiously. It is possible, and indeed almost easy, for fear to become so intense that it burns out the wires of the communications system.

Coming now farther up the scale of complexity toward the human individual and his social organizations, we find many of the simpler principles operating with additional complications added. The principal difference between animals and humans is that humans can talk and are self-conscious. These two phenomena of speech and self-consciousness may be more closely related than is frequently recognized. In human society it is still true that the defenseless can and do survive. They survive for the same reasons that the defenseless survive in the subhuman world—fecundity and mobility. Self-conscious organisms and organizations may survive for an additional reason: they may be protected by armed groups because of some service which they perform. The classically defenseless position of women in this regard is a good example. The development of language also introduces a new dimension into defense itself. Whereas in the animal kingdom communication is confined to simple signs of warning or encouragement, among men communication takes the form of *symbols* which take on a life and a significance of their own in addition to the things they are supposed to represent. Consequently words themselves have the power of inspiring fear and can therefore be used as weapons. The fact of self-consciousness means also that human individuals and human organizations exist in the midst of a complex environment of beliefs, ideas, prejudices, desires, and aversions. This mental environment dominates human individuals and organizations as the physical environment dominates the animal kingdom.

What, then, does "defense" mean to a social organization? It is possible, of course, for an organization to be defenseless, in the sense that it does not possess specialized apparatus either for injuring others or for preventing others from injuring it. By far the greater number of organizations fall under this category: families, clubs, most business enterprises, most sects and societies. These organizations survive either because they are so prolific and fundamental, like the family, that nobody has the power to destroy them, or because those who have the power to destroy them do not have the will.

There are also, however, many organizations with both offensive and defensive weapons. Many organizations usually regarded as "private" fall into this category. The labor union clearly has weapons in the strike, the boycott, even sabotage. Business firms have corresponding weapons in the lockout, the blacklist, the yellow-dog contract. These are instruments designed to enforce the will of one organization on that of another through the ability to inflict harm. Advertising likewise is a weapon, in that it represents the use of resources to increase the sales of one business at the expense of others. Even religious organizations have not always been above the use of "spiritual weapons"—the use of the fear of hell, or even of social disapproval, as a weapon to force adherence. The organization for which defense is all-important, however, is the national state. It is no exaggeration to say that today the greatest crisis which mankind has to face is the crisis of national defense, the demands of which seem to be insatiable and the success of which is doubtful.

One aspect of defense among organizations which is of special importance is that the means of defense must be compatible with the spirit and purposes of the organization. The means of defense, that is to say, must be compatible with the general cultural framework in which the organization finds itself. A business, for instance, may use advertising and propaganda, or even deceit, in its defense; it seldom resorts to open violence, for violence is not culturally compatible with the exchange relationship. The market is an essentially peaceful institution, requiring a certain amount of mutual tolerance and good will (enemies are not supposed to trade!), and an organization which is set principally in a market environment cannot develop either martial virtues or martial vices. Violence as used by businesses, therefore, as in the days of the "goon" squad and the armed strikebreaker, has not proved successful, even from the point of view of its employer, and has in addition brought down upon it the almost universal condemnation of society and the law. Labor unions, on the other hand, are somewhat less "trading" institutions, and have some of the attributes of states in that a great deal of their ideology is based on the twin supports of intense loyalty to the group and struggle with the "outsider"; consequently the union is somewhat more of a "fighting" organization than the business. Even in this case, however, the overwhelming predominance of the market as the environment even of labor unions has led to the dominance, at least in countries of Anglo-Saxon tradition, of "job-conscious" unionism of a peaceable, trading nature rather than militant revolutionary unionism.

In the case of the nation-state, however, the market environment has almost entirely disappeared. In its external relations the state is not a "trading" organization so much as a "fighting" one; its mythology consists mainly of wars and its heroes are mostly military men. The idea of defense, then, is basic to its concept, and it is little wonder that a world of independent nation-states is a world of perpetual turmoil and war. Nevertheless, paradoxically enough, the real *object* of the state is not to fight wars but to provide peace. Its inability to find a method of defense which is compatible with this function creates a profound instability in the present world order.

Why, then, has a rise of the power of organization made the problem of defense so much more difficult? The answer runs along somewhat the same lines as the answer given in the previous chapter to the problem of the rise of economic conflict as a result of the development of oligopoly. Where there are many organizations, all in some sort of contact with one another, action of any one of them, even if it is aggressive, is less likely to "bother" any one of the others than would be the case where there are only a few organizations. If we take the extreme case of "duopoly," where only two organizations occupy the whole environment, so that each constitutes the principal environment of the other, any kind of defense position is extremely unstable. The only way in which each can feel secure is for each organization to be stronger than the other.

This paradoxical result can sometimes be obtained if the organizations are a sufficient distance apart. There is an important principle that the ability of any organization to do anything depends on how far from "home" (the center of operations) the organization wishes to operate. The farther away from home it operates, the longer the lines of communication and the greater the costs of transport. This principle applies with particular force to military action: the ability of a nation to inflict damage on others (i.e., its military strength) declines rapidly as the scene of operations is removed from the home base. Thus in, say, 1922, it might have been true that Japan was stronger than the United States in Japanese waters, and the United States was stronger than Japan in American waters. This would provide an example of true equilibrium in defense, each side being stronger than the other in the place where it most mattered. The temporary success of the Washington Naval Agreement may well have been due to the existence for a short time in the twenties of such a genuine equilibrium.

Unfortunately, however, the technical revolution has proceeded with undiminished pace, with corresponding shrinkage in the size of the world, until nobody is far enough away from anybody else to make an equilibrium of defense possible. The contrast between American-Russian relations now and in the nineteenth century is a case in point. It is doubtful that the two countries are more ideologically repugnant now than then; it is doubtful that either of them is fundamentally more aggressive. The principal difference in the situation is that they are much nearer together. It is somewhat as if a distant mother-in-law moved into the family. A relationship which can be tolerable at a sufficient distance becomes intolerable at close quarters. And both the growth of organizational size and the shrinkage in effective distances have brought the human race into almost intolerably close quarters.

There is another reason why defense has become so acute a problem in the present day. The lack of any true equilibrium in defense means that the demands of defense are inherently insatiable. That is to say, the attempt on the part of each organization to provide for its own defense results in an "arms race." A arms to be stronger than B; this makes B weaker, and so B must arm to become stronger than A; this makes A weaker, so he must arm some more. The race goes on until either there is some kind of monopolistic settlement—a cartel, for instance, in the case of firms or a federation in the case of states—or the tension becomes unendurable and there is an attempt on the part of each to render the other impotent, i.e., war.

Even if the demands of defense are inherently insatiable, however, they must reach some sort of limit at the level which the organization can afford. If this limit is fairly low, defense may be an inconvenience, but it will not reach far down into the life of the organization. Such was the case with war in the eighteenth and nineteenth centuries. It is doubtful that any country turned more than 5 per cent of its resources into a war effort in the eighteenth century, and even the Napoleonic wars could not have absorbed more than 10 per cent. The Second World War absorbed about 50 per cent of the national income of the participating countries, and reached down deeply into the life of almost every individual in them.

The first reason is that in the eighteenth century it took 95 per cent of the resources of most countries just to keep the economy going in food and necessities, so that relatively little was left to spare for luxuries such as war. In the twentieth century the United States, at least, could devote only 50 per cent of its resources to the civilian economy and still live pretty comfortably. The instability of the system of defense, however, means that every country must put as much of its resources into war as it can, because of the competitive situation. If it does not it will fall behind in the race for power. Consequently the defense system in a progressive economy absorbs an ever-increasing proportion of the life and activity of the country until it may well become intolerable.

The second reason is that the ability of nations to organize themselves for war has increased in consequence of increased skills of organization. As long as the military establishment is inefficient it can be tolerated; when it becomes efficient it becomes intolerable because of its insatiable character. The state has enormously increased its ability to control the lives of its citizens in recent years— through transportation, through rationing and price control, through exchange control and immigration control, and so on. The more efficient it becomes, however, the more it becomes alien to its own citizens—a monstrous leviathan, coercing them with ever-increasing efficiency toward its own ends. No aspect of the organizational revolution is more menacing than the growing efficiency of coercion.

The revolution in military technology which is part both of the technical and the organizational revolutions has had, and is still having, another profound effect on defense: it has enormously increased the minimum size of the defensible nation. All defense requires a certain amount of "depth"; that is to say, defense is something that takes place on the surface or at the extremities of an organism, and its activities must not encroach on the vital center of the organism or the life of the organism will be endangered. Even up till the opening of the twentieth century a nation still had something like a "skin," a line of defense, to which the destruction of war could be confined while the essential activities of the nation went on behind the lines.

The invention of aerial warfare has made the "skin" virtually obsolete in the case of nations of such size as Britain, France, or Germany; the atom bomb and the guided missile probably make it obsolete for Russia and the United States. War consequently invades the whole organism—something like what takes place in the body when the defenses of the skin prove inadequate and blood poisoning sets in throughout the whole body. Thus the improvement in human organization not merely permits, but forces, an increase in the size of the state; as gunpowder finally made the city-state impossible, so airplanes and atom bombs have probably made the nation-state impossible because indefensible. This presents mankind with an unprecedented crisis, because, while the organizational revolution has knocked the props from under the nation-state, it is by no means certain that it has proceeded to the point where the whole world, made up as it is of innumerable diverse cultures, can be united into one political whole. We may find ourselves in the frightful dilemma where organizations have become too few to live together, and not big enough to take us all in. This dilemma also afflicts many industries, where the firms are too few to live comfortably together, and yet a combination of them all is too big to *stay* together.

3. The Rise of Totalitarianism

These principles are seen exemplified with dreadful clarity in the rise of totalitarianism, whether Communist, Fascist, or democratic-militarist. There have been plenty of examples of totalitarian regimes in history, from Sparta on. There have likewise been plenty of examples of monolithic planned economies, such as ancient Egypt or the Peru of the Incas. What is new about the totalitarian regimes of our day is their size and their power of oppression. This size and power are largely a by-product of the same improvement in the techniques of organization which is the theme of this work. This is particularly true of the Communist state. The essence of communism is the monolithic economy; i.e., the economy in which there is only one "firm" and that firm is also the state. If we imagine, for instance, General Motors growing to the point where it absorbed the whole American economy, we would have something like a Communist regime, at least as far as its economic organization goes.

Such a monolithic economy is, of course, inconceivable in the absence of advanced techniques of organization and communication. Its weakness is primarily the organizational weakness of the brontosaurus—the inability to maintain an adequate communications system when the organization grows so large. For this reason large organizations are almost forced to become conservative and traditional in their approach. It is no accident, for instance, that there are so many superficial similarities between the organization and even the dogmas of the Catholic Church and of the Communist state. In both there is emphasis on conformity to a simple and rigid pattern of belief, so that less need for communication and adaptability arises. The analogy must not, of course, be carried too far—the Communist state by reason of its monopoly of all economic resources exercises a much greater power over the lives of its citizens than the Catholic Church does or desires over the lives of its communicants.

Again it is at first sight odd, but true, that almost all the problems of "big business" are reflected even more intensely in the Communist state. There is, for instance, the "divorce of ownership from control" which worries many commentators on big business. Nowhere is this more obvious than in Soviet Russia, where theoretically the people own collectively all the means of production, but in fact have even less to say about what is to be done with them than do the stockholders of A. T. & T. A corresponding proposition is the accusation that the directors of big business form a self-perpetuating oligarchy; nowhere can be found an oligarchy more self-perpetuating than that of the Kremlin. The impersonality and "soullessness" of big business are greatly exceeded by the ruthless impersonality of the Russian state. And the clumsiness and inefficiencies of big business are mild compared to the fantastic clumsiness and inefficiency of the Soviet economy.

Modern fascism in one of its aspects can be regarded as an

application of the organizational revolution to the political party. There are many analogies between the way in which the excesses of oligopolistic competition lead to monopoly in economic life and the way in which in many countries and areas the competitive strife of political parties has led to a one-party state. Not enough is known about the conditions under which a two-party or many-party system is stable. It is possible that it is stable only under certain conditions of political apathy and party inefficiency, in which case political competition becomes a kind of ritual, not seriously affecting the emotional life of the people. This is certainly the case in the United States; it is true to a lesser extent in Britain and the British Dominions. The success of democratic political organization in these countries may well be a by-product of their vices rather than their virtues. Continental Europeans take their politics seriously, and as a result democratic institutions result in the intense competition of political parties to the point where the case for political monopoly has some appeal. In support of the thesis that intense political competition produces a one-party system one might also cite the American South, where a pathological political and cultural condition, resulting from the institution of slavery and its abolition by violence, created a situation in which it was felt that party conflict would be too real to be tolerated.

Another problem of internal political structure which is in a sense a by-product of the organizational revolution is the rise of pressure groups, and of the organized lobby as a determinant of legislation. In spite of much abuse and criticism which the pressure-group system has received, it may well be that it is a more constructive political solution than its possible alternative—which is the multiplication of more or less homogeneous political parties. The essence of democracy is not parliamentary organization, or even representative structures, but *discussion*; it may literally be defined as government by talk. The great disadvantage of the homogeneous-party system, in which each party "means" something and stands for a fairly coherent and self-consistent set of ideas and principles, is that conversation among the parties ceases, or degenerates into mutual shouting or speechmaking. This is not conducive to the political *process*, which is essentially the process of discussion or conversation. The thing that is most fatal to the political process is conclusions; when once the train of thought has reached a terminus, everybody might just as well get off it. It is the great advantage of the American party system that neither party ever reaches a conclusion, and the political conflicts are worked out by discussion *within* each party rather than flattened out by the victory of one point of view or another.

It can be argued, therefore, that however agreeable to the tidy mind a homogeneous-party system may be, the sloppy arrangement of a tweedle-dum-dee system actually facilitates the essential political process much better. Curiously enough, however, the success of the system seems to depend on the fact that organizational energies are directed away from the political parties toward other organizations (pressure groups) which do not contemplate ever seizing the weapons of coercive power. This is a much more satisfactory situation than one in which the organizations in control of the coercive power are unified, ruthless, and efficient in its use, as in the case of the Nazi or Communist parties.

The theory of organization yields some insight on why totalitarian regimes universally turn out to be unstable and inefficient in practice, in spite of the glittering promise of a smoothly running monolithic machine. The explanation seems to lie in the basic incompatibility between the totalitarian structure and the maintenance of an effective communications system. Dictators arise because men get tired of the wearisome process of discussion, and want a quick answer to the difficult questions of political life. For this reason the dictator himself becomes insulated from discussion, surrounds himself with yes men, and loses contact with the realities of the world around him. He sits in a dark room looking at the world on what he thinks is a television screen, but is actually an old movie, made out of his preconceptions and previous conclusions. Consequently he does not have any machinery for becoming aware of the current consequences of his actions and for correcting his mistakes. Mistakes are not corrected, but suppressed. As time goes on, however, the mistakes become so gross that his regime is swept away by the very violence on which it relies. Violence seems like a short cut to the solution of problems; but when it becomes a substitute for the process of discussion it turns out to be a short cut over a cliff, and what looks at first sight cheap turns out to be costly.

5

Ethics and the Theory
of Organization

The theory of organization which we have briefly examined throws light on some of the basic problems of "practical" ethics and, indeed, on some of the most basic problems of man and history. I am not suggesting that the theory of organization as it exists today is adequate; indeed, it is scarcely more than in embryo. Nevertheless, the idea that a theory of organization is possible is one of the important ideas of our time. This statement sounds like an absurd exaggeration. Nevertheless, there is danger lest in an attitude of cautious deprecation we overlook magnificence when it is presented to us and by keeping our eyes close to the ground we fail to see the doors open to us.

The importance of the theory of organization is that it gives us some hints as to where to look for sources of the deep frustration of man. Why is human progress so slow, and so self-defeating? Why, in spite of all the ethical insights and vision of the prophets and saints, does man still dwell in poverty and insecurity, pride and lust? Why do his civilizations come to grief, and why does his technical progress exhibit such ups and downs? Why do his achievements turn to dust, and his very successes drive him all the faster to destruction? We know indeed that the spirit giveth life. But how is it that the letter killeth? Why do all our attempts to *organize* great moral insights turn out so badly: the Church of the loving Saviour producing the Grand Inquisitor, communism becoming enshrined in a vast instrument of exploitation, democracy and science working hand in hand to produce the horror of Hiroshima?

The answer is not in the inadequacy of our ethical ideas. Indeed, the great ethical ideas are so simple that man arrived at most of them early, even though he is still working out their full impli-cations. There has not been, for instance, substantial improvement on the Sermon on the Mount as a statement of ethical principles; and practically all that is in the Sermon on the Mount is at least implicit in much older writings, and in writings of many peoples and cultures. There is, indeed, in a phrase of Aldous Huxley's, a "perennial philosophy," a core of spiritual wisdom which is always being forgotten and constantly rediscovered, and which goes back in some form or other at least to the beginnings of writing, possibly to the beginnings of speech. Man ate of the tree of knowledge of good and evil very early. Where he does not seem to have been successful is in putting this knowledge to use.

The trouble lies, of course, in the "flesh"; that is, in organization. All bodies are corruptible, whether the body of literal flesh or the body of the state, the corporation, the trade union, the philanthropic organization, or the church. All organizations possess laws of their own being which they impose on their members, laws which may not be consistent with the purposes of these members. Nevertheless, man has been haunted by the vision of incorruptibility, whether it is the vision of St. Paul in the Fifteenth Chapter of I Corinthians or the vision of Marxism in the withering away of the state and the establishment of the final classless society. Whether the vision represents a terminus only time will tell; what it does, however, is to set a direction to human action. We cannot rest content in corruption, and there is a constant drive toward the less and less corruptible. In this movement the theory of organization holds out great promise. Unless we understand the laws of organization, at least in some degree, we cannot hope to create organizations which will serve the ends of man instead of frustrating them. And organi-zations—"bodies"—are necessary if the "word"—the ethical insight, the perception of good—is to be made "flesh"; if it is to be embodied in arrangements for the practice of right and for the righting of wrongs.

THE MACHINERY OF ORGANIZATION

Thus the relation of ethics to organization can be summed up in the question *how* wrongs are righted; what machinery exists in the world for the correction of conditions which are perceived to need correction. This machinery, however, is precisely what is meant by organization. We have already seen that the barest essential of any organization, whether as simple as the thermostat or as complex as the animal body or the human society, is a control mechanism consisting of a system of communication and transformation. It consists, first of all, of *receptors of information* (thermometers, sense organs, salesmen, operators, spies). They collect information about the environment and transmit it over a communications system (nerves, speech, letters) to an *executive* (furnace control, central nervous system, manager) whose business it is to take the information which he (or it) receives and transform it into *instructions*. These are then communicated over a further communications system to *effectors* (furnace, muscles, workmen, soldiers) who act in some way to change the environment. The change in the environment is picked up by the receptors and the whole process is repeated endlessly. Any apparatus for *correction* will have this form.

What the receptors pick up is information about divergence of the environment from some condition which is regarded as right, proper, or normal. If the machinery is operating correctly, this information will be transmitted accurately to the executive, who will in turn transform it into the "right" instructions to the effectors, who will receive these instructions correctly and put them into effect. The result of their action will be to change the environment in such a way as to diminish the divergence between the actual condition of the environment and the condition which is regarded as ideal. If in fact the divergence is diminished, this information will be transmitted to the executive and the former policy will be continued. If in fact the divergence is increased, or is unchanged, or is not diminished sufficiently to produce satisfaction, this information also will be transmitted to the executive, who will be faced with the problem of altering his instructions in order to provide for different ways of affecting the environment.

TECHNICAL DEFECTS IN THE MACHINERY

If now wrongs do *not* get righted—if things go from bad to worse instead of from bad to better—it must be because of some defect in the machinery itself. This failure can be at any or all points in the circular chain that leads from the receptors of information back to the environment which they probe. There may first be failure in the receptors. The thermometer may be broken, the eye blind, the ear deaf, the mind insensitive. There may therefore either be no information picked up about the environment or, what is worse, there may be false information. If the eye is blind the executive will be blind, the effectors will be blind, and the whole organization will fall into a ditch. The failure in the receptors may be twofold: there may be failure to perceive the actual environment, or there may be failure to perceive the ideal, or both. The thermostat may read the actual temperature, but may be set at the wrong level. The eye may perceive a ball where it is, but may not register where it is going. The mind may be accurately informed about the present state of the world, but may not perceive that this state is abominable.

In this regard the scientist and the saint have strictly complementary tasks: the scientist to show where we are, the saint to show where we ought to be. The activities of both frequently result in an increased awareness of divergence between the actual and the ideal—the scientist because he dispels our illusions about what is actual, and the saint because he gives us a new vision of the ideal. Thus the impact of modern psychology and sociology upon family life has been to dispel certain romantic illusions and perhaps to create a sense of a wider gap between ideal and reality; the shadow that the ideal cast over the real has been dispelled. From the other end of the scale, prophetic figures like John Woolman opened men's eyes to the evil of slavery and created an acute sense of divergence between the actual and the ideal, not by changing the perception of the actual, but by changing the perception of the ideal.

Even if the receptors of information are in good working order, there may be inadequate means of communication between the receptors and the executive. The thermostat does no good if the wire down to the furnace is cut; the most perfect eye is of no use if there is no optic nerve; and the most acute and realistic perceptions of divergence between the actual and the ideal at the lower levels of an organization will do no good if there are no means of conveying this information to the executive. This is frequently the weakest link in social organizations. The necessities of hierarchy in any organization larger than the family create a communications problem because of the social distance which separates the members of the executive organization from the humbler "receptors" at the end of the line. Communications are generally organized *down,* to carry messages from higher to lower levels of the hierarchy; they are not usually so well organized in the upward direction.

Nevertheless, a communications system from the receptors to the executive is essential if an organization is to continue. The discontents of the lower levels of society must be registered at the executive levels if organizations are to survive; otherwise the executive does not receive a realistic picture of his environment, and especially does not know whether or not his actions are taking effect. He creates, as it were, a spurious environment of his own—an environment, if he is a dominant type, of yes men who reflect the executive's own wishes rather than the realities of the world around him; what he thinks are windows are in fact mirrors. Something of this sort happens, I am told, in certain forms of mental breakdown, where the individual creates an inner environment of his own and is largely cut off from the messages which come through from the outside world. This is the danger of the absolute monarch, whether of a state or of a firm, or of the schizophrenic.

Failure may occur also at the level of the executive himself; that is, he may not know how to transform the information which he receives into the "right" instructions to the effectors, or even if he knows he may not be willing to undertake the role. An important question, therefore, is how the executive gains knowledge of what responses are "right"; i.e., what instructions to the effectors will produce "better" information from the receptors when carried into effect. The simplest situation is one in which information regarding a single variable is picked up by a single receptor, and in which the effector operates directly on the environmental variable. Then, as long as the instructions to the effector are in the right direction and the system has about the right degree of sensitivity, the executive can hardly go wrong; any error will be immediately reported and can be immediately corrected.

About the only example of such a simple system, however, is mechanical governors or thermostats. The moment we reach the complexity of the animal body and, still more, the social organism, the possibility of things going wrong becomes much greater. Complexities arise because there are many variables which are relevant to the organism, and there are likewise many effectors. What is worse, some of the effectors affect a number of significant variables. Thus the attempt to correct a "bad" variation in one of the variables may upset some others, and it becomes extremely difficult to correct all the unwanted deviations at the same time. A fever is a good example in the animal body: the rise in the temperature of the blood stream which may be appropriate to kill off a dangerous concentration of microorganisms also has the effect of upsetting a number of other bodily processes. It is almost a commonplace among social organizations that the solution of one problem frequently gives rise to three fresh ones. Indeed, it is frequently the mark of a good executive that he juggles problems rather than solving them, for it may be more important to keep a number of problems moving toward a solution than to find a final solution for any one of them.

An important problem in the construction of organizations, therefore, is that of specializing the effectors—to ensure as far as possible that something can be done about each of the many variables of the environment without upsetting the other variables. The precision rifle rather than the blunderbuss is what is needed; nevertheless, it must be admitted that most action leans to the side of the blunderbuss. This is particularly true of governments, whose general response to trouble is to fire off a monstrous charge of legislative or military shot and hope that at least something hits somebody. The so-called "loyalty" program of the United States is a prize example.

Even if the executive is well-informed and capable of giving the right instructions, things can still go wrong farther around the circle. There may be breakdowns in communication between the executive and his effectors; the larger the organization the more likely is this to happen. Or there can be breakdown or inadequacy in the effectors; that is, there may not be any kinds of action responsive to the executive's instructions which can in fact affect the environment in such a way as to bring it closer to the ideal. The thermostat and the furnace control may be in fine shape, but the furnace may be out of order—or there may not be any furnace. The eye may inform the consciousness that a train is approaching and that we are lying across the track, but muscles may be paralyzed or bound. Everybody with half an eye for the shape of things to come can perceive at the moment that the human race is rushing toward a disaster of unusual magnitude at unparalleled speed, but nobody, least of all the statesmen, seems quite to know what to do about it; the runaway car of civilization seems to have no brakes.

The situation is still more complicated in social life by inter-action, that is, by the effect which the behavior of one executive has on the problems which face another. The behavior of each organization affects the environment of others, whose behavior in turn affects the environment of the first. In the absence of any over-all machinery of control, then, the interaction of a number of organizations is always likely to produce "mass movements" whose direction is often quite at variance with the true interests of the organizations participating in them, like the famous march of the lemmings to their death in the sea. The movements of inflation and deflation in the business cycle are examples of such "infectious" changes. A decision to reduce output on the part of one firm leads to a similar decision by a second, which leads to similar decisions by a third, fourth, and fifth, and so on until the whole economy is moving toward deflation and depression. Like movements can take place in the opposite direction. Chain reactions are not confined to atomic physics; they are common in simple chemistry (e.g., a forest fire) and common also in social life. The "chain" frequently gets out of the control of any single executive or organization.

The key position of the executive in human organizations arises, not merely because he occupies a central position in the chain of the control mechanism, but also because he sets up new mechanisms. So different indeed are these functions that we may wish to call them by different names, and to call the creator of organization the "organizer" rather than the "executive." The mere executive functions within the framework of an existing structure; the organizer creates new structures. He is the creative entrepreneur, the innovator who organizes new combinations of factors. He is likewise the organizer of religious sects and orders, and of new social forms in all spheres of life. The organizations which he creates are by no means always "good," nor do they always survive. Nevertheless it is this constant "mutation" of the social organism under the impact of the organizer that provides the material for the process of social evolution.

OTHER OBSTACLES TO PROGRESS

The answer, then, to the question, "Why do not wrongs get righted?" can be given at two levels. On the one hand we can point, as we have done, to the defects in the existing structure of organization: the gaps in communication, the inadequacies of the executive, the clumsiness of the effectors. More fundamental, however, is the further, twofold question why inadequate organizations survive, and why organizations themselves are not corrected. We have seen that the main function of an organization is to "right wrongs," i.e., to correct discrepancies between actual and "ideal" values of some set of variables.

The criticism of organizations must center around two points. The first is *technical* criticism: that organizations are not able to do the things they set out to do because of the various defects in their structure listed above. The second is *moral* criticism: that the things they set out to do themselves are not right, and that either they concern themselves with wrong or trivial variables or the ideal values of the variables which govern their behavior are wrong values.

Two examples of such criticism may be given. The capitalist economy is an efficient machine for correcting changes in tastes of consumers, weighed according to income. If people decide that they want ranch-type houses and picture windows, these things spring up all over the place, even where there are no ranch and no picture. Every whim of fashion in ladies' clothing is followed immediately by the clothing trades. The slightest divergence, then, between the actual structure of output and the "ideal" which best satisfies the tastes of those who are willing and able to spend money to gratify those tastes is communicated to highly efficient executives who immediately set in motion action which corrects the situation. In Soviet Russia, on the other hand, there is an efficient machinery for getting rid of profit making by private persons, except a little peasant trade that is winked at on the side. Any growth of Kulaks or Nepmen calls forth punitive measures which will cut the growth back, and anyone who engages in buying and selling for a profit does so at the risk of serious discomfort. Both these systems may be criticized morally on the ground that they are efficient machines for righting the wrong wrongs. Capitalism is too efficient at satisfying trivial wants, and communism in the suppression of perfectly innocent productive activity. Both can be criticized technically when they do not do what they are supposed to do—when capitalism falls into depression, and hence fails to satisfy wants which could readily be satisfied but for a defect in the organization, and when communism falls into Stalinism and re-establishes a new bourgeoisie in the shape of a privileged managerial and political class.

In spite of the fact that all existing organizations are subject to sharp criticism, and always have been at all periods of history, the process of correcting them has been slow and difficult. Perhaps the main reason for this slowness is the difficulty of getting rid of organizations once they are established. Organizations which have been created for good purposes persist long after they have ceased to meet the needs of man. It may well be that the rapid rate of technical progress which has always characterized competitive market societies, whether of ancient Greece or of modern America, is due to the relative ease with which obsolete firms can be got rid of in such a society through the processes of bankruptcy. The innovator is not suppressed; instead it is he who is the suppressor, and old firms must either conform to the technical improvements made by the innovator or they go under. By contrast, a "protected" society, where established institutions are protected by the power of the state against the innovator who seeks to introduce new methods, has generally a low rate of technical progress. In Communist society an even more drastic equivalent of bankruptcy in the shape of the "purge" has been introduced in the attempt to get a high rate of technical progress. The purge, unfortunately, applies only at the lower and middle levels of the hierarchy, whereas it is generally needed at the very top. Consequently it is doubtful that it can ever be as efficient as bankruptcy as a method for getting rid of the less effective economic organizations.

The slow progress of man in political and social matters, by contrast with economic matters, may well be due to the absence of any simple equivalent of bankruptcy for political organizations. It is virtually impossible, for instance, to get rid of a county, much less a state, and much less again a country, short of a complete political cataclysm. Inefficient political units, therefore, are protected, and there is no clear path made for the innovator. Thus, even though the whole local-government organization of most countries was designed for the pre-automobile era, and contains far too many small units for present-day needs, amalgamation is almost impossible. In the whole history of the United States only three counties have ever been abolished and no states, in spite of the fact that both the county and the state are frequently too small for efficient government.

The problem of getting rid of countries is even harder. The attempts made to abolish Poland, Ireland, Greece, etc. have met very indifferent success. Even Luxembourg shows an astonishing persistence. Furthermore, new countries are being formed, like Pakistan, to the detriment of most of the people involved. If the bankruptcy, reorganization, and merger of countries could be effected as easily as that of corporations, a great stride forward would have been made in human institutions. Constitutional parliamentary machinery is of course an attempt to provide a substitute for bankruptcy in the case of the *internal* organization of a state; that is, it is a device for getting rid of executives whose usefulness to the organization is over by methods which are relatively painless. It has never been applied, however, to getting rid of the organization itself.

One of the main institutions which prevents the improvement of the organizational structure is coercion. By coercion I mean any device which involves the fear of injury rather than the hope of benefit as the motive in attracting support for an organization. The food of organizations, as we have noticed earlier, is human time and energy; the more time and energy an organization can attract from the human population around it, the larger and more powerful it will be. There are, however, two very different ways of attracting time and energy to an organization. One is by coercion and the other is by consent. Most organizations use a mixture of both. On the whole, however, the organizations of a market economy are noncoercive. Probably capitalism is the least coercive society which has ever existed. Its institutions survive by serving, or at worst by wheedling or diddling, the public; they do not, on the whole, survive because people are compelled by fear of injury to give these organizations their support. At the other extreme is a military, slave society in which organizations survive through their ability to create fear of injury. In a coercive society, then, organizations survive which do not serve the interests of man or attract his voluntary consent.

Also, coercive societies are not in fact stable in the long run, or even in quite short runs, because of the fact that no society can exist solely by coercion, and coercion tends to be cumulative. The more coercion is used, the more needs to be used as voluntary consent is withdrawn, until the society cannot find enough voluntary supporters to consent to coercion and it collapses.

It is clear, however, that one of the greatest obstacles to human progress is the coercive nature of political organizations. Yet there is no doubt that advance can be made, and has been made, toward lessening the degree of coercion employed by states. It is the greatest significance of democracy that it substitutes discussion for violence as the instrument for establishing the policy of the state. Discussion moves toward consensus, and consensus implies consent. One of the greatest tasks now facing man is the substitution of discussion for violence in the relations among states. The task of getting rid of coercion, however, is a difficult one. Coercion cannot be driven out by coercion, nor even by the opposition of a "good" coercion to a "bad" coercion. There seems to be no way by which coercion can be lessened except by the growth of persuasion, sympathy, and communication—that is, by the inherent power of communicability of moral ideas. This is the "more excellent way" which has been characteristic of Christianity in its most vital manifestations.

"Laws" of Social Change

It must not be thought, of course, that defects in organization are the only reasons why wrongs fail to get righted. There may be no organization capable of correcting wrongs because of a lack of knowledge of the causes of what is wrong. Much moral sentiment and effort are wasted because of an incomplete understanding of the laws of social change. This may be interpreted, in terms of the above analysis, as the absence of an "effector." If we do not understand the forces that determine the variables which we wish to change, there will not be much chance of finding a practical method of bringing about the change. Hence the importance of the search for laws of society and human relationship. No amount of trial and error would have been able to hit upon the exact method for the release of atomic energy, unless these practical measures had been preceded by an adequate body of physical theory. So, in the search for a reformed society, practical measures must arise out of an adequate body of social theory. These laws of society are in a sense "iron laws," in that they frustrate constantly all attempts at human betterment which overlook or deny them. The iron, however, is malleable at high temperatures, and it is from this iron that the engines of a better world must be built.

First among the "iron laws" is that of Malthus: that if there are no checks on the growth of population except starvation and misery, then the population will grow until the people are miserable and starve. Given the major premise, there is no escape from the conclusion, and the condition of well over half the world's people is a shocking testimony to its truth. If, therefore, a society wishes to have a high *stable* standard of living it must develop deliberate checks on the growth of population. There is an inescapable choice in the long run between low birth and death rates with a long expectation of life, on the one hand, and high birth and death rates with a low expectation of life, on the other. A society which is unwilling to limit its births must take the consequences, and has no right to expect to shift the burden of its fecundity to other societies. It is astonishing how many people seem to believe that technical progress alone can solve the population problem. In fact, unless technical progress itself leads to conscious checks on births—as it may not do—technical progress in the long run merely enables more people to live in misery than before, and any improvement which it brings in levels of living will be a mere prelude to a greater mass of misery.

The iron law of Malthus is closely connected with another iron law—perhaps a somewhat more malleable one. It is that culture patterns of a society are transmitted mainly through the instrument of the family, and that social changes which do not change the character of the family are not likely to be permanent. There is an intimate link between the economic success of a society and its over-all culture pattern. Indeed, the basic reason why one nation is rich and another is poor is not primarily to be found in exploitation, nor in a difference in natural resources, but in a difference in the patterns of culture. Some cultures produce wealth and some produce poverty; but all cultures are produced in the home. If poverty is to be attacked, therefore, it must be attacked in its breeding ground—those patterns of life and character which are established in the home. Probably the most important single factor here is the status of women; the wealth-producing and wealth-sustaining capacity of a culture depends strongly on the position of women in it. Cultures in which women have a high place are likely to develop positive checks on population and so avoid the Malthusian trap; they are likely also to develop a spirit of enterprise and are likely to be more capable of political democracy.

A third iron law is that organizations of all kinds have an optimum size, which in some cases is small, like the family, and in other cases may be large, like the Catholic Church or the national state. Attempts to push one type of relationship or one type of organization beyond its proper size result in breakdown. Furthermore, the nature of an organization itself will depend on its size; large organizations even with the same ostensible purposes as small ones will turn out to be unlike them, fostering different kinds of relationships. For instance, only small organizations can be personal. Where large masses of people have to be organized the relationship must be stripped down to its barest essentials. This may be why coercion is much more characteristic of large organizations than of small. A good deal of harm has been done by interpreting the moral ideal of the "brotherhood of man" (a phrase, incidentally, which does not appear in the Bible) to mean that all human organizations must be like a family, in its looseness of organization and its complexity of personal interaction.

Each type of organization has a structure which is most appropriate to it. Attempts to extend any particular kind of organization much beyond its most effective size will cause breakdown in its communications and executive system. Thus the problem of organizing the human race is something more than giving everybody a vague feeling of brotherhood, even though that feeling to some degree is a prerequisite to any organization. The problem of how to organize large masses of people without sacrificing liberty and even decency is one of the most acute which the world faces. Everywhere the large organization, whether it be a Communist or nationalist state, a great corporation, a great labor union, or even a large religious body, is in danger of becoming an ineffective instrument for the righting of wrongs or even an enemy of man's dignity and liberty. The problem here is not how to establish a full personal relationship ("love" in the deepest sense) but to establish an adequate minimal relationship. The first is the task of the family; it is not the task of the great organization.

The iron law of size has a corollary: the iron law of hierarchy. The larger the organization, the more elaborate will be its hierarchical structure, the more grades there will be in it, and the greater is likely to be the difficulty of direct communication between the lower and the upper grades. Hierarchy, however, conflicts with the ideal of equality. We cannot, therefore, achieve equality by establishing large, integrated organizations. The only hope for an equalitarian world is a world of small organizations held together in a network of contractual relationship.

Next there is an iron law of oligopoly: that if the number of independent interacting organizations is *few* a situation of acute instability and conflict will be created, because each organization has some kind of visible coercive power over the others and can act to injure the others. We see this situation today especially in some industries and in international relations, where it threatens to engulf our whole civilization in catastrophic conflict. It is only interaction among *many* independent organizations (something like the economist's "perfect competition") which can give us a non-coercive as well as a progressive society.

On the other hand, there may be also an iron law of instability in the uncontrolled interaction even of a large number of organizations. We see this manifested especially in the fluctuations of inflation and deflation in the ungoverned market economy. We see it also in the fickle tides of public opinion on all subjects, and in the cycle of war and peace. It arises because of a principle of "self-justified expectations"; that is, the individual action in anticipation of a general movement precipitates the general movement which is anticipated. Thus, if people generally expect inflation, each man will find it in his interest to act so as to *cause* inflation by trying to turn his assets out of the form of money into other things. Similarly, if a group of nations expect war, then by preparing for it they will precipitate it; arming brings on war almost as inevitably as spending brings on inflation.

The fact that society is an "ecosystem" of interacting populations means not only that it is subject to the instability of cyclical or apparently cyclical movements; it means also that the results of action, even of reforms, are often totally unexpected. The suppression of an "evil" kind of organization may encourage the rise of even worse kinds which the suppressed kind itself helped to keep down. The suppression of the saloon led to the rise of the speakeasy and the gangster; the suppression of Communists gives rise to underground movements and inhibits valuable as well as useless criticism and radicalism.

Finally, there is an iron law—or perhaps a plastic law—of the persistence of the role. An organization consists essentially of a bundle of roles tied together with communications. There is a complex interaction between the role and the person who fills it, and frequently the role dominates. Changing the person in the role often changes the personality of the newcomer rather than the role itself; getting one set of rascals out just gets another set in, because the role—the position, the job—creates the rascal, or the saint. A boss behaves like a boss, a policeman like a policeman, a professor like a professor, a Czar like a Czar whether his name be Nicholas or Joseph. Thomas à Becket, the worldly chancellor, becomes more priestly than the priests when he is elevated, for political reasons, to the post of archbishop. Consequently the organizer who creates roles, who creates the holes that will force the pegs to their shape, is a prime creator of personality itself. When we ask of a man, "What is he?" the answer is usually given in terms of his major role, job, or position in society; he *is* the place that he fills, a painter, a priest, a politician, a criminal.

This is the truth in the half-truth of the Marxist doctrine of the determination of personality by the social system. There is, however, another half to the truth. A square peg in a round hole will do something to square the hole. Each person who comes to a role does something to change it, however slightly. Consequently there is a real problem of promotion—how to get the right people into the right places. Both the persistence of hereditary monarchies over hundreds of years and the equally persistent democratic conviction that any fool can be President indicate a certain superiority of the role over the particular individual who occupies it. Too many fools in high places, however, can ruin an organization. The role does not survive a succession of inadequate incumbents. The problem of promotion becomes more acute the less opportunity there is for getting rid of organizations or for modifying the organizational structure itself. It is acutely important in totalitarian regimes of any stripe.

THE NEED OF MANY CENTERS OF POWER

The theory of organization, then, points clearly to the type of organization of society which is most likely to be effective in the righting of wrongs and in developing progress toward the ideal. It should be "polylithic" rather than monolithic; i.e., it should consist of "many stones," many quasi-independent organizations, with a considerable turnover among these organizations to permit constant experimentation with mutations. There should be many centers of power rather than one. Nevertheless, there is need for an over-all organization with limited powers to act as a "governor"—to keep an eye on the aggregate variables of the society which are not under the control of any one of its constituent organizations, and to have power to act "counterwise"; that is, to act so as to move the aggregates in the opposite direction to which they are going as they approach the limits of toleration.

National income, as we shall see in Chapter 10, is one of these aggregate variables which need governing, but there are many others in noneconomic fields; for instance, racial and international tensions, family disorganization, crime rates, mental health, and so on. With the development of techniques for measuring these aggregate variables—some of which are perhaps even more important for the ultimate survival of the society than the more commonly measured economic aggregates—the possibility of counterwise action becomes greater, though the problem of what to do is more complex than in the case of the relatively simple economic aggregates. It is easier to cure the business cycle than it is to create a society of happy families.

In economics, then, the theory of organization points to the governed market economy as the one which is most likely to be characterized by rapid and steady progress toward the universal satisfaction of economic needs. It lies between the rigidity of the planned, monolithic economy and the instability of ungoverned market capitalism. The economic governing mechanism needs to be applied especially to two sets of variables: to one, the aggregates of national income and prices, in order to prevent serious depressions or inflations; to the other, the power structure of the society, in order to maintain the wide diffusion of power and to check the growth of organizations at the point where they pass the tolerable limits of power, whatever that point may be.

In politics, the same view looks toward the establishment of limited world government on a loose federal basis uniting large numbers of subordinate states. The main variable which such government would seek to confine to tolerable limits would be armaments. It could not, unfortunately, confine its activities to the mere regulation of armament, for there are also other variables which could produce its breakdown if they passed certain limits of toleration—such things as population pressures, economic discontents, trade disorders, and so on. The problem here is how to transform the competition of states from destructive into constructive forms; much study needs to be given to this point. One sees clearly the vision of a world of small states competing, within a framework of federal government, in progress, in freedom, in the arts and sciences, and in the pursuit of happiness; but how one gets there is another matter! And, as noted previously, states may be too small to perform their proper functions separately in the modern world.

There are implications of this view of society also for many other aspects of life—for the family (how do we encourage "good" families to be large?), for religion (how do we encourage competition in goodness?), for the arts, for education, and indeed for all other activities and aspirations of man. Many of these, however, wait upon the development of techniques for identifying and measuring the significant variables before even the framework of a governing mechanism can be suggested. Our information system in these respects is crude, and consequently the apparatus for improvement is crude also. Nevertheless, the possibilities for progress in these fields are enormous. In spite of what I have called the "iron laws," then, and in spite of the dismal spectacle of human history, the conclusion seems to be that there is *some* hope for man, though it is not all a foregone conclusion.

FREEDOM, JUSTICE, AND LOVE

It has been one of the major weaknesses of ethical thinking and preaching that its concepts have had such vague intellectual content. This is particularly true in the ethics of society, where ideas like "freedom," "social justice," and so on frequently have much more emotional than intellectual content. It is well, of course, that they should have emotional content; it is the prophet who calls down the wrath of heaven on the sins of his society, who awakens men to a sense of their need, and who creates that perception of divergence between the actual and ideal which is the beginning of creative action. Nevertheless, it is not enough to be against sin, even social sin. There must be some intellectual content in the ideal, and in the means of achieving the ideal.

The theory of organization can throw a good deal of light on these problems and should be of great assistance in clarifying the intellectual content of ethical ideas. We have noted already, in Chapter 4, some of the difficulties involved in the concept of "freedom"—its negative character, and the fact that it has no content unless it is specified *from what* freedom is desired. These negative concepts always cause trouble. (Compare, for instance, the trouble which the concept of "saving" has caused in economics, because it involves "not doing something"; the concept of consumption is much safer because that involves "doing something.") Thus, freedom means "not having obstacles" to the exercise of power. The concept of power and its distribution is, therefore, much less likely to be confusing, and freedom, as we have seen, may most satisfactorily be defined as the wide distribution of power.

The concept of justice also is frequently lacking in intellectual content or, what is even worse, is given different intellectual content by different people, so that the word leads to confusion of communications with consequent frustration. Here again the difficulty seems to be that "justice" is a negative concept; that is, it is not justice which leads to action, but injustice or discontent. We have seen how it is the perception of a difference between an actual and an ideal value of some variable which leads to "adjustment"; that is, which sets in motion machinery, if the machinery exists, for correcting the deviation. The study of justice, therefore, is the study of discontent, and especially of particular discontents. Discontents are "justified" if they can become part of a total apparatus (organization) for adjusting—that is, correcting—them. The apparatus, however, must be all-inclusive. It is easy to satisfy one discontent by creating others; the simultaneous minimizing of all discontents is a much more difficult matter. Here again coerciveness turns out to be a villain of the piece, for coercion involves the suppression of discontent, not its alleviation. Coerciveness therefore involves minimizing the discontent of the exerciser of coercion, but at the cost of perpetuating the discontent of the coerced.

One of the difficulties in minimizing discontent is the difficulty of measurement. There is no simple scale like the monetary scale by which discontents can be measured; still less are there any accurate devices for comparing the discontents of different people. In practice discontent is measured by the amount of action which it calls forth. The distribution of the ability and the inclination to act, however, is not equal, with the result that people who are adept at making a fuss are more likely to have their discontents corrected than those who suffer in silence.

Even if discontents could be measured and if agencies existed for minimizing them, the ethical problem would not be disposed of, for the question of "divine discontent" would remain. Adjustment, as we have seen, can be accomplished either by moving the actual toward the ideal or by moving the ideal toward the actual. Even the most persistent failure to carry out the ideals of Jesus, for instance, has not deterred people from striving after them. The "adjustment" which consists of resignation to imperfection is not the kind of adjustment that drives man forward. The feeling, therefore, that there is something which transcends justice—a feeling which has been characteristic of all the higher religions— finds confirmation in the theory of organization. Our machinery of "justice" is the machinery for the minimizing of discontent, and as such is a necessary part of social organization. The achievement of real justice, however, is only proportionate to the ideal which is cherished. No matter how good the machinery in society for the satisfaction of discontents of all kinds, if the ideals are inadequate the society will be less than ideal. Better Socrates dissatisfied than a pig satisfied! The society of Aldous Huxley's *Brave New World* was a "just" and certainly a well-adjusted society; it was an abomi- nation unto the Lord for all that, and it cracked under the impact of a simple prophetic figure.

The ultimate ideal which has most attraction for Christians is of course the ideal of love. This ideal has frequently been felt as a liberator from the bondage of organization. Thus we have St. Paul's constant contrast between the Law—which represents careful organization of the moral life—and the Spirit, which represents spontaneous life itself. There is also the famous remark of St.

Augustine, "Love God and do what you will." The history of Christianity is a constant testimony to the liberating and creative impact of the rediscovery of divine love. Nevertheless, love is not a substitute for organization and does not itself constitute an answer to the problems which organization tries to solve. Moreover, there is an ever-present problem of *why* the spirit is killed by the letter— why an organization so often ends by smothering the very thing which it was created to embody.

The word "letter" itself perhaps gives the clue. Any organization, as we have seen, is essentially a system of communication. Its behavior can be interpreted in terms of action to prevent some variable from wandering outside its prescribed limits. The only variables which organizations can operate on, however, are the *visible* variables—and it is the letter which is visible, the spirit invisible. Thus an organization which starts out to embody the spirit of love finds it difficult to identify this spirit in the information patterns which it possesses. Consequently its information patterns conform more and more to the things which can be easily observed, that is, conformity to a "law"—prescribed ritual, dress, habits, customs. The spirit somehow eludes the information system; hence the "executive" is not aware of its decline and becomes increasingly aware of the external items of information which pass more easily into the information system and can more easily be influenced by the effectors.

Consequently the "pure" Christian society is always a flower that withers almost in the moment of its blooming. The early Church at Jerusalem, the Franciscans, the Anabaptists, the Quakers, the Methodists—all have been subject to the law of organizational hardening, the replacement of the subtle and evanescent flower of the loving community by the hard, dry seed of organization, or by simple decay and death. The only hope of love is that the seed into which it passes has the power to generate new flowers. It is only by constant death and rebirth that loving societies can exist. The only possibility of a permanent organization embodying a spirit of pure love would be a much more subtle system of information and much better stimulators of love than we now seem to possess. Aside from this, the only recipe for a loving society seems to be a constant new birth, and this implies constant death of the old. In this sense, then, the less existing organizations are protected and the easier it is for them to die, the better the chance of the new birth and the flowering of the loving community. It is because we give our love to the organizations which are only the apparatus of life, and not to God who is the author of life, that perfect love comes so rarely into flower; the worst enemy of the greater love is the lesser.

This concludes, except brief references, the more theoretical part of this discussion. In the next few chapters, I shall examine some examples of the organizational revolution in various fields—labor, agriculture, business, and the national state (the latter taking two forms, Communist and social-democratic). This does not pretend to be an exhaustive survey. Indeed, each of the fields selected is worthy of a volume in itself. In a single chapter on each field only points peculiarly illustrative of the thesis of this work can be dealt with. There are also some fields which have either not been covered at all or treated only sketchily. Thus the field of professional associations has been omitted altogether. The problem of international organizations (international cartels, commodity agreements, and the various international agencies both inside and outside the United Nations) has not been given the attention which it deserves. No attention has been given to organizations such as those of veterans, lodges, women's clubs, and the like, which have some economic implications, but which do not affect economic life to any direct degree, or which involve principles which are covered adequately by the treatment of other organizations studied.

PART II
Some Case Studies

6

The Labor Movement

The labor movement is essentially a movement among wage earners to improve their position in society. It develops along with the development of a class of wage earners, i.e., a group of people who derive their income mainly from the sale of their labor and who expect to go on deriving their income from this source during most of their lives. Wage earners appear at early stages in the development of society. Nevertheless, as an important element in society they are in a sense the creation of the technical revolution: first, of the revolution in agriculture which, by creating a surplus of food over and above the needs of the agricultural population, permitted the enormous increase in nonagricultural industry; and second, of the revolution in industrial techniques which gave an important competitive advantage to large-scale enterprises.

PERSISTENCE OF THE WAGE SYSTEM

A wage-earning system in which there is almost complete specialization between the management on the one hand and the wage earner on the other is not, of course, the only conceivable way of organizing large enterprises. There have been many attempts at other forms of organization, such as the simple communism of communities like Oneida and Amana, and the many experiments in producers' cooperation. Through all these experiments, however, the wage system has proved astonishingly stable and persistent, and it is interesting to observe that it seems to be increasingly dominant in Soviet Russia, in spite of a long tradition and encouragement of other forms such as the "artel" (craftsmen's cooperative).

There are good reasons for the dominance of the wage system, and in any appraisal of it they must be taken into consideration.

Perhaps the main reason is to be found in the weaknesses of other forms of organization. Once the organization reaches beyond the smallest size there begin to be great advantages in the *specialization* of management, which of necessity involves a separation of those who give instructions from those who receive them. This is something like the specialization of the nervous system in the biological organism. The wage system is the easiest way to achieve this specialization, because of its impersonality.

In what might be called a "pure" wage system (which, of course, has never existed but which is a useful "extreme case"), labor is regarded as a commodity like any other; the relationship between the worker and the employer is a pure exchange relationship, just like the relationship between the employer and his supplier of raw materials. In this extreme case labor is regarded simply as a raw material of the process of production; it is "organized" passively by management and pushed around just as materials or machines are pushed around. From the point of view simply of the enterprise as an organization one can see the advantage of this arrangement over the system in which complex personal relationships exist. It is again an advantage of specialization; the enterprise can get on with its business, limiting its relations with the workers solely to what is essential to the conduct of the business, and *not* trying to be a "family" in which complete and therefore complex personal relationships are maintained among all the members.

The producers' cooperative, as a form of enterprise, almost inevitably involves an attempt to extend the informal but complex type of relationship which is involved in the family into much larger organizations. It breaks down on the point of the sheer incapacity of the human mind to cope with complex relationships with large numbers of people. The internal limitations of this type of organization begin to appear with even a handful of members, mainly because of the rapidity with which the number of possible relationships increases as the numbers increase. A couple have a single relationship, which can be rich and complex without overburdening the capacity of each to absorb and translate the kind of information which the relationship demands. In a group of three there are six relationships—three couples, and three relations of one to a couple. In a group of four there are twenty-five relationships, and the number of relationships skyrockets in more than geometric progression as the number of persons in the group increases. If large groups are to function at all there must be *economy* in personal relationships, or the organization will break down through its sheer inability to run its switchboard of communications. Historically the almost uniform failure of cooperative communities and producers' cooperatives is a testimony to this "iron law of organization." Even the success of consumers' and farm cooperatives is a testimony to it, for they have been successful in direct proportion as they have become impersonal and "business-like."

Paradoxically enough, however, impersonality—which is the chief reason for the success of the wage system—is at the same time its principal weakness. The wage system has been a success because it has been convenient to treat labor as a commodity; and, in spite of all the protestations of the unions and of the Clayton Act and the International Labor Organization, labor *is* a commodity. But it is also much *more* than a commodity, and the worker-employer relationship is more than the relationship of the employer to the supplier of his raw material. It is, for one thing, a more continuous one; it involves more time, and it involves more "life." What the worker is selling is a part of his life, and inevitably the relationship must be more complex and more personal than the relationship of pure material exchange. The employer likewise is selling the worker a piece of his "life," as well as a money wage. The specialization between management and labor can never be complete, for the worker cannot help being involved in the fortunes of the enterprise for which he works, no matter how temporary the relationship may be.

The rise of the labor movement must be interpreted in large part as an attempt to resolve this basic dilemma of the wage system. It aims to preserve the immense organizational advantages of impersonality—advantages which are by no means confined to the employer, for the worker too gains in individual freedom to have a "personal" life apart from his job. Yet at the same time it aims to recognize that the worker-employer relationship cannot be wholly impersonal, and that it is in some degree a "domestic" or human relationship.

In this sense the labor movement can be compared with the feminist movement. The feminist movement is a movement for equality of *status* of the sexes and for a reconstruction of the family away from a paternalistic dictatorship toward a more equalitarian democracy. Likewise the labor movement is a struggle for equality of status on the part of the wage earner and a reconstruction of the industrial relationship away from paternalistic dictatorships (even when benevolent) toward a more equalitarian system. The analogy is not as fanciful as it might seem at first sight, for in a sense labor represents the "feminine" passive element in the industrial process while the employer is the "masculine," more active element. What we are witnessing both in the case of women and in the case of the labor movement is a revolt against passivity. The same interpretation can also be placed on the farm movement, insofar as it is a revolt against passive subjection to the vagaries of an impersonal market.

The labor movement, especially in the English-speaking countries, is, however, not a revolt *against* the wage system but an attempt to live with it and to control it. In these countries revolutionary unionism such as that of the I.W.W. was never a serious threat to the society and it is now virtually extinct. It was all very well to emblazon the abolition of the wage system on the banner; but when all was said and done the worker still had to live within the industrial relationship. Mama may resent the institution of the family and preach against it, but if she has a nest and a brood she is obliged to live with it somehow. So it is not surprising that the type of unionism which has proved by far the most successful is what the Wisconsin school calls "job-conscious" unionism, the main object of which is control of jobs through collective bargaining agreements. This type of unionism has survived even a major split within the labor movement, for the C.I.O. unions today, though in a different context, are just as "job-conscious" as the A.F. of L. unions, and follow much the same practices in seeking to get contracts. Wages are often a relatively minor issue in the motivation which leads men to become members of a union. In a recent survey[1] the investigators were astonished to discover that out of 114 union members questioned not one gave higher wages as a reason for joining the union.

[1] Joel Seidman, Jack London, and Bernard Karsh, "Why Workers Join Unions," *Annals of the American Academy*, March 1951, p. 75.

THE MANY-SIDED LABOR UNION

The labor movement cannot be understood unless it is realized that a labor union is a many-sided organization. It is, in fact, something like a state, something like a church, something like a lodge, and something like a cartel. It is something like a state because, while it is not (except in Communist societies) an agent of "the" government, it is an agent of orderly government in the broad sense. Some recent writers (notably Arthur Ross) have argued that the internal political aspects of union organizations are dominant. A union visualizes itself much as a state does; it is an organization built around the two poles of service to its members and struggle against the world outside. The world outside in this case consists of not only the employer but also the rival unions and at times the national state itself. The service to its members consists mainly of "grievance procedure"—a kind of semilegalized industrial government whereby the arbitrary will of the boss is replaced by an elaborate step-by-step procedure along well-defined channels. The grievance procedure is based in turn on the contract or trade agreement, which is a sort of working treaty between the union and the employer. It contains usually a large number of provisions centered around the rights of the worker in his job, and includes usually a legalistic machinery for regulating dismissal, transference, or promotion (seniority).

Because of the job-centered nature of the relationship (the job is to the union what *Lebensraum* is to a nation) and the fact that the job is largely under the control of the employer, we find the curious phenomenon of "union security"—i.e., the union using its "enemy" (the employer) to police its own membership. Under the "closed shop" (outlawed under the Taft-Hartley Act), the union attains such complete control of the job that in effect it becomes the hirer and firer; that is, the employer can employ only men previously approved by the union as members. Under the "union shop," the employer, oddly enough, becomes the recruiter for the union; the employer is free to hire whom he will, but one of the conditions of the job is that the men hired immediately join the union. Even under the form of union security known as "maintenance of membership," the union uses the employer to force people who have joined to stay in the union during the period of the contract.

The wide acceptance of union security in contracts is itself a testimony to the "ritualistic" nature of the struggle between unions and management. In popular imagination, of course, the struggle is seen as a real one, in the sense that unions are supposed to make their gains at the expense of management. In fact this is rarely the case. There are cases in which unions and management in effect "gang up" to exploit the consumer of their product. There may then be some dispute about the division of spoils. But even these cases of genuine monopoly are rare, and, as we have seen, there is little evidence that the rise of unionism has had any large effect on the distribution of the national income. In fact, as I have tried to show in my *Reconstruction of Economics*,[2] the distribution of the national income between wages and nonlabor income is much more a matter of decisions about investment and dividend distributions, both of which are largely in the hands of management, than it is a matter of anything which can be brought about by collective bargaining. As far as wages are concerned, with the exception of the monopolistic corners, the strictly economic gains of unionism are what workers as a whole would have got anyhow.

In any case, since the employer provides the jobs which are the real building blocks of union structure, the relationship of the union to the employer is a peculiarly dependent one. The union dares not generally push the fight against the employer to the point where the employer "loses" and is forced out of business. In this sense the employer may have a certain advantage: whereas unions could not possibly exist without employers, employers can, and do, exist without unions. Nevertheless, employers are finding in increasing numbers that in fact unions are a useful adjunct as part of industrial government, and that an industrial marriage between the union and the employer, even though it occasionally takes place under circumstances reminiscent of a shotgun wedding, is by no means without mutual convenience and even advantage to both parties. "Mutual survival," in the phrase of Professor Bakke, becomes the order of the day. The worker gains status, a sense of dignity and a protection from the arbitrary use of management's

[2] Kenneth E. Boulding, *A Reconstruction of Economics*, New York, John Wiley & Sons, Inc., 1950, Chapter 14.

power; and management gains freedom from trouble, better morale, better discipline, and higher productivity. Union-management collaboration is a much broader and deeper relation than the famous experiments of the Amalgamated Clothing Workers.

The struggle against rival unions is frequently much more real and bitter than the struggle against management. The two hundred odd national or international unions in the United States can be thought of as quasi-independent states, all of them surrounded by Alsace-Lorraines. The story of jurisdictional strife is an oft-lamented one; nevertheless it is highly understandable when we see the union as an organization of jobs rather than of men—or perhaps, one should say, of men in their capacity as the occupiers of specific jobs. A certain sense of class unity (something like the "Holy Alliance") keeps the jurisdictional struggle in check, and the two federations help somewhat to keep it in check among their own members, though it is recurrently flaring up, especially in the A.F. of L. Jurisdictional trouble has been much less prominent in the C.I.O., largely because the separate C.I.O. unions have been carving empires for themselves out of the virgin territory of the unorganized, and hence have not bothered much about the boundaries between them. The "closing of the frontier" may well witness the spread of serious internal jurisdictional problems, especially as there are even fewer "natural boundaries" between industries than there are between crafts. The expulsion of the Communist-dominated unions from the C.I.O. has opened up an area of severe jurisdictional strife, though its sources are ideological rather than simply imperialistic. The United Mine Workers may not unjustly be regarded as an imperialistic union; its "District 50" involves it in jurisdictional conflicts with a great many other unions.

The fact that struggle is an important part of the ritual of unionism is an important element in the interpretation of the *strike* as a social phenomenon. In the strike the struggle of the union reaches its highest point of emotional content; it is in the strike that the loyalty to the union is either sealed or broken by suffering. Consequently the strike cannot be interpreted as an "economic" phenomenon, any more than war, to which it corresponds in the nation-state, can be so interpreted; its value is frequently symbolic and ritualistic; it is an orgastic relationship rather than a rational one.

Consequently the intensity of strikes has little to do with the matters apparently at issue; prolonged and bitter strikes have been fought ostensibly over a wage difference of a nickel an hour. They come, like war, at the climax of a period of emotional upheaval. This is not to say, of course, that no strikes occur which are cold-bloodedly planned as part of the strategy of the union leaders. Occasionally strike situations are created, like wars, to divert the attention of the members of the organization from dissensions and trouble within to enemies without, and a leader who is afraid of losing his position by an internal revolt may not hesitate to provoke trouble in order to unify the union behind him. This, however, is a risky game to play for all parties, and wiser counsels eventually prevail. Frequently, a strike, like a war, is not part of a carefully laid plan but is the outcome of profound emotional disturbances— a blowing-off of much pent-up steam. For this reason the strike is not to be condemned out of hand. Just as the family sociologists assure us that an occasional episode of dish-throwing, properly handled, may actually cement the unity of the family, so a strike, properly handled, may supply release for a lot of annoyance and frustration.

The strike is, after all, a lively and exciting episode in the otherwise humdrum life of the industrial worker; it gives him a certain sense of participation in the drama of history in a way that assembly-line production rarely does. It is important to distinguish between the essentially ritualistic strike and the bitter-end strike which leaves hard feelings and permanently lowered morale for a long time as its consequence. When coal miners get an urge to go on strike at the opening of the fishing season and when stocks of coal seem rather high, we need not necessarily feel that the foundations of industrial order are tottering.

There is, however, a real problem of strikes in "essential" industries. Certain groups of workers, such as railroad workers, elevator operators, truckers, sanitation workers, and so on, occupy "bottleneck" positions in the structure of society, and if organized may be in a position to levy a sort of highwayman's toll on the traffic of society. Strikes in these industries are not merely a domestic squabble between the union and the employer; they impose a substantial cost on the whole of society through the disruption of essential facilities. It is interesting to note, for instance, that there is an almost inviolable taboo in American life against striking against the government. This taboo is so strong, in fact, that the only way which has been devised so far to deal with some strikes is by government seizure of the struck properties. The reason why this taboo holds—in spite of the fact that government workers are frequently worse paid than workers of corresponding ranks and skills elsewhere—is mainly that another ritual and arena of struggle are provided in the legislative assembly. Postal workers, for instance, watch the progress of legislation on their behalf with somewhat the same kind of interest and excitement that steelworkers enjoy in the strike. Temporary nationalization, however, is a clumsy solution to this problem in nongovernmental industries. Yet it must be emphasized that the problem is to find a substitute form of conflict and substitute satisfactions.

If the individual union is something like a state, the labor movement as a whole is certainly something like a church. Behind the run-down little country church at the crossroads there somehow stands the Church militant and triumphant, with her saints and martyrs contributing their life to a great stream of history on which float the tawdry realities of the moment. Just so, behind the dirty union hall and even the shiftless or racketeering official there stands the Labor Movement, a stream of history which also has its saints and martyrs, its Mother Joneses and its Joe Hills, its songs and its stories and its traditions, giving a curious secret strength to its often commonplace embodiment. Alongside the job-conscious businesslikeness there runs a stream of idealism, expressed in the concept of a "good union man." There have been many unsung sufferers for the cause—people who have suffered loss of jobs, blacklisting, tarring-and-feathering, imprisonment, and even death because they have believed in the union, not as a means of personal advancement, but as a great movement in history for the betterment of the group.

It is this faith which ultimately gives the labor movement its strength, and which especially gives it strength to withstand the attacks of employers and of the state in periods when they have been hostile. Employers have a real competitive disadvantage in the struggle because they do not have so good a "mythology" as the labor movement, and because they do not have so vivid a sense of their purpose in history and their function in society. The myth of the self-regulating free market does not affect the springs of emotional life as deeply as the myth of a class struggle.

One may mention only briefly the lodgelike attributes of unions, as these are diminishing in importance. Nevertheless, it is not to be overlooked that one of the services which unions provide, and one of the motives for joining them, is the motive of simple fellowship; and in some unions the union hall serves much the same purpose as a lodge. Some unions have even gone in for "mysteries"— ritualistic ceremonies, initiations, even burials. (The painters, for instance, have a beautiful and moving burial service for their members.) In all this the influence of the Masons and similar orders can be traced. Some unions also have performed some of the functions of a "friendly society," with benefits for sickness, death, unemployment, and so on—mostly on a very casual actuarial basis. With the rise of social insurance these secondary aspects of unionism tend increasingly to be sloughed off, and unionism becomes increasingly job-centered. The recent growth of collectively bargained pensions is no exception to this rule, as these new industrial pensions are not paid foi by union dues, and are perquisites of the "job" rather than of the individual.

ASPECTS OF COLLECTIVE BARGAINING

Turning now to the economic aspects of unionism, the interest focuses on the impact of unionism on the wage-price structure, both relative and absolute. As the economist sees the union, from the pinnacle of his abstract world of commodities, it looks much like a cartel, that is, an organization of sellers for the joint sale of their product. Sociologically, of course, and psychologically, a union is very different from a cartel; in regard to its impact on the market, however, it is rather similar. A cartel is an arrangement whereby a number of producers retain the independent control of production but hand over to a central organization responsibility for sales and pricing. Similarly, a union is an organization of workers who retain their individual rights as workers (i.e., the union does not generally tell them where to go and what to do) but who turn over the responsibility for the terms of employment, in regard to both wages and working conditions, to the union. Even this analogy must not be pressed too far. In an industrial cartel, for instance, title to the product frequently passes to the central selling organization before the final sale is made. In the case of the union, the union does not, as it were, take title to the labor of the member and then sell that labor; the wage exchange is still an exchange between the individual worker and the employer, but the *terms* of the exchange are settled by the union.

The consequence of unionization, therefore, is *collective bargaining*. Attention is usually focused on the "collective" aspects of collective bargaining, emphasizing the point that for good or ill it represents the replacement of individual settlement of the terms of employment between the individual worker and the boss (or the boss's representative) by collective settlement of the terms of employment between the union and the employer. The main economic impact of the collective bargaining is that a much greater degree of uniformity in wages and working conditions is established over the bargaining area. This has the advantage that "hole and corner" exploitation due to ignorance and immobility is eliminated, and the market may even come to approximate more the "perfect market" so beloved of the economist.

Collective bargaining may have a certain cost in the suppression of individual differences in remuneration which might be justified on the basis of individual productivity; though if the market is as imperfect as many labor economists allege, there is not much machinery even in an unorganized market by which these differences can be recognized. It may have a more serious cost in conservatism, in the sense that the easiest thing to do in a collective situation is to do what has been done before. It may therefore operate somewhat as a brake upon technological change, though the factual evidence on this point is by no means clear in American society. Technological change takes place mainly in the unorganized labor market, and it takes organization a long time to catch up with it. The potential danger here is not serious as long as the labor movement is a minority movement, though there are certain industries—for example, construction and railroads—where there is some cause for concern. In spite of these potential dangers, however, collective bargaining has achieved a respectable status as an instrument of industrial government. It is regarded as a necessary modification of the free market, imposed by the fact that the industrial relationship of management to labor is much more than an exchange or market relationship and needs some form of political administration, internal or external.

Less attention has been given to the "bargaining" aspects of collective bargaining, and yet this may also be of great importance. Generally speaking, there is not much bargaining in the unorganized labor market, and what there is is perfunctory and not time-consuming. Usually the employer offers a job at a price, much as stores offer a commodity at a price, and the worker, like the consumer, can either take it or leave it. The inability of a worker to leave it under conditions of unemployment and labor immobility is, of course, one of the principal generators of the desire for unions; nevertheless, under conditions of full employment and a mobile labor force the worker *is* free to take or leave what is offered to him. Under these circumstances, bargaining plays a small role in the labor market, just as it plays a small role in retail markets. It must not be thought, however, that under the conditions of an active market the absence of bargaining gives any necessary advantage to the price or the wage *quoter* over against the price or wage *taker*. Under genuinely competitive conditions the power of the price or wage quoter is practically nil. If the price is set even a little too high, nobody will buy; if the wage is set even a little too low, nobody will apply for the jobs.

In the study of collective bargaining, sufficient attention has not been given to the fact that bargaining itself is for a great many people a disagreeable, even immoral, occupation, and that it is always time-consuming. For these reasons bargaining, which used to be almost universal even in retail markets (and in oriental countries still is the rule), tends to die out in an advanced economy. Insofar as it is a bargaining, rather than a standard price situation, collective bargaining represents what seems to be a retrogressive step as far as mere price or wage determination is concerned, and many of its most important economic effects derive from the bargaining rather than from the collective aspects.

The most striking difference between collective bargaining and the unorganized labor market is that under the unorganized market the determination of wages is rather strictly "economic," accompanied by no publicity and almost a minimum of emotional tone; but under collective bargaining wage determination steps, as it were, from the market place into the football field, and is accompanied by an immense amount of palaver, play acting, game playing, and general emotional hullabaloo. The analogy of the football field is a close one; there are "sides," there is on the side of labor at least a desperate necessity to "win" something, and both sides have something corresponding to "rooters" on the sidelines—invisible, but a mighty presence nevertheless.

The difference between the positions of the union and the management representatives is also noteworthy. The union representatives are acutely sensitive to their constituency, and are generally in grave danger of losing their jobs if they do not "bring home the bacon." Their constituency is almost universally called upon to ratify their decisions, and not infrequently repudiates them.

By contrast the lot of the management representatives is much easier. Shareholders are notoriously difficult to arouse, and are particularly difficult to arouse by anything that happens at the collective-bargaining table. Management's motivation is one of responsibility to the business as such—that is, to keep the organization alive and growing—rather than to the shareholders as a collectivity. There may be some fear of displeasing the general business community (the managers who are too "soft" may get black looks at the country club); but even this is mild compared with the fierce displeasure which constantly threatens the ineffective union leader. Consequently, the collective-bargaining situation constantly looks like an advance on the part of the union and a retreat on the part of management. We have seen that the "gains" of the union are seldom made at the *expense* of management; nevertheless, it would almost seem that this fiction must be kept up if the ritual of conflict is to be maintained.

Perhaps the most significant feature of collective bargaining from the point of view of its impact on economic life and policy is the fact that it consumes a lot of time and energy. This means that its main economic result is to make money wages "sticky," i.e., unresponsive to the general movements of inflation or deflation in the economy. In an inflationary period such as we have been going through, this has meant that the wages of organized labor have risen on the whole more slowly than the wages of unorganized labor, especially in such fields as agriculture and domestic service. Unionization, paradoxically enough, has operated as a force to hold money wages *down* in such a period because of the time-consuming character of the wage-adjustment process.

In the unorganized markets there have been countless "rounds" of wage increases. As the purchasing power of employers has grown with the inflation and as labor has become scarce, innumerable employers have found themselves bereft of labor and have been forced to offer higher wages to attract workers, or have been forced to meet the competition of the higher wages offered by others in order to keep workers. The process is like the rising of the tide: it creeps up the channels almost invisibly and imperceptibly, but with the immense force of gravitational necessity.

In the organized markets, on the other hand, the channels are interrupted by the dams of elaborate contractual agreements, usually reopened only at annual intervals or under conditions of great stress. The tide of inflation rises against these dams at first without apparent effect; then when it rises far enough it goes over the top with a great deal of splash and fuss and publicity. Thus, over against the million imperceptible "rounds" of wage increase in the unorganized labor market, we have four "rounds" in the organized market, accompanied by a great deal of publicity and shouting. Actually, however, while the dams increase the visibility of the tide, they may actually diminish its flow.

When the tide runs out, of course, the story is reversed; in the unorganized markets (for example, in agriculture) deflation in the general economy results in a rapid decline in wages and not much change in employment. The tide runs out quietly, even if not painlessly. In organized markets the dams of contract hold, often for a long time, and money wages do not fall in the face of a generally deflationary situation and rising unemployment. When the dams "give," they do so with a great deal of excitement and distress, sometimes involving the destruction of the contractual arrangement, or even of the union itself.

The development of contracts of the General Motors type which involve automatic cost-of-living adjustments may modify these conclusions substantially. If such contracts were to become widespread money wages would unquestionably become much more flexible, especially in an upward direction. Experience with contracts of this type in the past suggests that they do not generally survive a period of deflation, so that it may be questioned whether the general conclusion, that organized markets introduce a long-run inflationary bias into the economy, is seriously affected. It is possible, indeed, that such contracts may aggravate the problem. The effect of these contracts is to insulate one group in society from the effects of inflation. This means first that the political incentive to avoid inflation is correspondingly weakened; it means also that the impact of inflation works all the more hardship on the nonprotected groups. It is still too early to judge the significance of this development.

ETHICAL PROBLEMS INVOLVED

The relationship of ethical standards and ideas to movements like the labor movement can be discussed at three levels at least. There is first the relatively simple level of "common morality," on which we need not spend much time. It is obviously desirable that union treasurers should not abscond with funds, that union officials generally should not try to sabotage the union, that union members should take some interest in the affairs of their organization, and so on. Interestingly enough, it is probably at this level that the Communist influence has been most resented. The unforgivable sin of the Communists is that they regard the union as a means to gain their own ends and not as an organization with its own life and purposes. The sabotage of unions by Communist officials in the interests of the current party line is what makes most union men among the most bitter of anti-Communists. The United Mine Worker uses "Comrat" almost as a technical term. It is probable also that the violation of certain common decencies by employing groups, especially through the use of the "stool pigeon" (it is difficult to cultivate any affection for either a Judas or a Caiaphas), the use of the "yellow-dog contract," and overt violence, had a great deal to do with the growth of the labor movement itself, and, what is perhaps even more important, with the growth of a prounion sentiment among large masses of the public which led to the enactment of the Norris-La Guardia and Wagner Acts.

A question which deserves some attention at this level, but which must be dismissed with a mere mention because it would carry us far beyond the scope of this work, is the problem of the attitude toward work itself. It is clear that what we call "work" (that activity for which we are paid by others) covers the whole moral gamut from the most soul-destroying drudgery to the highest and most ennobling activities of man. When the division of labor is pushed to the point where the price of more and better goods is worse people, it is time to call a halt. Curiously enough it was Adam Smith himself (in *The Wealth of Nations*, Book 5, Chapter 1, Part 3, Article 2) who recognized this problem more clearly than perhaps any economist before or since, and his vigorous denunciation of the division of labor as a producer of idiots is too little known by those who think of him as an apostle of laissez faire.

The moral quality of work depends on two factors: the nature of the work itself, and the attitude of the worker toward it. There can be little doubt that the rise of organization must have had some impact on both these factors, but it is not always easy to say in which direction. On the side of the work itself, labor organizations perform a valuable function in keeping society aware of hazards to health and character involved in particular jobs. On the side of the attitude toward work, the effect of organization is frequently to formalize—and hence perhaps to make more rigid—an existing set of attitudes. Thus studies of restriction of output among workers have shown on the whole that the philosophy of "ca' canny," which unions are sometimes accused of fostering, is developed by the uncertainties of the job experience itself rather than by organization, and is found among unorganized as well as among organized workers. Where the reward of hard work is unemployment, it is difficult to blame people for not wanting to work themselves out of a job. Unions may sometimes formalize these attitudes into restrictive clauses in contracts, but they do not generally create them. On the other side of the ledger, the slogan of "an honest day's work for an honest day's pay" is not to be taken lightly. Craft unions especially have done something to foster pride in craft and in doing a workmanlike job, and in all fields a constructive union-management relationship can do much to increase the sense of significance in work.

The second level of ethical discussion deals with those visible problems of personal conduct which arise specifically because of the existence of the labor movement. These problems are many and complex and almost always involve a conflict of goods, and therefore ethical dilemmas—dilemmas which there are no easy formulas to resolve, and which can be resolved only by the individual's making his decisions as honestly as he can in the light of such knowledge as he possesses.

The labor movement itself is tinged with ethical coloring, as we have seen, and has attracted a good deal of public support because of it. Nevertheless, it inevitably creates conflicts of loyalties. The fact that the "job" which is the "living space" of unions is created by the employer creates a certain moral tension between the loyalty of the worker to his role as an employee and his loyalty to his role as a union man. There is nothing necessarily undesirable about this tension. In fact all individuals are subject to it insofar as everyone is a member of many organizations and "in his life plays many parts." It can become destructive; it can, however, be creative, and there is reason to hope that in American life, at least at many points, these conflicts of loyalties are producing genuinely creative solutions. But either employers or unions who insist on "absolute" loyalty are headed for trouble. Just as a creative tension between husband and wife, if it is undergirded by a mutual respect and love, is about the best recipe for a satisfactory family situation, so a creative tension accompanied by mutual respect, on a lower level of emotion, can provide the basis for a satisfactory industrial situation. The achievement of such a solution is not easy, but there are many examples of how it can be done.

Many of the moral problems involving the relation of an individual to a union, or the responsibility of a union official to his constituency, or the democratic or autocratic structure of the union itself, arise out of the fact that unions grow up in an atmosphere of struggle and are, like national states, agencies of conflict. Because of this, more power must frequently be delegated to officials, with more secrecy and fewer controls, than might seem desirable in organizations which do not live in an environment of conflict. The intensity of the loyalty problem, and the intense moral disapprobation bestowed on "scabs," strikebreakers, and others who threaten the internal security of a union, reflect similar attitudes toward those who threaten the internal unity of states. When the union is recognized and respectable and has established its position vis-à-vis both the employer and society at large, these militant attitudes largely lose their meaning, and the more democratic ethical standards have a better chance of coming into their own.

Even under the best of conditions, however, there are real ethical problems raised by the bargaining process; it is difficult to conceive of it without something in the way of deceit, bluffing, and a lack of regard for the truth. Insofar as these things are part of a ritual, understood by both parties, some of the moral sting is taken out of them. Nevertheless, it is conceivable that a sensitive conscience might be a handicap to a negotiator. It is clear that the ethics of bargaining are far from being worked out, and that a great deal of the emotional difficulty which collective bargaining occasions is due to the lack of any agreed concept of the limits of integrity under such circumstances. The really skilled negotiator must almost of necessity be two-faced; he must present himself as a "bonnie fechter" to his constituency, and must appear as a "problem solver" to his opponent across the table. How to turn "fight" situations into "problem-solving" situations is one of the major problems of industrial relations—a problem which is itself pretty much in the "fight" stage.

The visible moral problems raised by unionism, however, because they are visible, at least are being worked on. By far the most difficult set of problems are the invisible ones—those that arise because the real effects of almost any action or institution in social life are apt to be very different from the immediately apparent effects. This problem can be felt at the level of a single industry in connection with the long-run price of industrial peace. Industrial peace itself is not too difficult of attainment, given a modicum of good sense and good will. The price of industrial peace is not always apparent, yet it may be substantial, in terms perhaps of featherbedding, of a slowing down of the rate of technical advance, perhaps of permanent discrimination against racial minorities, or perhaps of a ganging up of union and employer against the consumer on the one hand and the excluded worker on the other. Because of the hidden nature of these effects it is difficult to demonstrate that they are important; one certainly may doubt whether they are of great importance in the American economy.

The case of the railroads, however, indicates that a mature unionism collaborating with an equally mature management, in a well-established and for the most part peaceful industrial relationship, may be both insensitive to consumers and resistant to technical and social change, as witnessed, for instance, in racial attitudes. It may be, of course, that the ills of the railroad industry are due to the dead hand of government regulation; but it must be remembered also that unionism represents industrial government and may be as resistant to change, once established, as any bureaucracy.

I am not suggesting that these problems are necessarily of great importance in our present society. We need, however, to know much more about them and need to be watchful, as they may be much more important in the future, if organization continues to grow, than they have been in the past. It may be that one of the best checks on the evils of organization is the competition of the unorganized, and as society becomes more completely organized this check diminishes.

An even more important "invisible" problem is that of the impact of labor organization on the whole economy, and especially on the rate of "improvement" in many spheres of life and on the more pressing problem of the control of economic fluctuations. The general social attitude toward the labor movement, as expressed ultimately in legislation, depends either on the more visible aspects of the movement or on the movement of the shapeless tide of public approbation. This tide of public approbation (or disapprobation), which in a democratic society, at least, is the ultimate mover of legislation, and is the element in which all organizations live and move, is affected strongly by the moral ideas of the society.

We have seen this tide first run strongly against labor organizations in the nineteenth century, then turn and run almost equally strongly in the other direction in the era of the Wagner Act, then turn again, or at least hesitate, in the Taft-Hartley era. The preaching and teaching of moral and religious leaders—especially the leaders of the "Social Gospel" movement of the early years of the twentieth century—undoubtedly had a profound influence in bringing about a change in the public atmosphere. Perhaps even more important on the negative side was the irresponsible conduct of many leaders of business who, as we have already observed, violated many of the canons of common morality in conducting their war against the unions and by doing so created a great deal of sympathy for their opponents. Related to this was the inability of business spokesmen to come to grips in any way with the problem of depression. The Wagner Act would certainly never have come into being if it had not been for the depression of 1929-32. The "welfare capitalism" of the 1920s, which was quite successful as long as there was full employment, and actually seemed to be destroying the labor movement by a process of erosion, proved itself quite inadequate to cope with the problem of mass unemployment, and denials that there was any such problem did not look particularly convincing in 1932.

More important in the long run than all of these more obvious reasons—which determine the time of the tide rather than the tide itself—is the pervasive influence of Christianity in American and European culture. It is from Christianity that the "familistic" ideals come into our culture, that is, the idea of a full and intimate relationship of love and concern as the ideal human relationship. This is derived ultimately from the view of God as the father and men as brothers, and of the family therefore as the symbol of divine nature. The familistic ideal, as we have seen, constantly comes into conflict with the necessities of organizational life; nevertheless, it creates a tension which makes it impossible to accept the impersonal operation of a pure market system as an *ideal*. It is from the familistic ideal that the love of the underdog[3] ultimately springs, and this is a force of profound importance in any Christian-influenced society; it is impossible to explain the legislative history of Western countries without it. It should be observed, however, that the dog must belong to the family; other people's dogs do not call forth anything like the same amount of sympathy.

Serious difficulties arise for society when real problems exist that are not in the public consciousness, and which are not, therefore, part of the system of public judgment. It may be that one of these problems is the relationship of the organization of the market through the labor movement and other organizations to the problem of business-cycle control and long-run inflation or stagnation. This question has already been discussed in Chapter 3. The organized market, because of its slowness to react, is a positive asset in times of monetary inflation, for it means that inflationary forces take themselves out in increased output and employment rather than in increased prices. In time of deflation, however, it works the other way, for the inability to adjust prices and wages downward means that deflation takes the form of a decline in output and a rise in unemployment. Consequently a society with highly organized markets cannot afford to have a deflation, which means that it cannot correct an inflation. This almost inevitably introduces an inflationary trend into the economy which has profound effects on distribution, both among classes and among individuals. We have hardly begun to think about the ethical problems involved in inflation, much less to integrate these judgments into our general system of approbation.

[3] "Infracaninophilism," in the mongrel coinage of an eminent essayist.

7

The Farm Organization Movement

The rise of farm organizations follows closely the history of the rise of the labor movement, in the United States and in most Western countries, even though the two movements are in no way organically connected. In the United States the long depression after the Civil War saw the beginnings of both the farm and the labor movements as effective organizations. The depression of the 1930s saw both rise to positions of dominance in legislative policy. In spite of the absence of organic connection, therefore, and even the absence of much communication except in the sporadic growth of farmer-labor parties, the two movements may be regarded as different aspects of a larger movement, which in its social aspect is a movement for equality of status and mutual improvement on the part of the lower status groups and in its economic aspect is a "revolt against the market"—a determination to control the conditions of exchange for the product of the group.

COMPARISONS WITH LABOR MOVEMENT

The great differences between the farm and the labor movements can be traced mainly to the difference in the nature of the market from which the incomes of these groups are derived. The worker generally derives his income from the sale of a single product (his labor) to a single purchaser (the employer). The farmer derives his income from the sale of the *products* of his labor and of any capital which he owns. Except in the case of specialized producers of milk, poultry, or cattle he generally sells a considerable number of products to an even larger number of buyers. It is this difference which affords the principal explanation why the labor movement has concentrated on collective bargaining and has laid only secondary emphasis on direct governmental intervention to regulate wages, whereas the farm movement has concentrated mainly on direct governmental action to affect farm prices and has laid only secondary emphasis on collective bargaining.

The differences between the two movements, however, are of degree rather than of kind. Where the farmer's market situation approaches that of the worker—as it does, for instance, in the case of the milk producer selling to a single distributor—we find the same emphasis on a cartel form of organization and on collective bargaining. In this case the producers' cooperative often corresponds closely in economic form to the labor union; its main objective is to obtain a satisfactory contract with the distributor, covering not only the price but also all conditions of sale. Because the market relationship is much less intimate and personal between the farmer and the distributor than it is between the worker and employer, we find less emphasis on such things as grievance procedure and the detailed administration of the conditions of sale. Nevertheless all these features are generally present in embryo, at least, in the producer-distributor relationship. At the other end of the scale we find an increasing interest in direct governmental regulation of wages on the part of the labor groups, resulting in minimum-wage and social-security legislation.

It thus seems to be the difference in the opportunities open to the two groups which accounts for their different policies, rather than any fundamental difference in motives or needs. The troublesomeness of collective bargaining makes it impracticable as a means for controlling a many-product, many-buyer market situation, just as the uncertainty and remoteness of government intervention makes it less attractive than collective bargaining at close quarters when the nature of the market makes collective bargaining feasible. However different the means, however, the end is the same: to give the sellers some degree of control over the market and to abolish the "free market" so beloved of the economists.

Another important source of difference between the two movements is the different social and economic status of workers and farmers. It is virtually impossible to be a farmer without owning some capital; and the average farm is in one of its aspects a small business, corresponding roughly in size to a small-to-medium retail store. Consequently farmers are much less likely to be "proletarian" in their social attitudes than industrial workers. In the poorer industrial countries there is apt to be a sharp cleavage in political and social attitudes between the "peasants" and the industrial workers. In the United States, and in all countries as they get richer, this cleavage becomes less important. As industrial wages rise to the point where industrial workers find it possible to become home owners, car owners, and so on, their attitudes become much less proletarian; and as we have seen, in the United States at least, the attitude of the main body of the labor movement has always been strongly capitalistic. We find also with the spread of improved transportation that the patterns of life of rural and urban people converge, and that one is just as likely to find the conveniences of industrial civilization, even its ulcers and mental breakdowns, in farm homes as in urban.

Nevertheless, it is curious that in a sense the farm movement has been much more "socialistic" in the United States than has the labor movement. It has from its beginnings been interested in direct governmental controls of economic life, even to the point of submitting to a detailed regulation of individual economic activity in the shape of production and marketing quotas, soil conservation subsidies, and so on, which a worker would probably find very irksome. It is not unreasonable to suppose, therefore, that the differences between the two movements stem much more from the differences in market environment than from any basic difference in the social groups themselves.

Because the worker's life is involved so intimately with the conditions of sale of his labor, the control of these conditions of sale has dominated the labor movement; it is the protection of the "job" more than any sense of unjust incomes which is the driving power behind the organization. In the farm movement, on the other hand, the conditions of sale of the product have been relatively unimportant, as the farmer sells not "life" but the product of his life, and he is hence much freer than the worker to arrange the details of his life and work to suit himself. In the case of the farmer, therefore, the driving power behind organization is not so much the sense of personal subjugation to the purchaser of his product as it is a sense of unfairness in the price which he receives.

The "Parity" Concept

Thus the prime symbol of the farm movement is not collective bargaining for a good contract, but "parity"—a "just" price for his product and therefore a "just" income for himself, derived preferably from the free market; but, if the free market will not provide it, derived from governmental activity of some kind. The parity concept is a "terms of trade" concept. It is the ratio of the price farmers receive to the prices they pay, referred generally to some "ideal" situation as a base—which in practice means the situation as it existed in some past base period. Put in another way, it is the amount of nonfarm products which the farmer can purchase with one unit of his farm products, relative to some ideal base. Thus if farm prices are at parity a bushel of farm produce will purchase just as much industrial goods as it did in the base period; if farm prices are 75 per cent of parity a bushel of farm produce will purchase only 75 per cent as much industrial goods as it did in the base period. Because of the diversity both of farm products and of industrial goods these figures must be expressed as index numbers, with all the limitations as to meaning which index numbers impose. Generally speaking, the parity concept is meaningful only over short periods of time. It is virtually impossible, for instance, to compare the kerosene, buggies, and bustles which farm products bought in 1890 with the electric light, automobiles, and nylon dresses of today.

There are even more weighty objections to the parity concept as basis of policy. Being a concept of "terms of trade" or ratio of exchange, it takes no account of relative changes in techniques or tastes, and therefore in costs. Suppose, for instance, that the average cost of production of wheat halved while other costs were stationary. It is evident that a wheat farmer who obtained a "parity price" under these circumstances, with reference to a base period before the technical change, would be obtaining far too much. If there is a relative fall in the costs of production of any given commodity, this should be reflected in a fall in its relative price. A "parity" system therefore which sets forth a "parity price" for each commodity tends to freeze the base-date system of relative prices, which becomes increasingly obsolete under the impact of different rates of change of cost. The price system under these circumstances is unable to perform the function of allocating resources among the production of various commodities. Commodities which have been undergoing technical improvement in their mode of production will be produced in excess of consumption under the stimulus of a "too high" price, and surpluses will develop; and commodities with more stable or rising costs will be consumed in excess of production, so that shortages may develop. The surpluses of grains and potatoes and the shortages of meat and dairy products which have occurred in recent years are evidence of some such breakdown in the price system—only partly, however, the fault of the parity doctrine.

With all its weaknesses, however, the parity doctrine has an extraordinary hold over the imagination of farmers to this day. It may be worth while to digress for a moment to inquire into some possible sources of this particular expression of discontent. One of the principal general sources of agricultural discontent is the undoubted fact that over the long pull agricultural incomes are substantially less than industrial incomes for persons of like skill, capacity, and capital. It is not merely that all studies of income show this to be the case, for it is difficult to make qualitative comparisons because of the differing amount of nonmonetary income involved in the two cases. The conclusive evidence for the lower real incomes in agriculture is that there is a constant net migration from agricultural to industrial employment, which goes on year in and year out with the possible exception of years of deep depression.

It is this very migration from agriculture into industry, however, which gives us the clue to the reason for the disparity in income. A society in which agricultural techniques are constantly improving must inevitably suffer a decline in the proportion of the population engaged in agriculture, because the very basic nature of most agricultural commodities means that the demand for them is inelastic. Thus a savage society in which the productivity of food production is so low that a family can find or raise only just enough food for its own needs cannot possibly afford any "industry" whatever; the whole population must be engaged in food getting. A primitive agricultural society where the food producer can produce enough food for two families can afford to have only half its people in agriculture and half in other employments. This is why agriculture itself, in the sense of settled cultivation of the land rather than sporadic cultivation or food collecting (hunting, fishing, etc.), is an almost invariable producer of civilization. It is the food surplus from agriculture which feeds the cities and the armies.

An advanced society like that of the United States can produce all its food with perhaps 10 or even 5 per cent of its population, and so can spare all the more for industrial pursuits. In a society of advancing agricultural techniques, therefore, there must always be a relative decline in the proportion of resources engaged in agriculture. The only way of accomplishing such a decline, however, in a market economy is by "squeezing" the declining occupation, i.e., by making it less attractive than the industries which are due to expand. The "squeeze" is not of course a conscious one. It happens because resources (especially labor) do not get out of agriculture fast enough and consequently agricultural output is persistently greater than can be sold at prices which would make agricultural incomes equivalent to industrial incomes. The remedy for the "squeeze" is an increased mobility of agricultural resources out of agricultural and into nonagricultural employments. The faster the transfer takes place, the less will be the differential between agricultural and industrial income, and the better agriculture's real terms of trade.

There is a further special reason why the general discontent of farmers with their income takes the form of an obsession with "parity prices" rather than with the problem of equalizing incomes in the two sectors. The fluctuations of the business cycle affect the farmer not in the form of reduced output and employment, but in the form of reduced prices and less favorable terms of trade. This is because of the flexibility of agricultural prices and the inflexibility of the volume of agricultural output, as contrasted with the greater inflexibility of prices and flexibility of output in industry. A depression is generally characterized by a sharp decline in national *money* income, which may be roughly equated to the total dollar value of the net output of goods and services. This decline is usually distributed fairly evenly over the large sectors of the economy, so that, for instance, agricultural money income declines in about the same ratio as industrial money income. In each sector the total money income is equal to the net output of the sector multiplied by the price of that output. In agriculture, then, the decline in money income during a depression is brought about through a decline in prices, not through a decline in output. In industry prices decline somewhat, but not enough to account for the total decline in money income, so that the decline is accomplished through a decline in output (and therefore in employment) rather than through a decline in prices alone.[1] A depression therefore hits the farmer in the form of low prices; it hits the industrial worker mainly in the form of unemployment.

The "terms of trade" of agriculture—i.e., the amount of industrial goods which the farmer obtains per unit of agricultural produce—is the ratio of the "industrial surplus" to the "agricultural surplus." The industrial surplus is that quantity of industrial goods which is not consumed within the industrial population and which is therefore available for the agricultural population. Similarly, the agricultural surplus is that quantity of agricultural produce which is not consumed by agricultural people and which therefore is available for sale to the industrial population. In a depression the agricultural surplus remains about constant, as agricultural production does not decline and the consumption of agricultural products by the agricultural population is also pretty steady. The industrial surplus, on the other hand, declines sharply because of the decline in industrial output. Thus the farmer notices a depression mainly as a sharp worsening in his terms of trade. He turns out just as much food as before, and works as hard, or even harder, but he gets much less for what he produces in terms of industrial goods. The reason is of course that the industrial goods which he might have had are

[1] The following figures illustrate this point for the depression of 1929-33:

Year	Base (100)	1929	1930	1931	1932	1933
Agricultural output	1935–9 (100)	97	95	104	101	93
Agricultural prices	1926 (100)	104	88	65	48	51
Nonagricultural output	1935–9 (100)	113	95	79	60	67
Nonagricultural prices	1926 (100)	92	85	75	70	71
Agricultural income	(pre–1929, 100)	101	84	68	49	47
Nonagricultural income	(pre–1929, 100)	104	80	59	42	48

The "income" figures are obtained by simple multiplication of the price and output indices. They are not to be taken as particularly accurate, as the price and output series are not strictly comparable. They do show, nevertheless, that the fall in income was of the same order of magnitude in both agriculture and in nonagricultural industry. In agriculture, however, output stayed up and the whole impact of this decline was in prices. In industry output declined, so that the price decline was much less than in agriculture. The figures are taken from the Midyear Economic Report of the President, July 1951, and refer to the United States.

not being produced, and the workers who might have produced them are standing idle. It is not surprising, therefore, that the labor movement is "job-conscious" rather than "price-conscious" and that the farm movement is almost pathologically "price-conscious."

PATTERNS OF ORGANIZATION

Because the farm movement is price-conscious and policy-conscious rather than job-conscious, it does not face the jurisdictional problem to anything like the degree that is found in the labor movement. In place of the two hundred national or international labor unions there are only three important regular farm organizations: the American Farm Bureau Federation with about one and a quarter million members, the Grange with something over half a million, and the Farmers Union with about a hundred and fifty thousand. These organizations differ somewhat in form and function.

The Grange is the oldest (1867) and represents the "lodge" aspect of organization, somewhat as do the Railroad Brotherhoods or the Machinists in the labor movement. The Farmers Union is reputed to be the most "radical" of the three and has from time to time maintained an uneasy alliance with the C.I.O. Its strength is mainly in the mountain and plains states, and it is perhaps directed more toward the tenant farmer than to the owner-occupier, though the class line is by no means clear. The Farm Bureau is the most "businesslike" of the three organizations. It arose, curiously enough, out of the establishment of the "county agent," thus being an almost unique example of a private organization which was created, in its initial stages at least, by the action of a quasi-governmental agency. In some states the county agent is still in part an employee of the Farm Bureau, and combines organizational and promotional functions along with his educational work. There is nothing particularly to prevent any farmer from belonging to all three organizations apart from the scarcity of time and money, and appreciable numbers of farmers belong to two of them.

In addition to these regular organizations there are others with more specialized functions which also have nationwide significance and on occasion also "speak for the farmer." Of these the National Council of Farmer Cooperatives probably has the broadest interests.

There are many national organizations of people concerned with special commodities, livestock improvement, and so on, and coming down to the local level innumerable organizations running country fairs and shows, youth organizations, Four-H clubs, and so on, covering every phase of rural life. In the following discussion, however, attention will be focused on the "regular" farm organizations, as it is these which present the most important problems for economic policy and conduct.

All three organizations follow somewhat the same pattern, with differences of emphasis. There are three main lines of activity: social, commercial, and legislative. The first is important from the point of view of the organization itself as a loyalty builder, and from the point of view of society at large it may easily be the most important contribution of the organizations. It meets a real need for organized fellowship in rural areas. It acts as an important educational channel whereby new ideas and practices are spread, and it acts also as an important training ground for democracy, where important matters of national policy are threshed out among the people. This type of activity, however, beneficial as it is, is only indirectly connected with the main problem of this work, and need not detain us further.

The commercial activities of the organizations, and of the cooperative businesses which they have sponsored, are extensive, especially those of the Farm Bureau. All the organizations either conduct or sponsor wholesaling businesses of some kind on a cooperative basis; the Farm Bureaus especially have developed large insurance businesses. A curious example of a tail wagging a dog is the "Ancient Order of Gleaners," which started off as a Grange-like farm organization and now is a pure insurance company. The problems of cooperative business will be examined in greater detail in a later chapter; so we may pass on to the third and probably the most important activity of the farm organizations, which is the lobbying function.

Political Policies

Agricultural policy, where anything worthy of the name exists, is almost always a product of farm organizations in their capacity as pressure groups. This is particularly true in the United States, where we have seen a strange political paradox: a large increase in government aid to agriculture at the same time that the proportion of the population engaged in agriculture has been steadily declining and therefore its political power might be expected to be declining also. The political power of the agricultural interest can of course be explained in part by the disproportionate representation of agricultural areas in all legislatures—in the United States Senate, for instance, there are thirty-eight senators representing the nineteen least-populated states, all of them predominantly agricultural, as against two senators representing an equal population in New York State. Even in the so-called "industrial" states, such as New York, Pennsylvania, Massachusetts, and Illinois, the rural "upstate" or "downstate" area frequently holds the balance of political power. The agricultural interest is not quite so strongly overrepresented in the House, but is still overrepresented even there.

This overrepresentation does not explain, however, why before 1933 the United States had practically no agricultural policy to speak of, whereas since 1933 it would seem as if the agricultural interest had captured the organs of government. The overrepresentation has not been increasing enough to account for the change, and there must be far fewer legislators today whose seats depend on agricultural votes than there were a hundred years ago. The explanation must lie not in the increasing political power of the agricultural interest, but in the changed attitude toward government economic policy which resulted from the great depression and rendered the general resistances to agricultural policy much weaker.

The various agricultural policies which have been proposed and which can be regarded as typical of the thinking of the farm organizations cannot here be examined in detail. Nevertheless something should be said about the principles involved. During the 1920s the main emphasis was upon proposals for export dumping; i.e., for raising the domestic price of agricultural commodities by inducing additional sales on foreign markets, thus reducing the total quantity offered on domestic markets. This was the essential principle of the McNary-Haugen bills, which represented the main objective of farm organization lobbying in that period. One of these finally passed Congress, only to be vetoed by President Coolidge. The essential principle of this type of policy is to try to make agricultural produce scarcer at home by making it more plentiful abroad. In a sense, of course, the Marshall Plan embodies the same principle, though with different primary motives.

The failure of the McNary-Haugen proposals and the acute crisis of the great depression produced a change in the general tenor of agricultural policy proposals in the 1930s away from the export subsidy, except as a minor device, toward various devices aimed at production control. The disastrous experience of the Federal Farm Board from 1929-32 made it clear that the mere withholding of stocks from the market could not affect agricultural prices, in more than the very short run, if the result of the higher prices thus obtained was increased production and diminished consumption. So the broad principle of the first Agricultural Adjustment Administration, subsequently modified substantially in detail through unfavorable Supreme Court decisions and legislative revision, was that of attempting to raise agricultural prices by restricting agricultural production. Fortunately for the economy as a whole, production control in agriculture is extremely difficult. The device of acreage allotment (i.e., restricting the sown acreage of each farmer's crop to some percentage of a historic base) is frequently unsuccessful, because the more intensive cultivation of the smaller number of acres results in larger output per acre and sometimes even in a larger total crop. Thus a measure which was intended for the detriment of the consumer may actually turn out to his benefit if, through ignorance or inertia, resources were not being employed in the best way before the shift.

About the only successful restrictive device is that of the marketing quota, which unfortunately seems to be constitutional in a way in which production quotas are not. The two commodities to which the marketing quota has been applied most successfully are milk and tobacco, especially tobacco. The weakness of the marketing quota, however, is the fact that it must be based on some historic base, such as the sales of individual farmers in some past period. Insofar as it results in monopolistic gains, therefore, these gains tend to go to the original owners of the "quotas," which become marketable items of property. Any newcomer who wishes to start in the business must pay a tribute to the established producers by the purchase of a quota; the price of a quota being presumably, at a maximum, that which will reduce the expected returns of the newcomer to some "normal" level. If the commodity is produced on highly specialized and scarce land, the "tribute" may take the form of increased rent or land values; this seems to have happened spectacularly in the case of tobacco. The result, however, is the same: the benefits of the scheme to the industry are capitalized by the original possessors of the field, who take a continuous toll of the rest of society by reason of the artificial turnstile created by the scheme.

If it is difficult to defend the marketing quota, it is still more difficult to defend the other alternative method of price raising, which is the government purchase and destruction of surplus products. The case of potatoes has been recently in the public eye, and is a typical example of what happens when the price of a storable but perishable commodity is held above the level at which production and consumption can be equated. There are, of course, other more palatable methods of dealing with agricultural surpluses, such as food stamp plans for raising the consumption of surplus products among low-income groups. Methods for raising consumption are, of course, superior to methods for restricting or destroying consumption. Nevertheless as long as the surpluses are a result of agricultural price policy, there are grave weaknesses even in the more desirable methods of disposing of them. Any beneficial effects which they may have are merely incidental to the disposal of the surplus and are not geared to an over-all program of improving nutrition or raising the level of life of the poor. Things such as a school lunch program, for instance, should be justified, if at all, on general grounds of public support for nutritional programs, and should be relatively independent of agricultural policy.

The basic weakness of almost all agricultural policy is its price-centeredness. The price system is a *symptom* of the more fundamental distribution of resources among various lines of production. Price-centeredness therefore is "symptom-centeredness," leading to treatment of the symptoms of social disorder rather than to tackling the basic causes. The suppression of symptoms may make the patient a little more comfortable in the short run, but it frequently makes the cure even more difficult by suppressing knowledge of the adjustments which need to be made and so weakening the drive toward making them.

A further special weakness of agricultural policy is its "agriculture-centeredness." Most of the serious problems of agriculture in fact arise in other sectors of the economy—in the monetary system or in the industrial system. We have already seen that the "parity problem"—the worsening of the terms of trade of agriculture in depression—is primarily a result of the decline in industrial employment and output. The remedy is clearly an adequate stabilization policy which will keep the economy reasonably close to full employment.

The only remedy for the parity problem available to *agriculture*, however, is the restriction of agricultural production, so that the agricultural surplus will diminish in proportion to the industrial surplus, and we shall starve during a depression as well as suffer the inconveniences due to the decline of industrial output. It is clear that if there is an industrial depression, *no* policy short of restricting agricultural output can solve the parity problem save a degree of direct subsidization of agriculture, sufficient either to increase industrial output or to restrict industrial consumption to the point where an adequate increase in the industrial surplus available for agricultural purchase is obtained.

If there is no industrial depression probably about three quarters of the parity problem is solved anyhow. The other quarter—that which relates to the long-run poverty of agriculture as a result of the necessity for driving resources out of it in an era of technical progress—is also in large part a consequence of industrial depression, for it is not the difficulty of moving people out of agriculture that is the cause of the trouble, but the absence of job opportunities in industry. In a period of full employment people move out of agriculture at about the requisite speed; it is in depressions that the surplus agricultural population backs up on the farms. In deep depressions there is even a retrograde movement back to the farms from the cities—which indicates perhaps that people prefer low prices to no jobs.

There are, of course, special problems of agriculture which may require some specific agricultural policy for their solution. There is a case for government crop insurance against damage by hail, flood, and so on, though it may be doubted whether the case is any stronger than the general case for a state monopoly of insurance, or for state enterprise in insurance. There is a real problem of the "supersensitivity" of the organized commodity markets, in which prices are probably unduly sensitive to small changes in stocks and in which they are also liable to speculative disturbances which have little or no relation to economic realities. There is a case therefore for a modified "ever-normal-granary" program aimed at "desensitizing" the market, so that it will still reflect the underlying conditions of demand and supply but will not be so liable to short-run fluctuations. The futures market itself is in effect such a desensitizer, in that it permits a degree of specialization between the pure speculator and the holder of commodities. It is by no means wholly satisfactory in its operations, however, as futures contracts themselves suffer from the same kind of speculative instability of price which afflicts all organized markets; so there is a possible case for a substitute, if one can be devised.

The only other case for a specialized agricultural policy that I can detect is the case of the "agricultural fundamentalists" who argue that a nation cannot afford to let its agricultural population decline beyond a certain minimum (usually unspecified) without suffering serious cultural losses. Rural life is frequently regarded as the cradle of virtue as well as of most of the future population of the nation. In these days, however, when the advance of communication has so reduced the isolation of the rural areas, an isolation on which both their virtues and their birth rates so largely depended, it may be doubted whether this argument has much weight. The divergence between rural and urban cultures has been diminishing with great rapidity, and there seems to be no road back to Arcadia. Even if by the sacrifice of, say, 20 per cent of our industrial output we managed to double the number of people on farms, with a corresponding decline in productivity to prevent them from being unemployed, there is no guarantee that they would be much less perverted by automobiles, television, and birth control. Even in this case it would seem as if the problems of agriculture originate outside it, and can be dealt with only in terms of an over-all attack on the whole culture, urban as well as rural.

ETHICAL PROBLEMS

As in all our examples, the ethical problems involved in the growth of organizations can be tackled at three levels: common morality; special morality—special, that is, to the organization and the relationships particularly involved in it; and the "unseen" morality—the wider standards of judgment that look at the whole impact of the organization on the social ecosystem.

At the level of common morality there are not many serious problems; indeed, the farm organizations seem to be relatively free from the personal vices which so often plague the labor movement. Racketeering is virtually unknown, with the possible exception of occasional troubles in milk, and even these are generally connected with strategic labor unions. The standards of probity in the organizations seem to be unusually high. Their leaders are for the most part men of high personal integrity. Even the lobbying is carried on with a minimum of deceit and, as far as I know, without bribery. Nothing like the scandalous story of the business influence in Congress is here visible. The farm organizations depend on straightforward, honest propaganda, on the power of the votes behind them, and on their ability to gain sympathy for a cause and to present a convincing case for their program in terms of the prevailing standards of judgment as to what government policy should be.

At the level of special morality also there do not seem to be many serious problems. There is nothing like the conflict of loyalties, for instance, which exists in the labor movement; there is practically no problem of violence except in rare cases of "milk strikes" or resistance to foreclosures. There is, however, the ever-present conflict between responsibility to the "inner" and to the "outer" group. To what extent should farmers, and especially leaders of farm organizations, feel a responsibility to society as a whole, and especially a responsibility for advocating policies which make sense for the whole society rather than policies which are for the advantage of their special group?

The problem is a difficult one both in practice and in theory. In practice farm organizations have felt less interest in the welfare of the larger society of which they are a part than in the struggle for the "rights" of their own constituency. This is astonishingly true even in wartime, when the farm organizations seem to be much less willing even than labor organizations to transfer their struggle from an internal to an external one. Consequently farmers in wartime are apt to become a highly privileged class, in regard to the impact of conscription, of price control, and even of taxation. There is a striking contrast, for instance, between the acceptance of the "little steel" formula by labor during World War II, grudging as it may have been, and the insistence of the farmers on 110 per cent of parity. In international relations also the attitude of the farm organizations has been one of irresponsibility, or at least indifference, to anything but the obvious and apparent interests of their own group. Thus the original McNary-Haugen plan, while in fact it would probably have benefited foreign countries at the expense of the American nonfarm population, would unquestionably have made the international relations of the United States much more difficult, and was based essentially on the philosophy of trying to get out of our own difficulties by piling them on the heads of foreigners. The present agricultural policy, with its export subsidy provisions, is one of the major handicaps to the development of multilateral, freer international trade, which is one of the ostensible objectives of American foreign policy.[2]

The attitude of the farm organizations in this respect is no different from, and no worse than, the attitude of most special-interest groups affected by international trade policy, in both labor and business. The problem is made more serious in the case of agriculture by the size and political power of the agricultural group. The ethical problem for the leaders of these groups is an acutely difficult one. Each group represents, as it were, a nation within the nation, striving for its own ends against the others, with the legislative process as the battleground. This is, of course, a preferable battleground to the field of war, but it produces a curiously difficult conflict of loyalties. The "farmer" is an "American" in a sense in which an "American" does not feel himself to be a "human." Consequently he feels less easy in a policy of "farmers first" than he

[2] For an excellent study of this problem see Gail Johnson, *Trade and Agriculture*, New York, John Wiley & Sons, Inc., 1950, *a study of inconsistent policies*.

The following quotation from a semiofficial history of the American Farm Bureau Federation is instructive. Describing how a group from the Farm Bureau went as advisers to the Inter-American Conference on War and Peace at Mexico City in March 1945, the author continues: "But one point the farmer advisers at Mexico City kept their eyes on—in addition to the development of hemispheric solidarity, of course—was to try to avoid any commitments by our government that would work to the disadvantage of our anticipated sales of farm products abroad or undue acceptance of competing agricultural products from other countries" (O. M. Kile, *The Farm Bureau Through Three Decades*, Washington, D. C., Published by the Author, 1948).

would in a policy of "America first." Nevertheless, it is with other farmers that he feels the closest ties and interest, and it is as a farmer, not as an American, that he elects and follows his farm leaders. The farm leader therefore faces the same dilemma as the labor leader, that if he is too virtuous he will lose his job. The role of the farm leader is to get things for farmers, not to serve the general interest. Nevertheless almost everyone will admit, if cornered, that he should serve the general interest, especially within the limits of the national state, and both farmers and farm leaders get extremely angry if they are accused of being unpatriotic.

The dilemma is usually resolved by always regarding one's own pressure group as a "counterpressure"; i.e., something which must be opposed to the already existing pressures in other groups in order to keep the general interest in its proper center. Uprightness thus comes to be regarded as an equal tendency to lean toward all sides, and if society leans too much to one side a pull must be exerted on the other side in order to right the balance. The idea of a counterpressure has been particularly important in the ethics of the farm movement. Much of its emotional "steam" has been generated by a feeling that other groups in society have certain natural or artificial advantages and that the farm group is correspondingly disadvantaged, and must therefore press itself for special privileges in order to gain "equality." Thus in the 1920s the idea of "equality for agriculture" found expression mainly in the agitation for an "equivalent for the tariff" in export subsidies or dumping—tariffs obviously being not of much use to a predominantly export industry. The "parity price" and later the "parity income" ideas are likewise an expression of the desire for "equality"—this time through direct governmental subsidy or government-granted monopoly powers.

It is probably the appeal of the idea of equality, in terms of a fair deal for an unfairly treated group, that has "sold" agricultural policy to the rest of the people; it must be emphasized that agricultural policy is a result of an act of salesmanship rather than an act of coercion. Unless farmers could win sympathy for their cause, their numbers would never permit them to impose so extensive a program of assistance upon the rest of society. Unfortunately, however, the sympathy has frequently been based on inadequate information, both as to facts and as to causes. Aid to agriculture has generally been justified in terms of the argument that (1) the poor should be helped, that (2) farmers are poor, and that therefore (3) farmers should be helped. The trouble with this argument lies in the second proposition. The truth is that some farmers are poor while some are not. Moreover, in practice, the proposition that farmers should be helped has frequently meant helping the rich farmer rather than the poor farmer. Furthermore, assistance to *agriculture* cannot be justified on the ground of helping the poor because by no means all the poor are farmers, and it is obviously unjust to help a poor farmer when we do not help the equally poor bootblack. The poor should be helped because they are poor, and not because they are farmers.

In framing attitudes and proposing policies with regard to farm organizations there are also certain "invisible" moral problems. They involve consequences of the growth of these organizations which are not in the consciousness of those who are affected by them, but which may often be the most important aspect of the problem in the long run.

The main results of the growth of farm organizations in the United States have been political rather than economic. In some countries, it is true, the farm organizations have succeeded in replacing the machinery of the competitive speculative commodity markets with governmental wholesaling and negotiated prices; Canada is a good case in point. And in all countries there is a strong tendency for certain commodities, such as milk, to be sold under conditions of collective bargaining. The result of these changes is likely to be similar to the results of similar changes in the labor market: a decline in the flexibility of prices, probably without much over-all change in the over-all pattern of distribution.

It is almost certain, for instance, that the Canadian wheat farmers in the past few years have done much worse than they might have done, as a result of the destruction of the grain exchanges and the fixing of the price by government, and of "collective bargaining" between governments. However, this "stickiness" of prices in inflation is tolerated because it is hoped that the price will be equally sticky in a subsequent deflation and that the wild price swings of the free-market era will not be repeated. If, however, there is another deflation, the development of price rigidity in these storable agricultural commodities will result in the piling up of quite unmanageable stocks, because of the inherent inflexibility of agricultural production. If the end product of agricultural organization is indeed a freezing of the agricultural price system, then we are doubly committed never to have a deflation.

Generally speaking, however, it is only the small countries with a predominance of export or import of agricultural produce that are able to attempt much in the way of monopolistic control of the market. Britain probably achieves a certain amount of exploitation of Denmark, and Argentina of Britain, by reason of the peculiar market relationships existing between the monopolized trade of these countries. Within a large country, however, like the United States, and in what remains of a world market, it is difficult for agricultural organizations to have a large impact on the nature of the market, except in the case of certain commodities like milk or lemons which retain strong geographic market limitations. In the event of another deflation, therefore, it is probable that agricultural prices would still be much more flexible than industrial prices in the actual markets. The result of the government program of price supports in such a case, however, might be to accentuate the problem of agricultural surpluses which always characterizes a severe deflation. The support of agricultural incomes by direct subsidy, as proposed in the Brannan Plan, has something to be said for it as an antidepression measure. Nevertheless, here again there seems to be no justification whatever for singling out agricultural incomes as deserving of support when we do not give such support to other incomes. One can only reiterate that, as agricultural problems almost all originate in the instability of the whole economy, attempts to solve this problem of instability through agricultural policy not only are doomed to frustration but are basically unjust.

The ultimate test of the value of farm organizations may well depend on the degree of their political power. There is a real conflict of interest between the agricultural group and the rest of society, in that the interest of society at large is always in favor of a rapid rate of technical progress in agriculture, and in favor of a highly competitive and adaptable agriculture. The interest of agriculture itself, especially as expressed in political programs, may require technical change to be concentrated in industry and require agriculture itself to stagnate (technically), for only thus can the farm population be prevented from declining, and only thus can the farmer obtain better and better terms of trade for himself. The results of such a policy for society at large, however, are a slowing down of the general rate of economic progress. They may be seen demonstrated in the history of France, where the protection of an out-of-date agriculture has meant both economic backwardness and political impotence.

It is clear, then, that the agricultural interest can be a serious menace to the progress of a society if it becomes powerful enough to demand protection from change, or at least from that amount of change which necessarily follows from a rapid rate of economic development. Fortunately, in the United States there are no signs that the agricultural interest has the power, or even the will, to demand such protection. The worst that can be said of American agricultural policy is that it causes a certain loss of national income through waste and maldistribution of resources. It is not possible to estimate the size of this loss. It is doubtful that it amounts to more than 1 per cent of the national income—about equivalent to the cost of industrial strife.

Agriculture presents a most interesting case of the situation where the interest of the individual conforms, but the interest of the occupational group conflicts with that of society as a whole. It is generally to the interest of the individual farmer—and of society—to employ improved methods of agriculture. The interest of most agricultural *groups*, however, is in concentrating technical improvement in industry rather than in agriculture; by so doing there would be more farmers and there would be more industrial products to buy with every unit of farm produce. In the past, however, the greatest source of industrial development has been the labor liberated from agriculture by the improvement in agricultural techniques. Fortunately the agricultural group does not threaten to become well-enough organized to realize its interest as a group. The individual interest still prevails enough so that the agricultural societies actively support colleges and research stations, the end product of which is better methods, fewer farmers, and lower terms of trade for agriculture.

For all the potential dangers, therefore, the farm organizations of the United States cannot be regarded as constituting much of a threat to the progress of the whole society. The policies which they have sponsored are difficult to defend as legitimate in any over-all scheme of economic policy. They can at least put forward the defense that this baby, at least, is a little one. And, on the positive side, there is always the vital benefit of status. The farm organizations give the farmer a voice, a self-consciousness, and an improved status in society. They give him therefore the capacity to accept responsibility; they have shown already a capacity to learn from their mistakes and a developing sense of wider responsibility. Like the labor unions, they cannot escape being instruments of government (with a small "g"). They have arisen to fill acute needs which the existing structure of organization was not filling. Unfortunately the basic sources of the needs out of which they have arisen do not lie within their province or peculiar capacities; consequently the solutions which they offer are piecemeal and largely inadequate in themselves. Nevertheless, by constantly calling attention to the need, they direct the large organization of Government (with a capital "G") to larger and more satisfactory solutions.

One of the principal obstacles to such solutions, however, is the Department of Agriculture itself; and a word must be said in conclusion about this extraordinary institution. One result of the political power of agriculture has been the growth of the Department of Agriculture to the point where it has become itself a lobby for the farm interest. In this it differs sharply from other government departments, such as Labor and Commerce, which are much more objective and less apt to act as pressure groups. A great deal of agricultural policy, however, originates in the Department of Agriculture, and its officials to a great extent regard themselves as representing not the general interest but the special interest of the agricultural group. Hence there is a strong pressure, arising from the way in which the executive branch of government happens to be organized, against the framing of over-all policies and toward attempting to solve problems sector by sector—an attempt which is doomed to failure. It is a misfortune that Departments of Agriculture, Labor, and Commerce were ever organized; there is plenty of opportunity for the expression of group conflicts within the legislative branch of government without deliberately introducing them into the executive. If we had had instead, say, a department of scientific services, a department of statistics, a department of stabilization, and a department of social security, each covering the whole economy, we would have had a much better chance of solving the basic problems not only of the economy as a whole but also of each sector within it.

Because of this organizational structure of government, and also because of the excessive political representation of agriculture in the legislatures, one gets an impression sometimes that the political power of agriculture has actually run away with the machine itself. We find increasingly the spectacle of the farm organizations asking for *less* than Congress wants to give them, and showing more self-restraint and more consideration of the general interest than Congress itself. That this is so is much to the credit of the present leadership of the farm organizations. The errors of the past, however, hang heavily around their necks, and some radical rethinking of agricultural policy—and some re-education of congressmen—will be necessary before less vulnerable policies become politically feasible.

8

Business Organizations

When we come to consider business as an economic "group" we find that it possesses many peculiarities. We saw that there were substantial parallels between the labor movement and the farm organization movement, in spite of their differences. The parallels are much fewer as we move toward business. Farm and labor organizations are part of a "movement" which is affected with moral tone, and consequently have a certain churchlike aspect. This is much less true of business.

There is, of course, a good deal of moral tone connected with old-established businesses, especially family houses. The du Pont family, for instance, even has its martyrs in those du Ponts and others who have lost their lives in the pursuit of the hazardous business of making explosives. There is a certain ethical tone connected with the trade association "movement"—at least to the extent that it seems to be a characteristic function of a trade association to issue a "code of ethics." In the interest of the business with which they identify themselves large numbers of executives work themselves into an early grave with a single-mindedness of devotion not excelled by the missionary or the C.I.O. organizer. Rotarians and Lions gather weekly to sing (or roar) the praises of Service.

Nevertheless, business is business; and the countinghouse is not the Meetinghouse. The countinghouse is where things are counted, and the essence of business is calculation; what is not arithmetical is not of its substance. The Meetinghouse is where things are met with—the uncountable, the unaccountable, the immeasurable, the intangible. There is inevitably, therefore—and properly—a certain tension between the businesslike and the Godlike—the one abstracting from life that which is subject to the measuring rod of money, the other attempting to read into life the unreadable, the unknowable, the ineffable.

FACTORS OF GROWTH OF "BIG BUSINESS"

At a less exalted level, business suffers by a comparison with the labor and agriculture movements because it is generally on the defensive. The labor and agriculture movements are aggressive, challenging the existing order of things, seeking rather consciously a "better" state of affairs, and seeking improved status for their group. They consequently have the morale of an army on the march. The business group, on the other hand, has been in almost constant retreat, fighting a continual rear-guard action for the preservation of a previous status as the dominant group in society. This is, of course, a phenomenon peculiar to the past hundred years. In the previous century it was the business group, as represented, say, by the "Manchester liberals," who represented the vanguard of progress against the retreating power and privileges of the landholding aristocracy, and who felt that they were fighting on behalf of a new and better order of society; it was the business group who stood for the "technical revolution" against the stand-pats and the fuddy-duddies. The dialectical processes of history have largely reversed the role, and it is now business who stands as the representative of an established order against the attacks of other groups.

Nevertheless, the role of the conservative in society is an important one, and a great deal depends on the skill with which it is performed. The orderliness of change depends largely on the skills of the conservative; if the established leadership group in society can absorb the challengers, change can be orderly and peaceful. If the established groups either resist the challengers too vigorously or do not resist at all, change is likely to be violent and discontinuous and much of the benefits of a broadening society is likely to be lost. The English-speaking countries seem to have a genius for orderly and continuous change which the larger continental European countries especially do not seem to possess. The reasons for this are obscure. There may be more than a passing connection with the nature of the English language itself, which by reason of its diverse sources is not conducive to sharp verbal distinctions and which therefore may be a positive aid to communication among different social groups. Whatever the reason, however, the historical fact is clear.

The aristocratic class, especially in England, responded to the challenge of the rising business class by marrying its heiresses. The business class is likewise responding to the challenge of the rising labor and farm group, not perhaps quite in the traditional manner of the earlier aristocracy, but by developing a working relationship of industrial government through collective bargaining and by submitting to the economic encroachments of the social-democratic state.

FACTORS OF GROWTH OF "BIG BUSINESS"

It is not my task to pursue in detail the question of the ethics and morale of the business community as such, especially as another volume of this series is concerned with this problem. Rather are we concerned here with the form and the consequences of the organizational revolution as it has affected business enterprises and the business community. It has two aspects. One is the growth in the size of the business organization itself, especially as reflected in the rise of the giant corporation. The other is the development of a variety of forms of organization among separate business enterprises, such as the pool, the cartel, and the trade association.

These two movements are by no means independent. Within the sheltering framework of a large corporation formed by the merger of many small ones, the component units frequently keep a good degree of independence, and in its structure the large corporation may be something like a coral colony of a number of semi-independent departments knit by a common financial skeleton. On the other hand, business units which are not formally integrated may have in fact a close coordination of executive policies and a great deal of communication among their various executives of an informal nature, which makes them act for all practical purposes as if they were a single body. The growth in the size of the formal business unit (e.g., the corporation or partnership) and the closer integration of formally independent business units in associations of various kinds are part of the same movement which we have traced in so many other fields—a movement which results primarily from certain improvements in the skills of organization.

What territory is to the state, and jobs to the union, capital is to the business firm; its domain is staked out essentially by the capital which it owns. Consequently, the growth in the size of the firm is a growth in the size of the capital-handling unit; it is a growth in the power to manipulate large masses of capital—land, buildings, machines, stocks of goods, stocks of money, financial instruments. This skill has grown up as a result of three principal "social inventions": the corporate form of financial organization, the specialization of management, and the improvement in accounting and in other methods of obtaining information.

The corporate method of organization has some advantages over the partnership, especially in that it permits continuity of the organization. Whereas a partnership must be dissolved if one of the partners wishes to withdraw his capital, the corporation is a "body" the continued existence of which is independent of the whims—or the decease—of its stockholders. The corporate form of organization is particularly suitable for the large business, which is enabled thereby to draw upon the resources of great numbers of people for its capital, far beyond the resources of any single individual proprietor, and at the same time is able to preserve a certain independence from its owners and to maintain therefore a "life" and existence of its own.

The specialization of the executive function, and the accompanying improvement in the techniques of getting and sifting information, is the device which has enabled large aggregates of capital to function as organizations with survival power. It is not enough to aggregate capital; there have been many large aggregations of capital which have turned out to be quite unsuccessful because it has been found impossible to manage them properly and they have diminished. We have seen earlier that beyond a certain point in the growth of any one kind of organization there are diseconomies of scale, and that if these are to be postponed there must be a change in the *form* of organization. In the case of the business firm the change which has permitted its great growth has been the development of an executive hierarchy, coupled with improvements in the methods of obtaining and transmitting information about the current position of the enterprise.

As was suggested in the Preface, the executive hierarchy acts as a kind of stratified sieve. Information which is relevant to the policies and behavior of the firm is constantly coming up from its "receptors"—the salesmen and purchasing agents and operators who are in immediate contact with the external or internal environment in which the firm lives. Much of this information is "stopped" and acted upon at the lowest executive rank—the foreman, or his equivalent in other departments. Some information, however, is abstracted and goes through to higher levels of the hierarchy; at each level some information is stopped and translated into instructions, and some is passed on—usually in a more and more highly abstracted form. Thus, paradoxically enough, one of the main functions of the hierarchy is to prevent information from reaching its upper ranks except in highly abstract and condensed form, for the individual human mind can deal with only a certain amount of information. The top executives must be spared the knowledge that machine X in shop Y needs oiling or that customer Z was dissatisfied with his purchase and returned it.

We thus see the importance of the accounting system, and especially of more recent developments in cost accounting, quality control, and business-machines operation as essential parts of the executive system of a business, especially of a large business. Both accounting and statistics are methods of *abstracting* and *condensing* information; i.e., of taking out of a vast mass of reality only those elements which are essential for the purposes of executive decision. Accounting does not, of course, conform to this function perfectly; a great deal of accounting procedure is traditional and is not closely devised with a view to fulfilling its function. Nevertheless, recent developments in accounting are all in the direction of making the information system more sensitive to the needs for control. The days when the striking of an annual profit-and-loss account and balance sheet was considered all that an accountant need do are gone, and we are increasingly finding a kind of marriage of accounting and statistics, looking toward an over-all system of information and control. This perhaps is the real significance of the so-called "scientific management": that it broadens the concept of the information system and ties it much more closely into the function of control, setting up, as it were, a whole series of "thermostats" and alarm signals which will give prompt information when things are going wrong.

The weakness of the information systems of business is their heavy concentration on those things which can be measured in terms of dollars. It is natural, of course, that information systems of this kind should be the first to develop; for, as we have already said, capital is the "domain" of business, and capital consists mainly of things which can be evaluated in terms of dollars. Hence, if there is something wrong with his dollar costs, his dollar earnings, or his liquidity position, or with anything else which is revealed by an accounting system, the businessman is likely sooner or later to find it out and to try to frame some appropriate action for dealing with the situation.

Things which are not so easily measured in dollars, however, such as morale, good or ill feeling, public relations, government sentiment, and so on, do not find such ready entrance either to the information system or to the consciousness of the businessman. These things may be just as important in the long run for the survival of his business, however, as the accounting magnitudes on which he is so fully informed. In better-managed businesses there is increasing awareness of the importance of these magnitudes and of the necessity of setting up adequate information systems regarding them; hence we get an elaborate growth of public relations departments, personnel management and labor relations departments, grievances procedures, and so on, the main business of which is to deal with the nonaccounting variables. The difficulties of measurement, however, and the absence of any clear notions as to how an over-all information system should be constructed, have hindered development in this field, though the potentials for the future are great.

There seem to be some alarming potentialities in the development of information and control systems. We are in the middle of a period of great improvement in these systems, the end of which is not yet in sight. If the relatively crude information-control and transportation systems of a generation or more ago permitted the rise of such vast aggregates as the American Telephone and Telegraph Company, General Electric, General Motors, du Pont, and so on, the potentialities for further growth in the size of individual business organizations opened up by the development of better information and control systems are alarming, at least to those who are already alarmed by the growth of giant business. There is not much evidence of increasing size of the business firm, relative to the rest of the economy at least, over the past forty years; the rapid rate of growth seems to have been in the second half of the nineteenth century. Nevertheless, if the theory of organization followed in this study is correct, it would seem as if we are once again in a period when the *internal* limitations on the size of organizations are being pushed back still farther.

It may be, of course, that the great corporations have now reached the point where the external limitations, in the shape of more and more imperfect buying or selling markets, are seriously limiting their growth, and that hence a further reduction in potential internal limitations will not greatly affect their size. This is particularly true of the noneconomic limitations. Even where the market would permit further growth, the fear of public opinion or of antitrust action may produce a voluntary limitation. In the United States, however, we still operate in a predominantly market economy, and it would be a little surprising if some leader did not arise to take advantage of the new opportunities which the developments in information and control systems seem to open up.

ATTITUDE OF PUBLIC AND ITS AGENCIES

The position of business in regard to the growth of its basic units differs sharply from that of labor or even agriculture in that, for the past twenty years at least, during which the organizational revolution has been proceeding, government in the United States has been generally unfriendly to the growth of large-scale businesses. In a period when the attitude of government toward the growth of labor organizations has changed from mild hostility to active support, and when in the Department of Agriculture the farm organizations have had an agency within the framework of government itself actively espousing their cause, the antitrust laws have remained on the books and have been pushed at times with considerable activity by an aggressive Department of Justice. It is true that trade associations enjoyed a brief holiday under the "codes" of the NRA, and that in the 1920s the attitude of government might be described as one of passive acquiescence. But with these exceptions the American government has been unfriendly not only to "big business" as such but also to the association of businesses in trade associations, except for the most innocent and impotent of purposes.

It is a curious paradox that the United States, which is reputed to be the most capitalistic of countries, should in fact have been so unfriendly to capitalistic enterprise; whereas in the supposedly more "socialistic" countries of Europe there were no antitrust laws to speak of, the growth of big business was unhindered by law, and monopolistic arrangements and organizations were frequently not only allowed but even sponsored by the state. The success of capitalism in the United States, however, may be due to this very paradox. The spirit both of the people and of the government was hostile to those methods of business survival which depend on the "gentlemanly" code of business ethics—live and let live, don't undercut, and so on. As a result, the only way in which business could survive in the American environment was by devoting a large proportion of their energies to technical improvement. There is something, perhaps, in the application of Toynbee's idea of "challenge and response" here; the slightly difficult and unfavorable environment in which American business found itself constituted a "challenge" to which the "response" has been an amazing rate of technical improvement and a phenomenal rise in productivity and in general standards of consumption.

The hostility of the American government to big private business and to business associations is not quite so hard to understand if the nature of the ideal of American democracy is considered further. The American Revolution is the "small businessman's revolution"; its ideal of society is one of many small independent units bound together in a market economy, in which every man is his own "boss" and in which political relationships are therefore reduced to a minimum. Big business apparently threatens this ideal from two sides: it threatens the successful operation of the market relationship by the administration of prices and the threat of monopolistic exploitation, and it creates a kind of "socialist" *imperium in imperio* in which political relationships among the hierarchy of control become of immense importance. It is because a big business is in fact something like a socialist state that it does not sit comfortably with the American ideal.

On the other hand, the technical advantages of big business are sometimes so great that they cannot be ignored. In some cases (the public utility and the railroad) the answer has been sought in public regulation by commission, or in other cases by public or semipublic ownership, as in the case of municipal utilities or the Tennessee Valley Authority. In still other cases, the answer has been sought in antitrust action, which might almost be described as regulation by irritation—the very inconsistencies and uncertainties of antitrust action acting as a fairly effective deterrent against the grosser forms of business Napoleonism. In any case the problem arises because large organizations through their very size and the number of people involved in them become "affected with the public interest."

The fact that big businesses probably do not discourage but even encourage the growth of small businesses clustered around them as suppliers and distributors really intensifies the problem; for it makes the big business still more like an agency of government—an environment in which large numbers of individuals and other businesses live and move, and which therefore cannot be "private" in the sense in which a small business can be. The larger any organization within a society, the more dangerously disturbed is the society if the organization fails to perform its proper function.

The ordinary means by which the market gets rid of ineffective organizations, however, seem too violent in the case of the great corporation. There is an uneasy feeling that the processes of bankruptcy and reorganization do not necessarily get the right people in control of the resources involved, and do not even always get the "rascals" out. In the case of small businesses, bankruptcy usually means that such resources as are left are reorganized into presumably more efficient organizations. In the case of large businesses, however, the resources involved are frequently too great to be dispersed, and must be held together in some form or other; so reorganization—or even socialization—actually makes little difference to the organization itself, which goes on its elephantine way almost indifferent to its succession of riders. The problem of "bankruptcy" also is in no way solved by socialization. There is no guarantee that state enterprise will not get into the hands of incompetent managers, and the problem of getting rid of them may be even more acute than it is in the case of private organizations.

ETHICAL PROBLEMS

The ethical problems which have arisen as a result of the growth of big business, as in the cases of labor and agricultural organization, can conveniently be divided into three groups: the problems of common morality, the problems of "special" morality, and the problems of "invisible" morality. Unlike the labor and farm movements, where the "invisible" morality perhaps presented the most difficult problems, it is in the realm of common and special morality that the most acute problems are raised by business organization.

A business civilization is inconceivable without the extensive practice of the "minor virtues"[1]—honesty, truthfulness, punctuality, faithfulness in the fulfillment of promises, sobriety, attention to business, and so on. The business world is one in which relationships are based mainly on faith and hope, and, if it seems to be deficient in the warmer virtue of charity, it must at least be given credit for the other two. The maintenance of personal integrity is consequently a vital problem for any business society in which the relationship that binds the society together is that of *contract*. It is for this reason that the connection which has often been traced between the rise of business civilization and the growth of evangelical and "perfectionist" Protestantism is so plausible. These Protestant societies developed a culture within themselves in which personal integrity was a deliberate and highly valued product. To a large extent capitalism was raised on a foundation of trust and personal honesty which was built up by these religious societies. In the absence of this foundation the characteristic institutions of capitalism, and especially of finance capitalism—banking, insurance, the organized commodity and security markets—either cannot develop at all or if they do develop become instruments of exploitation rather than of economic progress.

It is, of course, the main business of the legal system to see that a failure to live up to the requisite standards of personal integrity is punished, and hence to create artificially a situation in which "honesty is the best policy." No amount of law, however, can ensure honesty if the culture itself does not produce it, for if the culture is corrupt the judges will be corrupt also. We have therefore a curious paradox. The institutions of a business society do not always *in themselves* produce the kind of character which is necessary for their survival. Business institutions set up great temptations for individuals to deviate from standards of personal integrity; for when one man deviates in a society that is generally honest, he can frequently make great gains for himself at the expense of the honest majority. Furthermore, the abstract nature of the operations of

[1] I call these "minor," not in any way to depreciate them, but to distinguish them from the major virtue of love.

business does not in itself produce that richness of character which is probably the best ground for the growth of integrity. The cliché "We are not in business for our health" illustrates the curious nature of the problem. The businessman deals with an abstract universe—i.e., that part of the universe which can be measured in dollar terms—not with a real world. He is constantly tempted to the illusion that his abstraction, or part, is the real—i.e., the whole. If he falls for this illusion he is apt to find all too literally that he is not in business for his health, and because he has sacrificed wholeness for a part his health breaks down and he takes refuge in ulcers, alcoholism, riotous living, or marital or mental breakdown. It seems, therefore, as if the moral foundations for business must come from outside—from family loyalty or from religious faith.

It is not satisfactory, however, to establish too sharp a division between the various aspects of life, and to say that "business is business, and charity is charity." It is not satisfactory to encounter those experiences which build character in one sphere of life— the home, the school, or the church—and to encounter those experiences which put character to test mainly in another sphere, that of business. We here face a fundamental dilemma of which there seems to be no easy resolution. We have seen that it is only the abstract nature of business relationships which makes large-scale economic organization possible. If we are to have relationships with large numbers of people, the relationship itself must be pared down to the minimum necessary, and we have seen in this fact the explanation for the persistence of the wage system as over against producers' cooperation. On the other hand, in the paring down of the relationship something vital is lost—something which makes for the wholeness, and therefore for the health, of the individual.

The special moral problem of the businessman is precisely *how* to be in business for his health; to make his business something which yields rich and satisfactory relationships and which is in itself a creative and satisfying experience, and yet something which can survive in a market economy. The worker finds a partial solution to this problem in his union, one of the main functions of which, as we have seen, is to make complex and dramatic the job relationship which in itself is drearily simple and abstract. The businessman seems to have developed no such organization. The country club, the Rotary Club, the trade association, or even the National Association of Manufacturers or the U.S. Chamber of Commerce does not succeed in giving him that sense of "mission," of wholeness in his chosen occupation, or of vocation which seems to be an essential ingredient of the full life.

It is probably for this reason that the question of "incentives" constitutes such an acute problem in big business. One of the aspects of large-scale organizations which comes in for a good deal of moral criticism is the large salaries and bonuses which are paid to top executives. The size of these incomes is a fairly direct reflection of the number of stages in the business hierarchy, as the incomes in each stage of the hierarchy must exceed those in the stage before by a certain minimum proportion if incentive for advancement and the prestige of the hierarchy are to be maintained. Thus, suppose a firm in which there is a 30 per cent differential in salary between the grades in the hierarchy. If there are 10 grades, the top salary will be about 11 times the lowest; with 20 grades, the top salary will be about 146 times the lowest —such are the operations of geometric series. Thus a seemingly moderate differential between one grade and the next compounds to large differences over a number of grades. This creates problems both of general social dissatisfaction and of internal communication, as the top executives get into income classes which remove their lives from the comprehension of the worker on the assembly line. One solution for this problem is the reduction in the number of grades in the hierarchy; the other is a reduction in the differential between each grade. A study of the actual practices of large organizations in this respect would be instructive.

Another dilemma in regard to big business might be phrased as the dilemma of power and efficiency. Probably the aspect of big business which is of most concern to those who attempt to assess its value to society is the aspect of power—the fact that big business represents a great concentration of economic power in the hands of a few men who are not *directly* responsible to society at large through political processes. We have seen already that competition is a substitute for the political process in the control of power, in that if it is effective the inefficient holders of power lose their positions through the adverse impact of the market on their organizations. There is fear, however, that big business may grow to the point where it can control the competition which is the only effective check on its power. To what extent this is actually the case is a highly debatable point.

I have indicated earlier, as a personal estimate of the situation, that the gravity of the monopoly problem has been much exaggerated because the increasing substitutability of products in a highly technical society has been overlooked. Nevertheless there are informed people who disagree with this diagnosis, and the question must be kept alive; for even if the monopolistic power of big business is exaggerated as a present threat, it always exists as a potential threat. The dilemma arises when power grows as a *result* of productive efficiency. Are we then going to subsidize inefficient producers in order to create at least the semblance of competition—and perhaps increase the profits and indirectly the power of the feared monopolist by so doing—or are we going to attempt a solution in terms of public regulation or public ownership? If the latter, what machinery is there for creating an information-executive system which will register public dissatisfactions and create the proper amount of insecurity of tenure for the executives? There are no easy answers to these questions.

The principal "invisible" question relating to the growth of big business is much the same as that relating to the growth of other organizations—its effect on price stability. There is no doubt that one of the principal economic consequences of the rise of large-scale enterprise has been an increasing lack of flexibility in prices. The most striking difference between industry and agriculture is that in agriculture the income cycle is still largely a price cycle and not an output cycle, whereas in industry it is becoming increasingly an output cycle rather than a price cycle, thus entailing disastrous consequences of unemployment and social disorganization. The reason again is fairly plain: the removal of internal limitations on growth has caused businesses to expand to the point where their selling markets have become imperfect, and consequently they react to declining sales not by a cutback in price, for that has become relatively ineffective, but by a cutback in output. Again the solution is clear: as we cannot get rid of organizations or price stability, we must get rid of the income cycle, and again we must raise the question whether the cost of output stabilization is not an inflationary trend. These questions have been discussed earlier, however, and need not be raised in detail again, except to notice that if "blame" is to be apportioned for price inflexibility, business must bear a large share along with labor and agriculture. "Blame," however, is not a useful concept in deciding what to do about the inflationary trend, as it is not a situation which can be remedied by preaching; it can be remedied only by compensatory action.

It must be pointed out also that in our society, at least, businesses have grown to be large not so much because they are exploitive and have used coercion as because they have been productive. The organizations which have been responsible for the rising standards of life of the Western world on the whole have been businesses, not labor or farm organizations. Labor and farm organizations are *corrective* organizations, and as such are necessary. If they were abolished, however, our society would not be essentially different. There would undoubtedly be some changes in the distribution of income and power; but it is doubtful that there would be any revolutionary effect on rates of technical progress, on the rise in real standards of life, or even on the general spirit of the society. Business organizations, however, could not be abolished without a complete revolution, and without finding a substitute for them in state enterprise.

It is well to remember also that it is from business organizations that the technical revolution has mainly come. It has not been the professed revolutionaries nor even the reformers that have produced the great revolution; it has come from the unconscious operations of innumerable men of business. Few if any of them have been aware that they were part of a "movement"; most of them would indignantly repudiate the idea that they were reformers, still less revolutionaries. Yet because over a large area of life "better" ways of doing things have also been profitable, the pursuit of personal profit has in fact produced an enormous increase in the power of man over nature. Whether this is reckoned good or bad depends on our estimate of the ability of man to control the genies which he has unleashed.

OPERATIONS OF TRADE ASSOCIATIONS

A chapter on business organizations should not, of course, be concluded without some reference to a further aspect of the organizational revolution as it has affected business. This is the rise of the trade association, the history of which parallels closely that of labor and farm organizations. Trade associations begin in somewhat sporadic fashion in the period between the close of the Civil War and the First World War, receive a substantial boost during the First World War period, go into something of a decline in the 1920s, and revive again following the great depression. The latest estimate (1949) indicates that in the United States there are about 1,500 regular trade associations, covering practically the whole field of industry. Most of these are small organizations, with a handful of paid staff, or even with nothing more than a part-time secretary. They cover a wide variety of functions. They all act as collectors and disseminators of information about their respective industries. Practically all of them have some kind of legislative program, have some trade promotional program, and set up standards of trade practices ("codes of ethics"). About half of them go in for the collection of statistics, cost surveys, and various specialized services to their member firms.

It has not been easy to draw the line between what have been regarded as the legitimate and illegitimate or even the legal and illegal aspects of trade association behavior. On the one hand, trade associations can be regarded as a kind of industrial self-government, protecting both the consumer and the industry from fraud in both obvious and subtle forms, and educating their own members to a better understanding of their environment and their businesses. On the other hand, there is always the suspicion of an attempt to exercise monopoly power, and the trade association shades quite imperceptibly into the cartel and the trust. Even such apparently innocent activities as the collection and publication of statistics, especially of prices and of inventories, can be used to foster output adjustments rather than price adjustments in response to a condition of general deflation. Some form of organization of the market, however, may be a legitimate alternative to a condition of acute oligopolistic price instability, especially where the price cutting comes from firms which are not aware of their true cost situations.

It would certainly seem as if the effect of the antitrust laws (and prosecutions) has been a healthy one, in that it has made the trade association chary of the more obviously monopolistic activities.

Attitudes toward price competition are confused by the fact that it performs two unrelated functions. On the one hand, it is a method by which the benefits of improved methods of production of particular commodities are spread through the whole society, and by which producers using inferior methods are forced to adopt the superior ones. The innovator of a superior method who lowers the price to accord with the new level of costs either forces the old high-cost producers out of business or forces them to adopt the low-cost methods. If there is no price competition in the face of lowered costs, the advantages of these improvements will not be spread through society, and the inferior methods will not be so easily displaced.

On the other hand, price competition is also a method of bringing about a *general* decline in the level of money prices, i.e., a general deflation. Deflation manifests itself first in increasing imperfection of the market for individual sellers; they find it more and more difficult to sell at the old level of prices, and it is the "price cutter" who forces the whole price level downward. There is a strong "subconscious" feeling abroad in the whole business community that general deflation is a meaningless phenomenon, creating all sorts of difficulties without performing any real function. As far as the short run is concerned, this view is corroborated by modern economic theory; general deflation has nothing to do essentially with that type of *relative* price competition which is so necessary to economic progress. From the point of view of the business community, it is not the structure of relative prices of which its members are aware (and which is the most economically significant price structure) but the structure of money prices. A general decline in money prices then seems like much the same phenomenon, whether it is an expression of a meaningless general deflation, which could be avoided by appropriate monetary policy, or is an expression of economic progress.

It is not surprising, therefore, that there is much confusion in judgment regarding the matter of *preventing* price competition through trade associations or cartels. Times of general deflation produce a much more favorable attitude toward restrictive trade associations and policies than do times of general inflation. The trust and cartel movement itself as a large-scale movement was largely a product of discontents arising out of the long deflation of the 1870s and 1880s. In Germany, and to a lesser extent in England, this movement actually won social approval and received the support of the state. However, the only substitute for competition is socialization, and it is not surprising that these countries took a road toward increasing socialization and governmentally controlled price systems.

In the United States—I myself think fortunately—history took another turn, with the result that in all probability a more rapid *trend* of economic progress has been maintained, at the cost of serious fluctuations. The great deflation of 1929-32 produced the NRA, which represented a version of the old German policy of encouraging the cartelization of industry. However, the antitrust laws remained on the statute books and, with the long inflation following 1933, the "price cutting" problem passed into the background and the sentiment in favor of price competition reasserted itself. In the past decade the antitrust laws have probably been enforced as vigorously as at any time in their history, and there are no signs of a return to an NRA type of policy in regard to trade associations.

In this respect the situation in regard to business contrasts sharply with that of labor, where the NRA again provided the first legal encouragement of collective bargaining. The Wagner Act picked up the pieces that were dropped when the Supreme Court invalidated the NRA, and even the Taft-Hartley Act still maintains that the organization of the labor market through collective bargaining is a basic principle of national policy. Justification can be found for this apparent discrimination in sociological terms, because of the contribution of the labor movement to the rise in status of the worker and to his integration into the general fabric of society. There is also, however, some economic justification, which has not generally been made clear, in that money-wage reductions are almost invariably a sign of a general deflationary movement and are not a sign of economic progress. Consequently they are much less meaningful from the point of view of the economy as a whole than price reductions due to technical improvements. The famous chapter in the Webbs' work, *Industrial Democracy*, on the "Higgling of the Market,"[2] is a clear description of the deflationary process, though they do not recognize it as such, and it is this process against which the market is organized by trade unions.

Somewhat related to the general fear of price cutting is the protective tariff. Most protective tariffs are engineered by trade associations, whether formal or informal; for generally government seldom does anything so specific as imposing a tariff on a particular commodity unless some organization of that commodity's producers has been agitating. The case for free trade is reputed to be the only thing which the average student learns in his economics classes, and he doesn't believe even that, so it would be inappropriate at this point to expound it at length. It is worth observing, however, that unless a group of producers have some monopoly power within their country a protective tariff will not do them much good in the long run. If it results in abnormal profits, new producers will enter the field and profits in it will return to normal; indeed, as the tariff makes everybody a little worse off because the gains due to international specialization cannot be realized, even the protected group will be a little worse off in the long run.

In the long run, however, as Keynes so aptly remarked, we are all dead; so it is little wonder that the prevention of disagreeable but ultimately desirable short-run adjustments looms large in the eyes of those who make and influence public policy. There is also an antidepression case for tariffs or other trade restrictions, in that a country may "export unemployment" by achieving an export surplus. This is neither a particularly ethical nor even a particularly cheap way of raising the level of employment, and it seems difficult to justify it. Nevertheless, the relation of protection to the fear of deflation is a real one. One can see the connection by comparing the condition of the United States in the deflationary 1930's and in the inflationary 1940s. The removal of the United States tariff in the 1930s might have been accompanied by a good deal of localized distress and by a rise in unemployment. In the 1940's the complete abolition of the tariff would have been of almost universal benefit. Any workers displaced by imports would have gone to relieve the acute labor shortages, some material shortages would have been alleviated a little (like wood and meat), and virtually no serious unemployment would have been created.

[2] Sidney and Beatrice Webb, *Industrial Democracy*, London, 1898, Part III, Chapter 2.

The "mythology" of protection, like the mythology of agricultural policy, is an interesting example of the creation of a general myth in the interests of a special group. Large numbers of people in all countries believe that free imports from lower wage areas would lower real wages at home, oblivious of the fact that low wages are generally due to low productivity and rarely confer much competitive advantage. The persistence of this myth is a striking testimony to the difficulties of economic education; it is perhaps still more a testimony to the inadequacy of economics itself. The free-trade argument has fallen on such deaf ears largely because protection is the wrong answer to a real problem—that of general deflation. As long as economists denied that there was any such problem, one could hardly blame the layman for seizing on an obvious answer that seemed close to hand, especially as it was an answer which permitted him to express that dislike of the foreigner which seems to be an almost universal accompaniment of love of country.

A discussion of trade associations should not conclude without mentioning what the Germans call *Spitzenverbände* ("peak associations"), the national federations of all businesses, such as the National Association of Manufacturers in the United States and the Federation of British Industries in England. These are apt to be more expensive than they are impressive. They engage in a great deal of propaganda, and they engage also in extensive lobbying operations, some of which are effective. The National Association of Manufacturers, for instance, is generally credited with fathering the Taft-Hartley Labor-Management Relations Act. Generally speaking, however, they have been rather ineffective politically over the long pull in the social-democratic countries. Even where they have given some support to fascism, as in Germany and Italy, they have generally found their power clipped by the rising economic power of the state.

A striking feature of these organizations has been their inability to achieve intellectual respectability or public sympathy. There has been a serious failure of communication here between the organized businessmen and other groups, especially the academic community—a failure which, if long continued, holds a serious threat to the maintenance of a business civilization. The breakdown of capitalism in Europe can be traced rather directly to the inability of the organized capitalists to win the respect of the intellectuals. It is this lack of communication more than any other factor which has swung the intellectuals toward socialism. Not being able to understand the reality of the world around them because of the wall of noncommunication between them and the business world, the intellectuals turned easily to an abstract but unreal system which they could understand.

In America, fortunately, there are signs that real two-way communication between the business and the academic groups is opening up. The Committee for Economic Development, founded by Paul Hoffman and others, has been a valuable instrument for mutual understanding, and is in striking contrast with the other business organizations. It is successful mainly because it is an instrument for discussion rather than propaganda. The long and frequently painful meetings at which businessmen and academic economists sat down together to hammer out documents on important public issues have been much more effective in breaking down the barriers of communication between these groups than any amount of slick-paper propaganda put out by public relations departments.

COOPERATIVES

The cooperative society is a form of economic organization so closely akin to businesses that it must be considered as a form of business organization. It differs from other forms of business organization such as the stock corporation or the partnership in certain technical matters of law and practice. It differs from them also in that it is usually more charged with ethical tone, and is the object of much ethically motivated activity. So much is this the case that some church groups appear to believe that the cooperative form of organization represents a peculiarly "Christian" form of business, and that it is their duty to foster it.

The position of the present author in this respect is peculiarly difficult. Cooperatives have been supported by the resolutions of numerous church bodies. Moreover, the cooperative movement has attached to itself a sincerity of devotion which in itself is worthy of the highest praise. It is with reluctance, therefore, that I have come to the conclusion that the cooperative form of organization in itself is not the basis of the highly ethical aspects of the movement, that it makes but a minor contribution to the solution of our economic problems, and that on the whole I believe the time has come for a reexamination of the basis for the concern of many church people for cooperatives. With these conclusions many will disagree. I believe also that further study of this problem is needed. Nevertheless I have come to this conclusion for reasons which are at least convincing to me.

The essential characteristic of the cooperative form of organization is that the finance and especially the control of the organization are in the hands of people who are associated with the organization in some other capacity, either as buyers from it, as sellers to it, or as workers in it. There are three main types of cooperatives, corresponding to each of the above categories: consumers' (purchasers') cooperatives, marketing cooperatives, and producers' or workers' cooperatives. Consumers' cooperatives are ideally owned and operated by people who buy from them; marketing cooperatives, by people who sell to them; workers' cooperatives, by their employees. Workers' cooperatives have had a long record of failure in Western countries. The only country today where this form of organization exhibits much life is France.[3] Even the French communities, though interesting both sociologically and spiritually, represent an insignificant fraction of total economic activity. Consumers' cooperatives have been successful in England and Sweden, relatively unsuccessful in North America. Marketing cooperatives have been successful in Denmark, and moderately successful in North America and in some other parts of Europe.

The main technical difference between a cooperative and a stock corporation,[4] in regard to the form of organization, is in ownership and finance.

The ownership of stock corporations is legally vested in a body of shareholders who are not necessarily connected with the enterprise in other capacities, either as purchasers, workers, or even managers. These shareholders elect the directors and through them the managers of the enterprise, and the residual earnings of the enterprise may be distributed among them as dividends. Both

[3] See Claire H. Bishop, *All Things Common*, New York, Harper & Brothers, 1950.

[4] Most cooperatives are legally incorporated, and hence are strictly "corporations." I have used the more formal term "stock corporation," therefore, to distinguish the conventional type of corporation from the cooperative.

the voting power of the shareholder and the proportion of the dividend which he receives are proportional to the nominal value of the shares which he owns: a man who owns $1,000 in shares has ten times the votes, and receives ten times as much in dividends, as the man who owns $100 in shares.

In the cooperative, on the other hand, ownership is vested in a body of "members" who obtain membership by purchasing one or more so-called "shares" in the cooperative, or in some cases by merely paying a membership fee. The "shares" of a cooperative do not entitle the owner to a given share in the dividends ("rebates") distributed. They generally carry fixed interest, or no interest at all, and are hence more like the "bonds" of a stock corporation. A member also usually is entitled to a single vote in the election of officers, no matter how many shares he owns. The residual earnings of the enterprise may be divided, in whole or in part, among the members, just as the earnings of a stock corporation are divided among the stockholders. In the case of the cooperative, however, the dividend is divided not in proportion to the capital stock owned by the members, but in proportion to the *degree of participation* of the member in certain other aspects of the enterprise. Thus in the consumers' cooperative, dividends are in proportion to purchases: a member who purchased $1,000 worth of goods from the cooperative will receive ten times as much as a member who purchased only $100 worth. In the marketing cooperative, dividends are generally in proportion to the value of commodities sold to, or through, the cooperative. Most marketing cooperatives take title to the goods which pass through their hands, in which case the members can properly be said to "sell" to them; some allow the title to remain in the hands of the members until the goods are sold to the final purchasers, in which case it is more accurate to say that the goods are sold "through" the cooperative; but the principle of distributing earnings is essentially the same in both cases. Workers' cooperatives generally distribute earnings in accordance with some agreed measure of participation in the work of the enterprise.

The reasons for the success or failure of cooperatives in different environments are sociological rather than economic, and much more work needs to be done on this problem. The growth of cooperatives, like that of any organization, depends on their ability to attract resources unto themselves and away from competing forms of organization. In the absence of coercive power they can do this only by satisfying human needs better than their competitors. Their success therefore depends on two factors. The first is whether the "participant-ownership" characteristic which distinguishes them from other businesses fulfills a need in itself—that is, can the cooperatives attract human time and energy into their service motivated by the simple desire to participate in their ownership and control? The second is whether the participant-ownership feature enables the cooperatives to be more efficient in the satisfaction of other needs—cheaper groceries as well as participation. In regard to the first there seems to be little doubt that in some circumstances the cooperatives can satisfy a need for participation in itself, particularly among people who for one reason or another, their class status or personality difficulties or moral scruples, find it difficult to participate in other organizations. In regard to the second there is much more doubt. The participant owner is sometimes more of a liability than an asset, and there seems to be nothing in the cooperative form of organization as such which would make it necessarily more efficient in the satisfaction of the need for goods and services.

Besides attracting human time and energy, an organization must also attract or accumulate capital if it is to grow. Cooperatives often find difficulty in attracting "outside" capital in the form of loans or debentures. Moreover they are quite properly loath to finance expansion in this way, because it violates the essential principle of "participant finance." This means that on the whole the expansion of the cooperative can come from three sources only: the acquisition of new members, assessments on members, and the plowing back of earnings. The latter has been of especial importance in the British consumer cooperatives, and has led to a curious and anomalous situation in which the cooperatives possess large sums of capital as a result of conservative dividend policies in the past, capital which does not strictly belong to anybody. It is clear that internal growth by the retention of earnings can take place only if earnings are sufficiently high, and that the higher the rate of earnings the greater the possible rate of growth. It has been the small earnings of American consumers' cooperatives, faced as they are by the competition of a highly efficient system of chain-store retailing, which have been mainly responsible for the lack of growth.

The explanation of the striking difference in the success of the urban consumer cooperative in America and in Europe is probably to be found in the differing social structures of the two areas. In European countries class lines are sharply drawn, and in Britain the line between the ruling class and the workers is still more sharply drawn by the language barrier. Consequently there existed in these countries a reservoir of unused managerial ability in the working classes, which was not tapped because the worker could not easily penetrate into the ruling-class culture, with its different accents and customs. The consumer-cooperative movement in Europe has been almost exclusively an indigenous working-class movement, owing practically nothing to intellectuals. It has therefore been able to obtain good management very cheaply, and it has been able to draw its morale from the sense of working-class solidarity. In America, on the other hand, consumers' cooperation has been largely a product of intellectuals, seeking to copy something which they had read about. These cooperatives have found it difficult to obtain and retain good managers because class barriers are flexible enough so that there does not seem to exist, except in remote places and among immigrant groups, and perhaps in the spare time of the intelligentsia, any striking reservoir of unused managerial ability. The good managers are all too readily snapped up by the chain stores.

A form of consumers' cooperative which perhaps deserves to be classified by itself is the service cooperative, which sells not goods but services to its members. There are cooperative organizations providing credit (credit unions), insurance, medical services, electricity, housing, cold-storage lockers, and even burials. On the whole these have been much more successful in the United States than retail cooperatives, though they represent only a small percentage of the service industries. The rural electrification cooperatives deserve special mention as an example of imaginative combination of public and private enterprise.

By far the larger part of cooperative enterprise in North America is in agriculture. Agricultural marketing cooperatives account for about 20 per cent of the income from sales of farm produce in the United States. Rural purchasing cooperatives have been even more successful—in marked contrast to the urban consumer cooperatives. The success of rural cooperatives may be attributed mainly to a peculiar characteristic of the farm group—that it is both "business-like" and sociable. Those areas where the cooperatives have been most successful are the areas of commercial rather than of sub-sistence agriculture, where the farm is essentially a business and farmers cultivate businesslike attitudes. Rural life also develops attitudes of neighborliness and a tradition of joint action. The cooperative can be regarded in part as a joint extension of each farmer's business enterprise toward the consumer or, in the case of purchasing cooperatives, toward the producer. It requires both businesslike attitudes on the part of the members and a certain willingness to put time and effort into a joint undertaking. Both these attributes seem to be commoner in rural than in urban life, which goes far toward explaining why the cooperative movement, in America at least, is so largely rural. Part of the success of marketing cooperatives may also be attributed to the development of the "revolving-capital" method of finance, by which members are assessed contributions (loans) in proportion to their sales until the net worth of the cooperative has reached a desired level, after which the contributions of one year are used to repay the "oldest" contributions. Perhaps because of the more businesslike attitudes of their members, marketing cooperatives have suffered from shortages of capital rather than from the surpluses which are characteristic of the British consumer cooperatives.

There is a certain danger that marketing cooperatives, when they have grown to cover a large proportion of the total market, may develop monopoly power and may be tempted to use this power by restricting the output of members through quotas or other devices. When it gets to this stage the cooperative becomes more like a cartel, with all the social disadvantages that are implied. In fact, however, few marketing cooperatives have ever achieved such a degree of control of the market. Perhaps the best example is that of the California lemon growers, who succeeded by restrictions of output in maintaining the price of lemons during the depression, thereby depriving the American public of some desirable vitamins. Some of the milk marketing cooperatives have also tried to obtain a monopoly position by controlling output. Agricultural output, however, is difficult to control because of the large number of producers, and though the motivation to obtain monopoly power has often been important in the formation of agricultural cooperatives, it has rarely been achieved except for short periods.

The cooperative movement claims that the cooperative form of organization is ethically superior to other forms. Its enthusiasts claim that it is also economically superior. The claim to economic superiority is not difficult to assess. In certain times and places the cooperative form of organization has made a good deal of sense, especially where it has tapped hitherto unused sources of human energy and ability. It has, however, no intrinsic superiority to other forms of organization as a means of making people richer. Indeed, the circumstances under which it is likely to be most successful are rather special, and it cannot claim any general superiority over other forms. Furthermore, the cooperative movement makes only a small contribution to the solution of the major economic problems of our day. If all cooperative enterprise were to be replaced by private enterprise, or if cooperative enterprise were to expand to cover a large part of the economy, all our major economic problems would remain—instability, lack of economic development, and so on. The extension of cooperative enterprise may have a desirable effect in equalizing incomes. The social conditions which would permit this, however, are likely to give rise to more equal incomes under any form of business organization.

The claim to ethical superiority is, of course, more difficult to assess. Some of the belief in the ethical superiority of cooperatives is due simply to the name. Resale price maintenance laws made no headway until the movement was labeled "Fair Trade," and cooperatives would probably be much more difficult to organize under the name of "Participator-Financed Businesses." Some of the stigma attached to the word "uncooperative" sticks to anyone who doubts the virtue of "cooperation."

There are, however, more valid grounds for the ethical claim. It is not unreasonable to attach a high value to *participation* in organizations, and to suppose therefore that there is a value in itself attached to organizations which are participator-owned and financed. I cannot avoid the conclusion, however, that much of the ethical value attached to cooperatives on this score is a result of confusing the desirability of participation in the life of the community as such with participation in particular forms of organization. Some people find ethical satisfaction in extending their personal enterprise through the cooperative form of organization, whether it is the family participating in the ownership of a store or a farmer participating in the ownership of a marketing association. For many others, however, such effort would be a waste of time and energy, and would divert their attention from other forms of participation in community activity which might be more productive.

Perhaps one of the most powerful ethical judgments involved in the cooperative movement is the attitude toward profits. Cooperatives are frequently supposed to derive a good deal of their ethical value from the fact that they are "nonprofit" organizations. This attribute was legally recognized prior to the Revenue Act of 1951 in the exemption of agricultural cooperatives, complying with certain conditions, from the corporate income tax. The question here is partly one of semantics; it is apparently quite respectable to have "earnings" but disgraceful to earn "profits." Where the question is more than a semantic one it involves essentially the further question whether the cooperative is to be thought of as a "business" existing in its own right, with a life and being of its own, or whether it is to be thought of simply as an extension of the personalities of the members, a sort of collective tool by which the members get things cheaper or sell them dearer.

If a cooperative is a business, then its earnings are essentially indistinguishable from profits; they represent an increase in the net worth of the business entity, which can be disposed of pretty much as the business sees fit. If the cooperative is simply a way of getting things "at cost" for the members, then its earnings may properly be regarded as income of the members rather than of the cooperative. In point of fact, however, a cooperative will never be successful unless it is regarded as a business entity in its own right. The members of a consumers' cooperative must be interested in owning and running a store rather than in getting things cheap; the members of a marketing cooperative must be interested in running a marketing business, not just in "eliminating the middleman." Otherwise the organization simply will not function. I would argue, therefore, that in order to be successful cooperatives must behave as if they were essentially profit-making organizations.

To my mind this is nothing in their disfavor, for profit—in the sense of a surplus of incomings over outgoings—is an essential characteristic of *any* healthy and growing organization. It does mean, however, that the ethical distinction between cooperatives and other forms of organization which is based on their being "nonprofit" organizations is shaky.

Perhaps the basic question at issue in both the economic and the ethical evaluation of cooperatives is the desirable extent of specialization in society. Cooperatives represent in a sense a movement away from specialization. The housewife who trades with the supermarket is leaving both the worries and the benefits to be derived from owning and running a store to someone else. The housewife who is a good cooperator has to be interested in owning and running the store she trades with. The case for cooperatives therefore is closely bound up with the case against specialization. The case against specialization in turn is closely bound up with the question of the degree of integration of the society: if specialization proceeds too far it may lead to social disintegration and to a decay in the character-building institutions in society. Adam Smith himself, it should be remembered, made a vitriolic attack on the division of labor as a producer of highly skilled dolts.

It should be clear, however, that the strength of the case for cooperatives depends greatly on the nature of the other institutions in the society. Under some circumstances cooperatives make a great deal of sense; under other circumstances they represent a sheer waste of effort. They make sense where this particular form of organization is able to liberate the spirit of enterprise—the spirit that expresses its dissatisfaction with the status quo not by trying to get something easier but by trying to do something better. It is the enterprising spirit, however, which is important, not the particular form of organization in which it happens to be best embodied at particular times and places.

9

The National State: Communist

The national state in our day has come to occupy something of the position that the Church occupied in the Middle Ages, in that it is an institution which is accepted without question, and which therefore is not generally thought of as a subject for inquiry. Many may be a little surprised, therefore, to find a discussion of the ethics of economic organizations which does not stop at those organizations subordinate to the national state—labor, farm, and business organizations—but which goes on to include the national state itself. Nevertheless, practically all the economic and ethical problems which have been discussed in connection with "private" organizations arise also in connection with the national state, which is the largest, most powerful, and most inclusive organization of all.

Under the impact of the organizational revolution the national state itself has become much "larger"; not only has the average population of the national unit been rising steadily, but the state has been extending its activities deeper and deeper into the life, and especially into the economic life, of its citizens. Indeed, the rise of the state as an economic organization is a phenomenon of much more importance than the rise of any of the organizations which we have considered in the previous three chapters. It would leave a one-sided impression of the nature and impact of the organizational revolution, therefore, if the national state were not discussed.

The rise of the national state as an economic organization has taken two forms, which are so different that they must be treated separately: the Communist state, on the one hand, as represented mainly by Russia, but now also by her adjacent satellites, as well as by China and Yugoslavia; and the social-democratic state, on the other hand, as represented by the United States, Great Britain, the Scandinavian countries, and the British Dominions. The fascist state represents a third variety, now fortunately in eclipse though not, alas, extinct. Some may object to lumping together states as diverse as "capitalist" United States and "socialist" Britain. The differences among the Western democracies, however, are due more to differences in size and age than to any basic divergence in their philosophies.

One hardly needs to say that the rise of communism is one of the most striking features of the past century; that it presents acute ethical problems for individuals, both those who accept it and live within the framework of a communist society and those who oppose it and seek to liberate mankind from its influence. It is perhaps less obvious that the rise of communism and of Communist states is a result of the impact of an ethical system (Marxism) on the organizational revolution. Without the ethical system the organizational revolution would not have taken this form; without the organizational revolution the ethical system would never have found expression in Communist states.

The discussion must begin, therefore, with a discussion of Marxism. I have described Marxism as an "ethical system." I do this not in any sense of approbation; but unfortunately there is no word in the English language which means "pertaining to judgments of good and bad" which does not carry virtuous overtones. I mean simply that it is a system of criteria of judgment, of standards according to which the conditions of society, the acts of men, and the movements of history can be judged. It is not a system which I myself believe to be true; in considering its impact on society, however, its essentially moralistic nature must recognized.

FOUNDATIONS OF MARXIST THEORY

Marxist theory has two principal foundations: the first is the labor theory of value and the second is the materialistic interpretation of history. Both are worth examining in the light of the principles of organization, because they illustrate the danger of the combination of inadequate social science with appealing ethical insights.

The labor theory of value in Marx is often misunderstood because it is thought to be a theory of relative values—i.e., of prices. In the third volume of *Das Kapital* (whether we regard this as Marx or Engels does not much matter) it is made clear that the labor theory of value and the theory of surplus value are not to be regarded as a theory of prices, and the theory of prices which finally emerges is practically identical with that of Ricardo and can easily be stated as a special case of modern value theory. Consequently attacks on the Marxian theory of value which point out the absurdity of supposing that in any system commodities will exchange in proportion to quantity of labor embodied are aiming at a somewhat irrelevant target. What the Marxian theory of value really amounts to is a labor theory of *output*, and of output as a whole, rather than a theory of value.

The roots of the idea come from Ricardo—the idea of the economic process as a "labor process" and of commodities as "jellies of embodied labor." Every commodity, say a loaf of bread, can be regarded historically as "caused" by a long series of acts of labor, or parts of such acts—the labor of the storekeeper, of the trucker, of the baker, of the miller, of the farmer, of the men who made the machines and tools, of the men who made the machines that made the machines—in a kind of house-that-Jack-built regression until finally we come back to Adam or the primordial amoeba, or at least to the point where the amount of labor involved is too small to be noticed. The whole output of a society can similarly be analyzed into past acts of labor. This idea is suggested in the first sentence of Adam Smith's *Wealth of Nations*: "The annual labor of every nation is the fund which originally supplies it with all the necessaries and conveniences of life which it annually consumes."

The theory of surplus value, which is perhaps the most essential feature of the Marxian system, is derived directly from the idea of production as a labor process. All that Marx means by surplus value is "nonlabor income." The Marxian value theory can therefore be put into the nutshell of a single syllogism: labor makes everything; labor doesn't get everything; therefore labor doesn't get what it makes—i.e., is exploited. The fact that Marx expounds the theory in terms of a single worker or a single commodity, probably for the sake of bringing the magnitudes down to dimensions where a working man could appreciate them, has diverted attention from the fact that the theory is essentially one of aggregate income and output. This essential simplicity perhaps explains how a book like *Das Kapital*, perhaps one of the worst-written and most unreadable books ever written, even in economics, has exercised such a great influence. In effect, the Marxist stands on his soapbox and says to his laboring audience, "Look at that top hat over there. Who made it?" And the answer comes roaring back, "We did." "Who's wearing it?" "He is." "Knock it off." And the little boy with a snowball takes on the features of David before Goliath. The infusion of a sense of righteousness into the common urge to bash things around has always proved to be a powerful stimulus to action.

The other pillar of Marxism is the theory of dialectical materialism. The dialectical interpretation of history comes, of course, from Hegel. It is the view that history consists of a succession of systems, each of which is a reaction against the previous one. Each state of society is a "thesis" which by its defects produces an "antithesis," and the interaction of both thesis and antithesis produces a new "synthesis" which in its turn becomes the thesis for the next cycle of development. Essentially, the dialectical view of history is a picturesque statement of the principles of ecological succession which were developed in the preface of this book. As such it naturally contains a good deal of truth. It is, however, a pattern which is too simple; history always refuses to fit into intellectual strait jackets. Its cyclical movements are never particularly neat; systems are not usually succeeded by their opposites; change is sometimes regular and slow, sometimes cyclical and violent; chance plays an important part at critical moments; history sometimes does and sometimes does not repeat itself; and so on.

In the hands of Marx the dialectical theory became even more of a strait jacket. Marx converted the broad dialectic of Hegel into a narrow dialectic based on class struggle. Marx conceived of history as a succession of systems, each based on the dominance of a particular class, each brought to an end by the overthrow of the ruling class, usually by the one immediately below. When the lowest layer came to the top the process would be complete and the golden age would be ushered in, exploitation then being impossible.

In this aspect of his theory the "dialectic" is not particularly "materialist," and it can be argued that the materialist aspect of Marxian thought is secondary to the idea of the class struggle. Nevertheless it is an integral part of the Communist system of thought in that it introduces the idea of an ultimately overriding *necessity* into the historical process. The "materialist" interpretation is that the institutions and ideas which prevail at any time are determined primarily by the techniques of production. As the development of techniques of production follows a law of its own, almost independent of human activity, the ideologies, religions, and institutions of man are not independently determined but are mere creatures of the techniques of production.

The idea that economic techniques could affect the ideas, beliefs, and organizations of society was a useful corrective to the kind of history taught by the "Great Men" school; it might even be a useful corrective to the "Great Books" school. We have already observed how the horse collar eventually abolished slavery, how gunpowder abolished the city-state, and so on. Nevertheless we have here a clear example of the Hegelian dialectic operating in the realm of ideas. The neglect of economic factors in the older views of history (the "thesis") led to its antithesis in the Marxian school of economic determinism, an equally one-sided picture, the two incomplete views now being synthesized in the ecological view of history.

From the point of view of Marxism as an ethical system, however, it is important to observe that the dialectical materialist interpretation of history plays much the same role as the concept of the will of God in Christian ethics: it is an omnipotent force which requires voluntary consent. Hence we see in Marxism the same kind of paradox that we view in Calvinism: a doctrine of predestination which results not in resignation, as it seems to do in Mohammedanism, but in great activity in efforts toward salvation. The message is not that there is a will of God—i.e., an absolute necessity or fate about which we can do nothing—but that men are fellow workers with God (or with History) in the accomplishment of His (or Its) purposes. Hence the call "Workers of the World, Unite!" which at first sight seems so incompatible with the automatic dialectic of history. This point has been argued in the Marxist theologies, and there have been heretical Marxians who have maintained that because the dialectical process was invincible there was no necessity to enlist in the class war—one could simply wait for the glorious revolution to happen. This view has generally been frowned on by the more orthodox.

The Marxist system is essentially an "adventist" system. Like the Jehovah's Witnesses, the Communists look at history as if it were a one-way street with a triumphal arch at the midpoint; before the arch (the second coming or the expropriation of the expropriators) all is dark and gloomy; afterward all is light and joy. Moreover, the closer the triumphal arch approaches, the worse things get—this is the Marxian doctrine of increasing misery— and it is precisely when things are at their worst that the revolution comes and we enter the classless society, the Kingdom of God on earth. One can see the appeal of this kind of doctrine when things actually *are* getting worse!

FALLACY OF LABOR THEORY OF VALUE

It is not too difficult to expose the fallacies of the Marxist system; or, one might say more kindly, to exhibit it as a special and unlikely case of a general social theory. The labor theory of value as a theory of the social output is the weak foundation on which most of the superstructure is raised. The fallacy of the labor theory of value is not, as many have supposed, that it is an inadequate and improper account of how prices are actually determined, for as we have seen Marx did not say, ultimately, that prices were in proportion to the amounts of labor embodied in the commodity, and even if he had, a labor-embodied theory of relative prices is after all a rough first approximation. If anyone asks us why an automobile costs a hundred times as much as a watch, it is at least a rough-and-ready answer to say that it is because it "needs" a hundred times more working hours to make it. The real trouble with the Marxian labor theory of output is that it is purely mechanical, and does not include any adequate theory of organization. It is almost like a chemical theory of man, which "explains" man in terms of so much hydrogen, so much nitrogen, and so on. The truth is that the productive process is a product of the *whole culture*, of all its institutions and ideas, and it is meaningless to separate out a single part of the culture (acts of labor) and say that labor "produces" the product.

Indeed, it is not too difficult to stand the Marxist theory completely on its head, and to expound the productive process as a "capital theory of value" instead of a "labor theory." We could argue, for instance, that labor is an amorphous mass which is incapable of producing anything unless it is organized into a process of production by the owners of capital. In this theory labor would be regarded as a kind of raw material of the process of production, much like any other kind of raw material; and as obviously iron ore and lime and coal would never of their own accord walk out of their mines and unite with each other to form steel, so labor (at least abstract labor of the kind contemplated by Marx) would never walk out of its lair in the unorganized human body and organize itself into processes of production. A "raw materials theory of value" then would seem on this view to be just as sensible as a "labor theory": for the real creator of the social product is the activity of control of capital—i.e., ownership—and it is the capitalist who is the source of the whole product.

From this a reversed theory of surplus value emerges: the capitalist *makes* the whole product, but, alas, does not get all of it. Labor persistently, because of its favorable political position in the society, is able to get more than is necessary for its maintenance, and is therefore in a position to exploit capital, to the detriment of the process of production, economic progress, and justice in distribution. The remedy for this sad state of affairs would seem to be a revolution (along the lines of that organized by Joseph—Genesis: 47) to establish a slave society, in which the exploitation of capital by labor would be abolished, and labor, like other cattle, would receive merely its maintenance and depreciation.

The absurdity of this theory should not blind us to the validity of its logic, nor to its basic similarity to the Marxist system. One suspects, indeed, that there are certain business interests which would not be averse to holding a capital theory of value. In spite of the fact that it is absurd in its conclusions and morally revolting in its content, it is actually a more realistic theory than the Marxist labor theory of value. Indeed, one has a depressing feeling that both theories of value come out to much the same practical conclusion—a slave society. Both of them are arithmetical theories rather than organic theories; they think of the productive process as if it consisted of simple addition rather than highly complex integration. At this level the more realistic nature of the capital theory of value by comparison with the labor theory of value is shown by the Russian experience. A society based ostensibly on the view that labor is the creator of all value has been forced by the necessity of its own inner logic into a highly "capital-centered" society. The working classes are organized ruthlessly into a process of production by the ruling oligarchy, who have obtained a unified control of the capital resources of the economy, and the society takes on increasingly the appearance of a slave state.

The basic fallacy of both the labor theory of value and the capital theory of value is the assumption that any single element in society is the "cause" of the output of the productive process. The ruthless economic planning of a communist society is testimony to the fallacy of the labor theory of value. Labor left to itself produces nothing; it must be organized, either by the unconscious processes of the market or by the conscious regimentation of a planned economy, if it is to produce anything. On the other hand, the economic weakness of slave societies is a testimony to the fallacy of the capital theory of value, as it is in slave societies that the capital theory of value finds its supreme expression.

The human being is not simply a machine or a piece of raw material. The productive process, as we have seen, involves interpersonal relations which are inevitably much more complex than the relations of a man to a machine or to a lump of clay. The capitalist entrepreneur—or the socialist planner—is not simply a potter molding the clay of labor into productive forms; or, if he is, the forms will be misshapen and much clay will be wasted. Human clay can be molded only by consent, and if this consent is obtained by coercion and by fear of punishment, as in a slave society, the resulting relationship is adequate only for subhuman tasks. Subhuman tasks, however, are continually being taken over by subhuman instruments, whether animal or mechanical; in our day, of course, even animal "slaves" are being superseded by mechanical "slaves." The highly complex machinery of modern civilization cannot be operated properly in an atmosphere of violence. We see this even at the level of the study of industrial accidents, most of which seem to be due to the absence of an attitude of inner consent on the part of the worker. It is inner resentment, whether of the boss or of a family situation, which seems to be the most important psychological root of human failures in an age of machinery.

FALLACY OF MARXIST INTERPRETATION OF HISTORY

The Marxist interpretation of history suffers from the same kind of defect which vitiates the labor theory of value. His view of the class structure is entirely too simple. There is in fact no such thing as a "working class," especially in the Western democracies. There is a complex stratification of society with many vaguely defined classes. (There is no agreement among sociologists, for instance, as to their number or exact boundaries.) There is also enough geographical and occupational mobility so that the "caste" structure of Western society, so far as it exists, is loose and ill defined, and is in any case very complex. The interpretation of history in terms of a class struggle, therefore, is a grand oversimplification—the over-simplicity of which gives it at once its persuasive power and its predictive weakness.

It is a commonplace that the past hundred years have falsified Marx's predictions in almost every particular. In the Western world, at least, the "law of increasing misery of the working class" has not operated. The proportion of the national product going to labor has been fairly stable, so that instead of technical progress all going into "surplus value" (i.e., nonlabor income) its fruits have been shared among all groups. The Communist revolution has come not in the factories of the West, but in the dispersed totalitarian societies of the East. Once it has happened, the state has not "withered away," but has become an increasingly effective instrument of oppression, until the exploitation of its people by the Communist state has exceeded the wildest imaginings of the most predatory capitalists.

Nevertheless it must be emphasized that the ethical strength of Marxism lies in the fact that it does have an interpretation of history, even if it is a wholly inadequate and misleading one, and that the weakness of "liberal" thought has been the absence of any interpretation of history. Incidentally, it is precisely their possession of a vivid and poetic interpretation of history which gives the fundamentalist and adventist Christian groups their strength as over against more liberal religion. There seems to be a clear need in the mind of man for some guideposts as to where he stands in the great stream of time, and a religion or a political and economic philosophy which stands wholly in the present, without either roots in the past or branches in the future, does not satisfy this need. It is not enough to confine religion to the psychology of everyday adjustment or to confine political and economic thinking to the solution of current problems. The need for a sense of direction in time is one of the deepest necessities of the human mind, and if the existing culture does not provide a good one, somebody will come along with an acceptable bad one.

PROBLEMS OF SURPLUS VALUE

The concept of surplus value is so important in the ethical system not only of Marx but of all socialists that it is worth some further examination. In its most general form the concept may be defined as that part of the social product or income the consumption of which is not necessary to maintain a continuing flow of product, and which is "surplus" in the sense that it can be devoted to uses, such as war, luxury, or redistribution, other than the maintenance of the continuing flow. The concept goes back earlier than Marx to the English classical economists, especially Ricardo, whose distinction between the gross and the net product is closely analogous. In the Marxian system, of course, all nonwage income is regarded as "surplus," in the sense that it is not "paid for" anything. This conclusion follows from the labor theory of value.

As we have seen, however, the labor theory of value, or rather of output, is inadequate, in that it gives no account of the contribution made by institutions to the whole productive process through history. It is clear from the study of comparative economic systems that the legal, religious, and social institutions in society profoundly affect the course of economic development and must therefore be considered "productive," in the sense that they affect the historical product one way or another. Thus a set of institutions which promotes a rapid rate of economic development may properly be considered more "productive" than a system which prevents or hinders economic development.

Unfortunately there is no easy answer to the question of the exact relationship between social institutions and economic development. Economic development is a product—one is almost tempted to say a by-product—of the whole culture pattern, and institutions which operate excellently in one setting operate poorly in another. Thus, in the setting of Christian America, the institutions of capitalism—banking, the corporation, private enterprise, organized commodity markets, and so on—have given us a phenomenally rapid rate of economic progress and a quite workable society in spite of many weaknesses and deficiencies. The same institutions in a culture setting such as the Chinese family system may give rise to hopeless corruption, nepotism, and social breakdown, in spite of the many admirable qualities of the family-centered ethic.

The main ethical presupposition of Marxism is that the private appropriation of economic surplus for private ends is improper, and that any income which is "unearned" in the sense that it is not necessary to provide for the further continuance of output should be used for public purposes—either for direct public purposes or for redistribution among the receivers of "earned" income. This is an ethical principle which has attracted a good deal of support in the past hundred years or so, and cannot be neglected in any appraisal of present situations. It is at the basis, for instance, not only of Marx's but of Henry George's critique of capitalism. Henry George identified economic surplus with Ricardo's concept of rent (an identification proper only in a static economy) and then went on to make further unjustified identifications of "economic" rent with actual land rents and especially with rising land values. It is at the bottom also of a great deal of non-Marxist socialist thought and feeling. Curiously enough it is also prominent in the military ideology. The economic surplus is the maximum amount of its resources which a nation can devote to war. Consequently, especially at a time of total war when it is believed that the maximum amount of resources must be devoted to the war effort, it is regarded as improper to devote economic surplus to private ends.

The problem of what shall be done with economic surplus is a problem in ethics rather than in social science. Nevertheless, social science can help to define and determine what the surplus is. The problem is particularly difficult when it is conceived, as it must be, in terms of a dynamic and progressing society. The problem almost has to be stated in terms of what social institutions are most likely to encourage creativity. If, for instance, private property in the means of production is more likely to encourage productive and creative uses of these means than is collective ownership, then private property as an institution may be considered creative. Income which results from the ownership of property, therefore, cannot necessarily be classed as "economic surplus," even though the contribution of an individual bondholder idling out his days in Florida may not be particularly apparent.

A classic example of the productivity of private ownership was provided by the history of the Jamestown and Plymouth colonies. The people who came over on the Mayflower were communist enough to warrant their exclusion under the McCarran Act, and it is ironic that the first successful British colonies in America started off as communist experiments, everything at first being held in common and the common produce being divided according to need. A near famine ended this idyllic situation (as it ended the attempt to impose "pure" communism on Russian agriculture in 1932) and the means of production were divided up among the colonists in private ownership. The simple change of giving each family title to what it produced and to the means with which it produced it began immediately to produce an abundance from which America has hardly ever looked back.

The community did not, however, cease being Christian, in the sense that it was profoundly influenced by the life and teachings of Jesus, and it did not, therefore, cease to recognize the responsibility of the community for the poor and the unfortunate. The rights of property were clearly bestowed upon the individual by the community as a matter of convenience in administration and not as a matter of inalienable right (the inalienable right of property, it may be recalled, tried to sneak into the Declaration of Independence and was promptly thrown out in favor of the pursuit of happiness). Nevertheless the convenience in administration is undeniable, especially when the right of property is placed in a cultural setting which emphasizes charity, stewardship, and the social responsibility of the individual.

"Exploitation"

The attack on the private use of surplus value can also be expressed as an attack on "exploitation." This word is so important in the ethical system of the Marxists that it is worth examination even at the cost of some repetition. There are two senses in which exploitation can be regarded as "bad." One is the sense of the *use* of human beings by others as if they were inanimate objects. The other is the sense of taking away from people something which they have produced without giving anything in return— that is, theft.

It is the second meaning which is of importance to the Marxists, for they regard all income as ultimately produced by the working class; hence, any income which does not go to the working class is exploitative. The working class is exploited in the sense that it produces goods (value) and then has its product forcibly taken away from it. The appeal of this doctrine as an explanation of poverty is not hard to understand, especially in those parts of the world where a small class of wealthy people exists side by side with great masses on the verge of starvation. It seems obvious to a poor man that he would be much better off if the riches of the rich were redistributed.

In brute fact, of course, it is simply not true that the main cause of poverty is exploitation. This is not to deny that exploitation exists. The main reason why people are poor, however, anywhere in the world, is not that they produce a lot and have it taken away from them, but that they produce so pitiably little. China, for instance, is poor and America is rich, not because China produces a lot and the wicked American capitalists take it away from her by force or fraud, but because Chinese produce so little and Americans produce so much. An even better case is India: in spite of the withdrawal of British rule and the amazing fact that Britain is now a debtor nation to India, so that actually India is now taking income away from Britain and giving "nothing" in return, the poverty of India is in no way alleviated and is steadily becoming worse. Nobody can now pretend that Indian poverty is caused by British "exploitation," however much it may be the cultural product of a long history of foreign rule. Even within the United States the South is poor and the North is rich, not because the South is exploited, but because it is relatively unproductive.

The Marxist has the best case in those countries where the capital is owned by a small indolent ruling caste, untouched by the spirit of enterprise and protected from the competition of the enterprising by their control of the state itself. The Near Eastern countries are a case in point. Hardly anywhere is the economic case for communism stronger, or the difficulties of a constructive capitalist revolution greater. There seems to be no answer to the problem of the concentration of capital into the hands of ineffective users except some kind of revolution. It is a tragedy that it is the wrong revolution that is being peddled most actively—wrong in the sense that it is a revolution based on a wholly inadequate social science and therefore doomed to frustration. It is not exploitation in the Marxist sense which is wrong with these countries; it is a lack of exploitation of opportunities for technical progress because of the culture pattern of the dominant class.

DEPERSONALIZATION

Although the first ethical criticism implied in the word "exploitation"—that of using men as if they were inanimate—is not such an important part of the Marxist critique of capitalism as the second, it is frequently an important part of the ethical dissatisfactions which people feel with capitalism. We have noticed this dilemma in Chapter 6: that any large organization involves a depersonalizing of human relationships, simply because of the number of person-to-person relationships involved. The lower ranks of the hierarchy then become mere "pawns" which the upper ranks move around, and lose any sense of identification with the enterprise of which they are a part.

Communism, far from solving this problem, actually intensifies it, simply because it involves bigger organizations. The naïveté of Marx in regard to the theory of organization nowhere stands out more clearly than at this point. In fact the Communist state has turned out to be more impersonal, more ruthless, and more exploitative than any capitalist system, simply because it involves larger organizations and greater concentrations of power. The invalidity of the Communist solution, however, should not blind us to the validity of the Communist criticism. The more we can make our attitude to the Communist's criticism not one of blind opposition but one of seeking to find *right* solutions—instead of the Communist's *wrong* solutions—to the real and important questions which he often raises, the more fruitful the interaction of the two orders of society is likely to be, especially if the Communist can also show himself capable of learning from his enemies.

We see therefore that the conflict, so important to our day, between communism and capitalism (or rather one should say social democracy, for a "pure" capitalism nowhere exists; the closest approximation to it is West Germany) is one which revolves around the theory of organization. To a considerable extent the basic disagreement centers around a question in social science rather than a question in ethics. This is not to deny that there are important ethical disagreements, particularly at the level of common morality. Communists have mortally offended Western sensitivities by importing the ethical standards of international conflict (the lie, the spy, the cheat, the swindle, and as much violence as is necessary to gain one's ends) into the field of domestic political conflict where normally higher standards are expected to prevail. Communists have also offended Western people by their exploitative attitude—regarding every aspect of life as a means rather than an end, and so destroying the multiplicity of ends which is so dear to the Western mind. It is this attitude, for instance, which has made them so unpopular in the labor movement, where they have sought to use as a means to their own ends the union which the good union man regards as an end in itself.

Nevertheless, in regard to the question whether a Communist society, once established, is "better" or "worse" than a capitalist or social-democratic society, the difference in view is not so much due to differences in ultimate ethical propositions as to differences in view in regard to the realities of social life. These differences may be summed up by saying that communism has no adequate theory of organization, and in effect denies that there is any such problem, with the result that in Communist society the development of organization takes place in defiance of that society's ethical presuppositions. In the Western world we have only the beginnings of a theory of organization, but we are at least not so handicapped in developing the practice of organization by false theoretical presuppositions. The critical problems of organization in both types of society are much the same. In Communist society, however, because of its monolithic character, the problems of diseconomies of scale are much more acute, the breakdowns of the communications system all the more important, and the problem of hierarchy becomes almost insoluble.

One can see the problem more clearly perhaps if one contrasts a large business enterprise—say General Motors—in American society with a similar enterprise (a state trust) in Soviet Russia. In structure of organization, the two are doubtless very similar. Each will have a hierarchy; each will have some kind of centralized executive. The problem of internal human relations may be made difficult in Russia by the existence of the Communist party as a kind of secret police, spying on workers and management alike for the first signs of heresy ("deviationism"). However, it is probably no worse than it was in many businesses in America in the days of the stool pigeon and the company "fink." The great difference between the two organizations lies in the nature of their environments and in their standards of success—i.e., in the type of results which lead to praise or blame, growth or decline.

In America the principal environment of the enterprise is a *market* environment—i.e., millions of customers with dollars in their pockets. The test of success of the organization is the market test—i.e., whether the organization is able to wheedle more dollars out of its customers than it has to pay out to its suppliers, workers, executives, and creditors. If the organization is efficient at transforming dollars paid out into dollars received it will be able to grow, both by plowing back (or rather, not distributing) its own profits, and by being able to attract new capital on favorable terms. Within the market environment the business is reasonably autonomous; i.e., if it is successful in coping with the market environment there is nobody much to say what it should do or what policies it should espouse. The market environment is not, of course, the only one. It operates also in a legal environment of antitrust laws, labor laws, pure food and drug laws, tax laws, fair employment practices laws, and so on, to which it must conform in some degree, and it will shape its policies accordingly. The legal and political environment is felt as a rather abstract and impersonal matter, however, in a way not unlike the market environment, but much less important. The legal environment merely places certain restrictions on operations within the market environment—a sort of boundary within which the business is free to move, and a wide and elastic boundary at that. Similarly there is an environment of public opinion, somewhat vaguer but of much the same general character as the legal environment.

Consider now the Soviet trust. This also operates to some extent under a market environment, in that it buys labor and raw materials and sells products. The results of operations in the market environment, however, are not crucial, because the trust is not an autonomous body but a kind of department of a much larger business, which is the Communist state itself. Consequently the executives of the trust must keep their eyes mainly not so much on the market environment as on their bosses higher up the line of Soviet hierarchy—the officials of the Gosplan, and higher still the Politburo. The main criterion of success is conformity with the plan—much as the criterion of success of a department within any large organization is conformity with the over-all plan of the organization. The political environment thus becomes the crucial one, and the market environment is secondary. If the trust runs into financial difficulties these can be cared for, if they do not conflict with the plan, by the simple application to the appropriate bank, just as the manager of a single plant in a large concern meets his payroll by simple application to the head office.

It is easy to see that the planned economy does not make for a rapid and effective communications system, and indeed is almost forced by its inner logic to suppress the transmission of information up to the centers of authority. The market on the other hand is a highly sensitive transmitter of information. If people decide that they dislike nylon shirts, this sentiment is rapidly reflected in sales figures, in inventories, in profit expectations, in all sorts of sensitive spots in the economy, and appropriate decisions are not long in forthcoming. The production of nylon shirts is slowed down and resources are turned to things more in demand. The weakness of the market is that it transmits only certain kinds of information; it transmits not general and political dissatisfactions, but only the kind of dissatisfactions and satisfactions which can be expressed by purchases and sales. It has the weakness also that through advertising and selling effort it may create demands rather than simply registering them. However, within the limits of its narrow vocabulary—taking into consideration also that its vocabulary may be distorted by the fact that communications from the rich carry more weight than those from the poor—the market does a remarkably effective job in providing a communication-decision system.

In the planned economy there is still, of course, something like a market and there is still something like a communications system. But the communications which are sent to the executives by market information do not have a sense of urgency about them. The executives tend to insulate themselves farther and farther from the ultimate sense organs of the organization (the people themselves), and live increasingly in a dream world of their own, peopled with "information" which they themselves create to suit their pre-existing notions.

In the Communist political world also there is atrophy of the communications system. As the rulers do not have to rely on the attempt to capture the votes of the electorate against organized opposition, there is no way for dissatisfaction to be communicated to those who have either incentive or power to do anything about it. Hence more and more reliance has to be placed on coercion and on pure "homeostasis," that is, on a strict conformity to the narrow limits of orthodoxy. A society with a poor communications system cannot afford to be flexible. The very logic of organization, therefore, seems to condemn the Communist world to a period of increasing sterility, for its poor communication system imposes on it the necessity for a rigid orthodoxy which cannot help having the ultimate effect of the suppression of growth and development.

In this respect there are striking analogies between the Communist and the Mohammedan worlds. Both, in their initial stages, were great revolutionary movements deriving their strength from the simplicity and single-mindedness of their ideas. Both, in their initial stages, acted as releasing forces for a great deal of human energy which could not come to flower under the systems which they displaced. Both, however, suffer from the fatal defect of an imposed "priestly" orthodoxy—a grand scheme of thought to which all aspects of life must conform. Both, in this sense, are essentially totalitarian. Just as Mohammedan culture dried on the vine after its amazing flowering, and became a kind of fossil society, insulated from the immense winds of change which were blowing over the Christian world, so it looks as if the Communist world is following the same pattern. In one field after another in Russia we see the suppression of free inquiry in science and the necessity to fit everything into the rigid strait-jacket of the Marxian dialectic, under the grim penalties of the police state. This is likely to insulate the communist world from the changes which are still in progress in the West, not merely in the physical sciences and in mechanical and chemical techniques, but in the social sciences also. It will be surprising if Communist culture—if it is left sufficiently alone—does not fossilize.

As an additional confirmation of the view expressed above, the nature of the cyclical movement in the Soviet Russian economy is worthy of attention. The over-all output of the Soviet economy has exhibited cyclical movements which, oddly enough, have strongly paralleled the cyclical movements of the capitalist world. There is first the period of "war communism" from 1917, ending in the utter debacle of 1921. This was followed by a recovery under the New Economic Policy, which permitted limited restoration of private enterprise. This reached a peak in 1928 with the beginning of the Five-Year Plan and the collectivization program; the collectivization "depression" resulted in the famine of 1932. After 1932 another kind of "new economic policy" was reinstated, though not under that name, with greater security of property to the collective farms, wider inequalities of income, Stakhanovism (a Soviet version of Taylorism), and so on. Since 1932 there has again been substantial economic development, in spite of the devastation caused by the war. We thus see that the economic cycle in Russia is not, like the capitalist cycle, a result of instability in the market economy, but is a result of instability in the political amosphere. One might almost say that Communist principles are applied until there is a famine; then when that information is obvious enough to get through even the Soviet communications system, some executive adjustments are made in the direction of a more relaxed system, with consequent recovery. When the recovery has proceeded far enough, however, the Communist rulers decide that the time has come for another application of Communist principles, and another severe setback seems to be the result.

PROMISE AND PRACTICE

One cannot study the history of Communist thought and practice without being overcome by an almost overwhelming sense of tragedy. The slogans are so appealing; the practice is such a nightmare. "Each for all and all for each"; "From each according to his capacity, to each according to his need"; "Production for use and not for profit"—it is little wonder that Western intellectuals who have thrown off what they imagine to be the shackles of Christianity, but who nevertheless retain in the very bones of their thinking the Christian ethic of love, should have found socialism—Marxist or otherwise—so attractive. It seems to promise a truly familistic society, in which the cold calculations of the market place and the inhuman niceties of property shall be dissolved in a joyous mutuality of common work and shared achievement. Why, then, does the attempt to put these golden promises into operation seem to result in the drab nightmare of the police state, the regimented society, the universal rule of fear, the destruction of friendship and of all simple, human relations, the enshrinement of hatred as the prime mover of society, the suppression of all free thought and criticism, and the sycophantic adulation of the almost divine dictator?

The answer lies partly in intellectual error, in the sheer falsities and inadequacies of Marxism as social science, and in the hardening of this essentially erroneous intellectual system into a dogma, providing in its completeness a hard shell for the mind which accepts it—a shell which gives an immense feeling of security and yet prevents all further growth.

The answer, however, also lies deeper, in the nature of the laws of organizations themselves. Organizations follow certain necessities of their own, almost independent of their ostensible purposes. The family type of intimate relationship which is the highest expression of the spirit of love in human life can be achieved only *in an organization* of family size—i.e., a mere handful of people.

This seems to be true even in war, where recent studies have shown that what a man dies for is not a "cause" but his "buddies"—it is the intimate relationships of a small group of men in common danger that are the ground from which a man may lay down his life for his friends.

As organizations grow larger and larger, relationships must of necessity become more and more formalized, and the most acute problem of society is to achieve the right degree and kind of formalization. A society whose theoretical structure has never faced this problem, and which tries to apply a familistic ethic to a brontosaurian organization, will end in a terroristic rigidity. In our present state of knowledge the only substitute for the cash nexus is the fear nexus: a society moved not by the hope of gain but by fear of the inquisitor. This is not to say that we can rest easy in a market-dominated society; this too has ills of its own, some of which will be examined in the next chapter. It does mean, however, that our thinking, both in social science and in ethics, must go beyond the alluring simplicities of socialism to a deeper understanding both of the organizational necessities of social life and of the prophetic impulses which drive us remorselessly onward either to damnation or to salvation.

10

The National State:
Social-Democratic

The organizational revolution has been felt in its impact on the national state not merely in the rise of Communist states, but also in a profound change in the character of most of the Western countries from the aristocratic-commercial state to what may quite properly be called the social-democratic state. This movement may be dated from about the middle of the nineteenth century with the Factory Acts in England and the beginnings of the extended franchise; it began to get under way vigorously in the 1870s and 1880s in Bismarck's Germany, a little later in Lloyd George's England, later still in Roosevelt's America.

It has come to involve a great increase in the proportion of national incomes absorbed by the central government, part of which is due to the expanded activities of government in social insurance, education, health, regulation of business, and so on, and part to the ever-increasing cost of warfare and of national defense. There has also been an increase in the amount of government-operated enterprise, especially in the more socialist of the social-democratic countries (e.g., England, Norway), but not enough to make a fundamental difference in the economy. Even in England only about 20 per cent of the economy is operated by government enterprises. Another marked characteristic of the social-democratic countries is the development of progressive income taxes to the point where a substantial redistribution of personal incomes has been effected, even to the virtual elimination of very large incomes. In all these countries also there has been an increasing degree of government control of the pricing system, through regulation of public utilities and railroads, through the control of agricultural prices and marketing, through minimum-wages laws, and, in time of war, through general price control and rationing.

1. FACTORS OF EXPANSION

The change in the nature of the state in the direction of extending its activities and powers is again a result of two sets of factors, one operating on the side of demand, the other on the side of supply. On the side of demand there is, as we have already noticed in the case of the rise of the labor and farm movements, an increased demand for status on the part of the low-status groups which has expressed itself in demand for legislation on their behalf. This demand has proved effective partly because of the extension of the franchise to these groups, and partly because of the rise of nationalist as opposed to class feeling and a consequent increase of the sense of community *within* the nation, developed through wars with other nations.

The last point is worth examining further. The establishment of the national state—i.e., a politically independent state covering a fairly homogeneous area—though it has increased conflicts between nations and has led to a progressive increase in the cost of defense, has developed a sense of responsibility of all for all *within* the national unit—at the cost of diminishing the sense of responsibility for "foreigners." It is probable that the general acceptance of the social-democratic state, even by the old privileged classes, is a result of the almost universal rise of nationalism. In America the poor are still "Americans," and we cannot let "Americans" starve or go naked; similarly Negroes are still "Americans," so that in spite of the legacy of hatred and prejudice left by slavery and the Civil War there is a constant governmental pressure, through fair employment practices legislation and court decisions, pushing toward racial equality. A sense of community or of "we-ness" among people is built mainly by engaging in activities together; the more dangerous and strenuous the activities, the stronger will be the sense of community. War, for reasons which we will go into later, has been increasing in intensity and has been reaching farther and farther down into the life of the people. The day is gone forever when it was an affair of professional soldiers and touched the life of the people only when battles were fought on their property. The people of all classes within each nation, therefore, have come to share experiences of increasing danger and emotional significance as a national group. Consequently they have been drawn together in a sense of mutual responsibility.

As the national government is the principal machinery for the expression of this mutual sense of responsibility, it is not surprising that the powers and activities of national governments have grown. It is interesting to observe, in further confirmation of this thesis, that the executive branch of government has grown in power and responsibility relative to the legislative branch in almost all countries. We saw this movement in its most extreme (and perverted) form in fascism, which represents in one sense a complete absorption of the legislative function by the executive, and the reduction of the legislature to a mere cheering section to applaud the acts of the executive-dictator. Even in democratic countries, however, the power and prestige of the legislature have declined, and the executive bureaucracy has expanded.

In part, this reflects the logic of organization. If government is going to play an active and positive part in organizing the life of the people, obviously only the executive branch can do this, and the legislature becomes increasingly a policy-making body whose policies become broader and broader. Finally most of the really significant decisions, even of policy, are made in the executive departments through executive orders and regulations rather than through legislative enactment. We seem increasingly to be moving toward a point where the legislature decides that something should be done and the executive decides what. Perhaps an even more fundamental reason for the growth of executive power, however, is the fact that the executive symbolizes the unity of the people, whereas the legislature symbolizes their diverse interests. In the legislature the pressure groups pull one against the other; it is the executive who speaks for the people as a whole. Consequently the growth of a feeling of national unity, and of group responsibility for the welfare of all within the national group, finds its most obvious expression in the growing power of the national executive.

2. The Problem of the Business Cycle

The critical problem of the social-democratic state is whether it can in fact deal with the sources of discontent which may undermine it and whether it can cope with the real problems of government in a market-dominated internal economy and in a world of independent states. The two greatest problems are undoubtedly the business cycle and national defense. The greatest technical weakness of a market economy is its persistent tendency to fall into periods of underemployment and deflation. The greatest problem of economic policy in the Western world is how to create an economic framework for a market economy which will prevent the level of employment from falling below tolerable levels, without at the same time diminishing the rate of economic progress and if possible without involving the economy in long-run inflation.

Fortunately our understanding of these problems has been greatly extended by the developments in economic thought of the past twenty or thirty years, especially those associated with the name of Lord Keynes. It is now almost universally recognized that large-scale unemployment is something which requires "policy" and is not self-correcting except over a period of time which is intolerably long. It is generally recognized also that an uncontrolled market economy has inherent tendencies toward fluctuation in the general level of money payments, and that the banking system accentuates these fluctuations. It is recognized also that these fluctuations can express themselves in two alternative forms: either in price fluctuations or in output and employment fluctuations. The more they express themselves in one, the less will they express themselves in the other. The increasing organization of the market, however, and the growth of economic organizations have made price fluctuations less and less possible, and the fluctuations in money payments and in money income have therefore expressed themselves in the worst possible form—that of fluctuations in employment and output.

The general nature of the remedy is clear. It is to install one or more "governors" in the system which will operate counterwise to the general movement of the system, just as a thermostat or the governor of an engine acts counterwise to the movement of the rest of its system and so stabilizes the variables under its control within tolerable limits. What is needed, that is to say, is not a "planned" economy but a "governed" economy; neither the regimentation of the monolithic state nor the anarchy of the ungoverned market, but a free, "polylithic" economy with a governing mechanism. Exactly what this governing mechanism should be and how it should be operated, and even more, how people can be persuaded to set one up, are critical questions of our day. It is clear that the only adequate governor is government; that, indeed, it is the prime economic duty of government to be a governor, to act counter-wise to undesirable general movements whether of crime or of prices. It has been the failure of government to be a governor that has led to the proliferation of unwise and unsuitable governmental interventions into particular phases of economic life—for instance, in tariffs and trade policy, in agricultural policy, even in labor legis-lation. As we have seen, most of the problems of particular sectors of the economy—of agriculture, labor, or business—in fact originate in the *general* instability of incomes, prices, and outputs and cannot be solved in the particular sectors themselves.

A. *The System of Public Finance*

It is clear also that the principal governor of the economy must be the system of public finance, for only this is powerful enough to affect the general levels of money payments and income. No private agency has the power to govern the monetary system, for this power of necessity involves the power both to create and to destroy money, and so is of the essence of sovereignty, or of delegated sovereignty. A mere regulation of the conditions of private creation of money or credit through the banking system is also not enough. Central bank activity can deal with small fluctuations, under cer-tain conditions which do not, in fact, obtain in the United States today, but it is not powerful enough to control fluctuations of the magnitude which a rich and unstable economy is capable of en-gendering.

The system of public finance, however, and especially the tax system, is potentially a powerful instrument for governing and stabilizing the total volume of money payments. The impact of gov-ernment on the total money stock in the possession of the people is directly equal to the "cash surplus" or "cash deficit" of government. The cash surplus is the excess of government collections of money (mostly in taxes) over the government payments of money to its employees and suppliers. If there is a cash surplus of, say, a hundred million dollars in a year, government has taken out of the "pockets" of the people a hundred million more than it has put in. From this source directly, therefore, the total money stock of the people will have declined by a hundred million. A cash deficit, on the other hand, puts money into the pockets of the people. If government pays out more than it takes in, the difference must represent an increase in the money holdings of the people.

The cash surplus or deficit can be regulated swiftly and easily through adjusting tax payments. It can be regulated also by changing government expenditures; but unless these expenditures are pure gifts (in which case they could be regarded as "negative taxes") they are not easy to change rapidly, for government *purchases* involve shifts in the employment of resources. Even if government expenditures are constant, however, the cash surplus or deficit can easily be changed by changing the total tax bill. It would be possible, therefore, to stabilize the total volume of money payments within wide but quite tolerable limits by instituting an "automatic tax plan."

Under such a scheme a decline in total money payments, as registered in the statistical information of, say the Department of Commerce, would be automatically followed by a decline in tax *rates*. If the tax rates refer to current income, as today they do in the case of the personal income tax, a reduction in the rates will immediately reduce the total tax payments and will reduce the cash surplus or increase the cash deficit of government. This will mean that people's money stock will be higher than it would have been in the absence of the tax reduction. People will therefore probably spend more, and a force will be brought into play tending to increase payments. Similarly a rise in total money payments, indicating a spontaneous inflationary pressure, would under this system automatically be followed by a rise in tax rates, which would drain money from the pockets of the people and so reduce the inflationary forces.

A progressive income tax itself operates in the same manner. In an inflation, many more people get up into the higher money-income brackets, and even if the rate structure is not changed the average rate of income tax paid is increased. In a deflation, on the other hand, incomes move down into the lower brackets, a larger proportion of income is exempt, and the average rate of tax falls. Thus limits are set to inflation and deflation as long as the tax system does not break down. The limits, however, are probably too wide for tolerance, and a system of adjustable rates is likely to be necessary in order to narrow the range of the "turning points."

No system of this kind, of course, would stand up under the strains imposed by a total war economy, which is virtually certain to result in inflation. For peacetime conditions, however, such a system would be an important safeguard against severe depression or serious inflation.

All the machinery for such a system is already in existence. We already have an information system which yields moderately accurate quarterly reports of national money income, prepared by the National Income Division of the Department of Commerce. We also have, in the deductible-at-source income tax, a powerful and flexible instrument for the rapid adjustment of tax collections. All that needs to be done is to hitch these two parts of the machinery together, and to link changes in tax rates quarterly with changes in national income. Then the budget deficit or surplus could be left to look after itself. A deflationary movement in the economy would automatically produce a budget deficit tending to offset it, as declining national money income forced a decrease in tax rates; an inflationary movement, on the other hand, would produce a budget surplus tending to offset it, as rising national income forced an increase in tax rates.

The reader who feels that this is all too easy is, of course, right. The problem of economic stabilization is a much more ticklish problem than that of holding fluctuations in national money income down to tolerable limits—though if that were all that could be accomplished, it would be something. It would prevent, for instance, the absurd debacle of 1929-32 when the national money income approximately halved. Within a stable national money income, however, it would be possible to have large fluctuations in output and in prices in opposite directions. Money income is equal to output multiplied by the price level; hence money income can remain constant and yet output could decline and prices rise. Thus an inflation of prices under a stabilized money income would lead to unemployment. This is something, unfortunately, that could readily happen, especially where there are disproportions in the amounts of resources employed in different industries.

There are some cycles which are not part of the general movement of the monetary system, even though they may contribute to it. There are, for instance, a long cycle in building activity and shorter cycles of somewhat similar nature in goods of shorter length of life. These are nonmonetary cycles in the sense that they arise

from distortions in the composition, and especially in the age distribution, of real capital. Individual cycles of this kind cannot be
dealt with by monetary or fiscal means; they must be treated, if at
all, by measures directed specifically toward them. Thus the building
cycle might be offset in part by a counterwise program of public
works. Obviously the sensible time to encourage the construction
of public buildings, dams, and roads is when construction in private
fields is lagging.

B. *Price and Wage Controls*

There still remains a crucial question whether a full employment
policy can be successful without some kind of price and wage controls. An attempt to raise employment by raising the national money
income will be frustrated if the rise in incomes takes the form of
price increases rather than output increases. There is no doubt that
inflationary pressure on prices and money wages can set in when
money incomes are rising but a satisfactory level of employment has
not been reached. A vigorous full employment policy may then be
faced with the dilemma of continuous inflation, or of direct controls
over prices and wages. Neither of these alternatives is particularly
attractive.

Continuous inflation produces great and usually unjust changes
in the distribution of income, shifting income away from pensioners,
bondholders, and people with sticky money incomes toward profit
makers—farmers and businesses. It renders the problem of caring
for the aged much more difficult, and it may have subtle but devastating long-run effects on the character of a people, undermining
their habits of thrift along with their faith in the value of money.
If continued for long it is likely also to disorganize the financial
system, as real rates of interest will probably be negative over long
periods. Thus a rate of inflation of 5 per cent per annum makes the
real rate of interest negative on all investments earning less than
5 per cent. A 5 per cent per annum rate of inflation does not sound
very much; nevertheless, it would mean, if steadily maintained, a
rise in the price level of 32 times in a single lifetime.

Inflation means that businesses have to rely—and are able to rely
—much more on self-finance out of inflated profits for their expansion, and much less on borrowing. While this has some advantages

it means also that one of the checks on the rate of expansion of businesses is removed—the difficulty of getting new capital from outside sources. Businesses find themselves in possession of additional capital which has not been yielded to them voluntarily, but is a result of the "forced saving"—i.e., the involuntary restriction of consumption—on the part of those caught with fixed incomes and rising prices. Those who restrict their consumption in this case, however, get no benefit from it. Their "savings" fall as windfalls over the neighbors' fence. This is a situation which cannot be described as just, and it creates profound social discontents. The rise of Nazism in Germany, for instance, is by no means unconnected with the experience of the German middle class in the great inflation of 1923.

On the other hand, price and wage control may be an even more unsavory prospect. The problem here is the inadequacy of administrative techniques by comparison with the sensitivity of the free market. What we want to do, of course, is to control the *general level* of prices and money wages. There seems to be no way of doing this, however, except by controlling particular prices and wages—an administrative problem of almost impossible complexity, particularly on a long-run basis. Our experience with price control in the two world wars consisted of freeezing all particular prices as of a given date (i.e., making some past price the legal maximum), and then making adjustments in the legal maxima as complaints arose. The difficulty is that price control freezes the *relative* structure of prices, which immediately begins to get out of date. In practice, the administrative machinery never catches up with the changes in relative prices which are demanded by changing conditions of demand and supply; consequently shortages and black markets appear for some commodities, and surpluses may appear in others. Eventually the structure of legal prices becomes so obsolete that it breaks down either through widespread evasion or through repeal of the price-control law. Even if the administration becomes flexible enough to deal with the relative price problem, evasion may become an almost insuperable problem unless there is a general willingness to conform to the regulations. Unfortunately, it seems almost to take a full-scale war to produce the requisite degree of conformity. There is no easy resolution of the dilemma.

C. *Other Stabilizing Devices*

A possible solution for the control of prices at the wholesale level which does not involve individual price control is the "composite commodity standard" proposed by Benjamin Graham.[1] This would provide a more sensitive substitute for the gold standard (which was, it must be remembered, a governing mechanism of sorts, though with a very delayed period of reaction). It proposes that the monetary authority shall stand ready to buy or sell "bundles" of warehouse receipts or titles to stocks of commodities at a fixed price per "bundle." The bundle of course would consist of certain fixed quantities of different commodities, say ten bushels of wheat, twenty bushels of corn, five pounds of iron, and so on.

If the total value of the bundle on the market was less than the fixed "standard" price by an amount sufficient to compensate for the cost of assembling the bundles, operators would buy up commodities in the markets to sell them to the standard authority. This would withdraw commodities from the market and add money, thus raising the prices of all commodities. If the prices in the market were high enough so that the market value of the standard bundle exceeded the standard price by a small amount, operators would buy standard bundles from the monetary authority and disperse them among the various commodity markets, thus bringing prices down. While there would be many practical difficulties in the administration of such a scheme, it does offer at least a hope of solving the basic problem of regulating the price level—how to regulate the *general* level without regulating prices. It is of course applicable only to a part of the price system—the prices of storable, standardized commodities. It would not therefore serve to stabilize money wage rates or retail prices. Nevertheless, the stabilizing of even a part of the price structure would be a valuable achievement, and would go a long way toward stabilizing the whole.

The technical economic problems of setting up a stabilization machinery for a market economy are not insuperable. The problem of convincing people that it can be done, however, is a far more difficult one. The main obstacle to the establishment of such a policy

[1] Benjamin Graham, *Storage and Stability*, New York, McGraw-Hill Book Company, 1937.

is a lack of understanding, among both voters and legislators, of the real nature of the problem.

Unfortunately there are profound reasons for this deficiency in the nature of human understanding. It is difficult for the human mind to make the leap from open to closed systems. Our personal experience is all of an "open system." For instance, in our personal economic life we find ourselves in an environment in which we receive money for the sale of goods and services, and spend money in the purchase of goods and services; our money stock looks to us something like a reservoir into which flows a stream of receipts and out of which flows a stream of expenditures. In our personal experience receipts and expenditures are very different items, which are under no necessity to equal one another! In a closed (i.e., a complete) monetary system, however, every receipt is an expenditure to someone else, every expenditure is a receipt to someone else; receipts and expenditures are exactly the same thing; hence an increase in expenditure is the same thing as an increase in receipts, which is certainly not true of individuals. There are many other instances of these "paradoxes of closure."

It is difficult, however, especially for individuals who are untrained in abstract thinking, to think in terms of a closed system; the tendency is to generalize from individual experience, by simple addition, to the system as a whole. Thus, because an individual can accumulate money by not spending as much as he gets, it is easy to conclude that all individuals can do the same. This, however, is not the case. *All* individuals cannot succeed in not spending as much as they get, unless somewhere in the system there is actual creation of money; for unless there is creation (or destruction) of money, the total amount of money in the possession of all people taken together remains the same. Any general attempt to accumulate money by not spending it results not in an increase in the money stock but in a decline in the total of both expenditures and receipts.

If government, therefore, is to act as a stabilizer, it must pay out more money than it receives at a time when people as a whole are trying to accumulate money by contracting their expenditures, and it must pay out less money than it receives when the reverse is the case. Many of the principles of financial management which are prudent for a private person or business therefore are not prudent for government; there is a common tendency, however, to judge the actions of government as if it were a private organization. Thus many people think that in a depression government should not be "extravagant"—meaning that it should contract its operations just like everybody else. It is precisely at a time of depression or threatened depression, however, that government should expand its operations to counteract the contractions in the private economic activity.

This does not mean, of course, that government should be extravagant in the sense of using resources wastefully or carelessly. It may be more extravagant, however, not to use resources at all than to use them carelessly, and a policy of "economy" which results in unemployment may in fact be the most extravagant of all.

3. CONSERVATION PROBLEMS

The control of fluctuations in employment is not, of course, the only problem of control which is faced by the national state. There is, for instance, an important long-run problem of conservation. To an alarming extent the high-consumption economy of the Western nations is based upon the use of "geological capital"—irreplaceable natural resources. We are like people who have come into a great legacy in the shape of coal, oil, natural gas, metallic ores, forests, and soils, and we are consuming this legacy at a rate which has already brought us to the verge of exhaustion of our best natural resources and which promises to use them all up within a few centuries. What is even more alarming, the present phenomenal rate of consumption of natural capital is almost all the result of the activity of not more than a fifth of the world's total population. If the standards of consumption of the rest of the world were raised to present American standards, the problem of exhaustion of many important resources would then be a matter of urgency.

It is true, of course, that the evil day is continually being postponed by scientific discovery of new sources of energy, new metals, and new crops. Up to now, however, this has been merely a postponement; we have not yet discovered a technical base for a *continuing* high-level economy that is not dependent upon geological accumulations. Such an economy is not inconceivable. It would have to derive its power mainly by direct use of the sun's rays, for even atomic power seems to depend upon a strictly exhaustible resource, and it would have to rely on processes for extracting metals and other elements from the sea or other relatively unconcentrated material. Fortunately there are signs that technical change in this direction may be taking place: two twentieth-century processes—the fixation of nitrogen from the air and of magnesium from the sea—may presage some reversal of the essentially dispersive forces of the modern economy.

What part the state should play, if any, in this process is difficult to say. There are some extreme conservationists who would freeze to death on top of a coal mine for fear of using it up. On the other hand one cannot view with equanimity the rate of consumption of many of our natural resources today. There may be a real dilemma here between full-employment policy and conservation policy. The only thing which can be said for a depression is that it is at least a period of slackening in the consumption of irreplaceable natural resources. What is certain, however, is that war—which is by far the greatest consumer of natural resources—is even more costly than it seems. Were it not for war we could feel a little more comfortable about our wasting natural capital and a little more hopeful that it would last until we could find ways of doing without it. In terms of resources, however, the cost of war destruction to the destroyer is probably as great, in terms of resources, as the destruction itself.

An advantage of full employment policy is that we have a pretty clear idea of what we want and have good alarm bells to indicate a divergence of reality from the ideal. In conservation policy, however, this is not so; there is no clear indication of what the "ideal" level of consumption of resources should be. Consequently there are no clear danger signals to indicate when the state should interpose to restrict the levels of consumption.

4. DISTRIBUTION OF INCOME

A similar difficulty besets policy in regard to the distribution of income and power among individuals and groups in the society. It is generally felt that the distribution of income which results from an unfettered market economy is too unequal. Consequently a great many measures are taken to rectify this defect: the progressive income tax, social security, minimum wage laws, protection of labor and agriculture groups, and so on. There is also a strong feeling in the Western nations that there must be some minimum standard of life below which its families should not be allowed to fall, and a complex apparatus of social service and relief is set up to meet this need. The difficult question here is what should be the minimum standard, and what degree of inequality is to be regarded as satisfactory.

In constructing policies aimed at decreasing inequality there is a further problem of the actual effects of these policies. Thus we have found that policies supposed to "aid agriculture," on the ground that farmers are poor, in fact frequently aid the richer farmers, or even more the landowners, and do little for the poor farmer. Similarly policies designed to strengthen labor unions may in fact help to improve the lot of the already better-off workers, perhaps even at the expense of the really poor. The real test of these policies, however, is a political one: it is the test of whether the masses of people in fact support the national state and feel that it is "theirs." On this score the modern national state can claim considerable success. No genuinely democratic country, with the possible exceptions of France and Italy, is threatened by any *internal* group who feel so little a part of it that they wish to destroy it. This is far from true in other parts of the world, and it must be counted one of the most remarkable achievements of social-democratic states that they have integrated into their society a large proportion of their citizens, in a way that each does feel some responsibility for all.

Probably the greatest weakness of the American democracy is its racial attitudes. As long as there is a large group of citizens who remain in some sense "second class" and who do not participate on equal terms in the life of the nation, a potential source of disruption remains. Fortunately there is real progress, intolerably slow though it seems at times, in the direction of a solution of this problem. It is, of course, not so much a "Negro" problem as a "white" problem; i.e., it is not the unwillingness of the Negro to become a full-fledged "American" which bars the way to an integrated society, but the unwillingness of the white to admit him to full equality. It is a sign of hope, however, that the ideals of America conflict with its practice, and that there is at least some machinery existing in the Constitution for making these ideals effective, or at least exerting legal pressure in that direction. Almost everything that happens in regard to race relations is a step, small though it may be, in the right direction. The growth of fair employment practices legislation, the slow equalization of educational opportunities, and rulings against segregation in interstate transportation and so on are not perhaps enough to give us cause for congratulation, but they are at least enough to save us from despair.

Examples might be multiplied, but enough has been said to draw a tentative conclusion: that in regard to its internal problems and policies the social-democratic state is a reasonable success as an institution, in that it does provide a machinery by which wrongs can be perceived and by which measures can be taken to right them. The information system is inadequate and the machinery is creaky, and much remains to be done; nevertheless, the machinery exists and the machine responds. In social progress it is not the rate of change which matters, but the direction: the slowest tortoise will carry us where we want to go if his nose is pointed right. The contrast is striking between the social-democratic societies in which, on the whole, things have been going from bad to better and the stagnant feudal societies in which things stay as they are—or even more the totalitarian dictatorships in which on the whole things go from bad to worse because of the insulation of the executive from an adequate information system, or because of the inadequacy of the ideals which they cherish.

5. Problems of Defense

The internal success of the social-democratic state points up all the more poignantly the utter tragedy of national defense. It is not internal economic breakdown, nor exhaustion of natural resources, nor social disintegration, but war, which is threatening our cities and our civilization with almost immediate destruction. It is the complete failure of the social-democratic state to solve the problem of its defense which threatens to suppress all its other virtues and to transform it into something different—a militarized garrison state—or to overthrow it altogether. There are, alas, good reasons for this failure, many of them inherent in the organizational revolution itself. The same forces which have led to an increase in the effective size of almost all organizations have likewise led to an increase in the effective size of the national state. The changes in military techniques, furthermore, have enormously increased the minimum size of the "viable" state—i.e., the state which can provide for its own military defense—so that now there are only two effective centers of independent power left in the world. The fact that military strength is of significance only insofar as it is *relative* to the strength of some potential enemy also means that in a situation of acute military rivalry there are no limits to the demands of national defense short of the absorption of the whole economic surplus of a country—which in modern countries means something approaching half of the total output. The revolution in transportation has furthermore destroyed the only possible situation in which an equilibrium of national defense is attainable—that in which the competing nations are so far apart that each is stronger than the other in its own home territory.

It seems to me (August 1952) that there is no terminus to the arms race at present taking place between the United States and the Soviet Union save a third world war, a war which would almost certainly involve the destruction of the world's major cities and the disruption of its economic life. It is a war, furthermore, which would leave the basic problem unsettled. It is unlikely that a world state would emerge from it, and the problem of national defense would be as unsolved as ever—as the First and Second World Wars likewise failed to solve it. As long as national defense remains, however, it will always be inherently insatiable, and the farther the technical revolution proceeds, the farther will national defense reach down into the lives of the people.

The insatiable character of military defense is not perhaps so important when the technical base of the economy is so poor that the maximum which can be spared from the production of basic necessities is a mere 5 or 10 per cent of the national output. This was the case even as late as the Napoleonic wars. When the production of basic necessities, however, can be accomplished by less than half, or perhaps even a quarter of the people, a system of national defense reaches so far down into the life of the nation that no family is unaffected. Such a system almost inevitably demands conscription—i.e., a form of temporary military enslavement—and even those families whose members are not reached by the long arm of conscription will find themselves in all probability involved in some form of activity connected with a war effort.

The moral dilemma raised by the problem of national defense

is almost intolerable. No other organization presents the spectacle of two-facedness as does the national state. On the internal level it is the most basic organization of social life, the framework of society, the suppressor of violence, the protector of the weak, the benefactor of the poor, the executor of justice. It is no wonder that men have seen in the state an expression of the Divine Will; it is a greater instrument even than the church for the expression of that concern of all for all which to the Christian at least is the most perfect symbol of the Divine. Toward its enemies, however, the national state is a monster, a liar, a thief, a murderer, a creator of orphans, a destroyer of cities, an immense machine to create pain, death, destruction, madness, famine, and intolerable woe. It is selfish; it cares for none but its own; its only objective is its own power and its own defense; it is sadistic, ruthless, inhuman, diabolical. Take the most evil, most piratical, most selfish private organization in existence; it has caused fewer tears than the most virtuous of nations. The most selfish of capitalists probably does more good than harm; he goes around the world inconspicuously providing little people with little things that they want, all under the wicked motivation of self-interest. The nobler the nation, the more self-sacrifice it can call forth from its people, the more likely it is to lay the world desolate and to consign to the maw of war everything that the patience of enterprise has built up.

What is the sensitive individual to do in this appalling situation? He can, of course, accept the national myth—that anything is justified if it is done in the name of the defense of his own nation, that the "other" nation is always the aggressor, that all virtue resides in his own nation, that no matter how aggressive his own nation may have been in the past, now all is different, and so on. The myth, however, is never quite convincing.

> In the small circle of pain within the skull
> You still shall tramp and tread one endless round
> Of thought, to justify your action to yourselves,
> Weaving a fiction which unravels as you weave,
> Pacing forever in the hell of make-believe
> Which never is belief.[2]

[2] T. S. Eliot, *Murder in the Cathedral*, New York, Harcourt Brace & Co., Inc., 1935.

Unfortunately the opposite, or lovey-dovey, myth is also unconvincing. Wickedness is a real problem, aggression and covetousness are real problems, not to be dealt with by smiles and handshakes. It is well occasionally to remember that the symbol of Christian love is a cross and not a Teddy bear.

Nevertheless it remains true that defense by essentially immoral means will eventually undermine the morale of the members of the organization which uses these means. Myths are long-lived, but not immortal, and eventually the pretense that an organization is "good" which devotes most of its energies to murder and devastation will be given up. As the members of such an organization withdraw their voluntary allegiance, however, because of the moral conflict which it involves, the organization is forced to use its coercive powers against its own members. Thus we find the national state increasingly relying on the coercion of its own citizens to achieve its ends. We see this most completely in the totalitarian dictatorships, but there is a terrifying increase in coercion even in the democracies. It is now a universal practice to raise armies not by appealing to the love of country but to the fear of it. There is an increasing appeal to coercion to force conformity also. We saw this in its most horrible form in Nazi Germany. The logic of Nazism, however, is merely the logic of militarism: if it is all right to get rid of foreigners by killing them, why not apply the same methods to internal dissidents or nonformists?

There is, therefore, an inherent paradox of national defense. We have stated in Chapter 4 that one of the essential principles of defense is that the means of defense must not be inconsistent with the over-all purposes of the organization. The national state violates this principle completely. Its essential purpose is peace and order, its defense is by violence and disorder; it must therefore inevitably destroy itself by its own defense. The alternative, however, is by no means clear. We do not escape the dilemma, as some pacifists try to do, by denying that there is any problem of defense at all. There is really no refuge in anarchism, attractive as the position may seem in a day in which the state has become such a monster. Good will is not enough; there must be organizations for putting it into effect, and these organizations face a real problem of defense. There is also a real problem of coercion. A voluntary organization, it is true, does not need coercion for its defense; i.e., it can rely wholly on its power to attract human effort into it by reason of the advantages which it offers. But there can be no voluntary withdrawal from the human race except by suicide, and an organization which is universal necessarily involves a certain amount of coercion. The problem of coercion is not solved, therefore, by simply rejecting it—because one of the tissues of society has become cancerous is not necessarily a reason for cutting it away altogether.

We do not really escape the problem, either, by establishing a monopoly of the means of violence. This is, it is true, a partial solution. It is one which has been very successful *internally* in the national state; the concentration of the means of violence in the hands of the state has materially reduced the use of violence among private persons and organizations. Nevertheless, as we have seen, it is precisely this concentration of the means of violence in the hands of the national state which is threatening to destroy it. The world federalists propose to solve the problem of war by essentially the same means by which the national state has established internal peace, by concentrating the means of violence in the hands of a single organization—i.e., the world state.

In the present state of things world federation seems to be the only way in which war can be avoided and the urgent and immediate problem of national defense solved. It does not mean giving up the internal benefits of the national state; it means merely giving up the right of mutual self-annihilation. In fact the existing national states would be much more secure under a world federation than they are at present, just as the forty-eight states of the United States are each much more secure, as organizations, than they would be if they were independent and each had a problem of "defense."

Nevertheless, the difficulties, and the dangers, of such a world government must not be underemphasized, and the problem of the world in 1952 is very different from that which faced the thirteen American colonies in 1789. A government must have ability to "govern"; i.e., it must provide means by which those variables which are essential to its existence can be kept within the limits of toleration. By far the most important of these variables is the degree of *acceptance* of the government by the people. If enough people feel that the government is not meeting their needs, whether these needs are economic, emotional, or "spiritual," the government will not survive. This is as true of a world government as of any other. We have seen, however, that coercion is an alternative to satisfaction, and that if an organization cannot survive by meeting people's needs it will be tempted to survive by invoking people's fears. A world government would be no exception to this rule. Indeed, as we have also seen, the larger the organization, beyond some optimum size, the more difficult it becomes for it to meet "needs"; for the more complex these needs are, the less efficient become the channels of communication to and from the executives. It would not be surprising, therefore, if a world government, no matter how well intentioned its origin, turned out to be a world tyranny. One merely has to visualize the problems of a government which can meet the needs, and so commend the voluntary acceptance, of the Americans, the Chinese, the Russians, and the Eskimos to see how difficult the problem is and how desperate is the plight of man.

Nor is this all. One of the most important means by which an organization secures the voluntary support of its members is by invoking the fear of an external enemy. It is only a mild exaggeration to say that all states are the creation of their enemies. The thirteen squabbling American colonies would never have come together had it not been for George III. Germany is the creation of Napoleon; and so on through history. The same is true to a greater or lesser degree of sects, parties, labor unions, and athletic teams. There are only two forces which bring people together— one is a common regard and a common need; the other is a common fear. Of these the latter is the easiest and most frequently invoked, especially in political organizations which unite diverse groups with diverse interests. A cynic might say that the only thing which unites the people of a nation is a common hatred of the foreigner; while this is not true, it is most deplorably true that any nation finds its highest expression of internal unity in time of war. A world state, however, would have no enemy, and could not use this simple device to weld its impossibly diverse people together. We have reached the pass now in the development of man where there is almost literally no choice but love; where the only basis of human organization which can function is that of common concern and common need. It is on this slender foundation that the future of man must be built.

In this situation the importance of the ethical vision can hardly be overemphasized. We are in a situation where we cannot live without the national state and we cannot live with it. The solution to the problem is clearly in view—a limited world government—and yet there seems to be no road that leads there. Our present reliance on national defense leads to the destruction of us all; yet to ask the national state to lay down its arms is like asking the brute beasts which symbolize it—the lion and the eagle and the bear—to give up their claws. It is not in the nature of a beast to be a man. Nevertheless there is always the possibility of redemption, and redemption takes place through the slow working of the idea of goodness in the beliefs and practices of men. It can be argued that the peculiarly diabolical quality of the national state today is due to the immensely rapid advances in the techniques of warfare and the consequent inability for moral ideas to catch up with physical power. Particularly is this true of air power. I believe that the unrestrained use of air power as practiced by all nations today will make them hated, not only by their enemies, but by their own citizens also, and that it threatens the national state with an almost universal loss of love. Perhaps one of the greatest dangers threatening the world today is that men should stop loving their country, because it has become so abominable. This threatens us with general moral breakdown and civil disorder as well as with international holocausts.

Nevertheless, there are some signs of hope. The redemption of the national state consists in a recognition of its responsibility for all men, not merely for those within its borders. It is the principle that one American (or German or Russian) is worth any number of Japanese or Chinese (or Americans!) that makes the national state an abomination. It is when national policies are regarded as morally justified if they benefit the citizens of the nation, without any regard to their impact on the rest of the world, that the state becomes a monster of irresponsible power. But there are a few signs of change. The British Commonwealth of Nations is an example of a limited area within which a slight tradition has developed of national policy justified on grounds wider than the national interest. Toward New Zealand, Britain acts with great courtesy and restraint; toward Denmark, with very little. Similarly the "good neighbor" policy of the United States toward Latin America is another "Commonwealth" tradition; UNRRA, the Marshall Plan, and Point Four represent similar recognitions of wider responsibility. These things will be of no avail, however, if they are done solely in the interests of national defense, for it is not merely what is done but why it is done that matters. A foreign assistance program which is a recognition of the world responsibility of the national state is a symbol of its redemption; the same program conceived merely as an aid to national defense is a symbol of its damnation.

6. IMPERIALISM

We should not leave this subject without considering briefly the Marxist theory of capitalist imperialism, both for its intrinsic importance as guiding the behavior of the Communist world and also because it raises the question of the relation between two aspects of the democratic national state which we have discussed here—the stabilization of its internal economy and its national defense. The Marxist view is that a capitalist society is forced by its inner logic to become imperialist because of the necessity for preventing the fall in the rate of profit and for supplementing the increasingly inadequate home market by seeking opportunities for investment and new markets abroad. War in this view is mainly a result of the clash of rival imperialisms.

That this is much too simple a theory of imperialism is clear when we reflect that imperialism is a much older institution than capitalism, and that states with all kinds of economic systems have been imperialistic, both states with planned economies, like ancient Egypt and modern Russia, and states with capitalistic economies, like England and France. It is much more realistic to regard imperialism as an essential part of the dynamics of national defense—wherever a "defense vacuum" exists in the world, some armed power may be expected to occupy it, simply as part of the "role" of the armed force. And war is an integral part of a system of national defense rather than a consequence of any particular economic system.

Indeed, it can be argued cogently that capitalism is much less likely to produce wars than socialism; the trader is after all a man of peace, and trade can only take place under peaceful conditions. It was the capitalist nineteenth century which was most free from wars, partly of course because there was plenty of room for the expanding Atlantic world to expand into, but also because in a predominantly capitalist society the state is a relatively weak institution. In a world of socialist states all trade would be in constant danger of degenerating into war, and there is a much greater likelihood of economic conflicts taking on a military cast than in a world in which most trade is "private."

Nevertheless there is a certain sting in the Marxist criticism. It is unfortunately true that in the absence of any adequate machinery for preventing large economic fluctuations one of the easiest ways for a social-democratic state to prevent unemployment is by devoting a large proportion of its resources to national defense, thereby, of course, promoting general insecurity. It was not until rearmament got under way in 1940 that the United States really recovered from the great depression, and there can be little doubt that the fear of depression is a potent factor making for an unwillingness to disarm, even if the other circumstances were favorable. Nevertheless, I have endeavored to show that this situation is not necessary: that an adequate stabilizer can be built into a market economy which will remove this fear and will break the evil link between prosperity and war preparations. This is, I suspect, a prerequisite to any world settlement on the part of the West. It would be fortunate if similar solutions could be devised which would take the threat of war out of communism and transmute it into a more "open" and less aggressive culture.

11

Summary and Conclusions

Since about the 1870s there has been a worldwide increase in the number, size, and power of organizations, especially those whose activity is directed toward the economic betterment of their members. So striking is this movement that it deserves the name of the organizational revolution.

This movement has taken five main forms:

1. There is first the rise of the labor movement. Labor unions have been increasing in power and membership, with some ups and downs, in most of the more "advanced" countries since about 1870. Today they are an important political and economic force in virtually all democratic countries.

2. Farm organizations have grown in numbers and in political power at about the same rate as labor organizations. They too have risen to great political influence, especially since 1930. In the United States nearly half the farmers belong to one or another of the three main farm organizations.

3. Professional organizations, such as the American Medical Association, have likewise grown greatly in numbers and power in the same period. They too are exercising increasing political pressure through their various "lobbies."

4. Organization in the business world has two aspects. Up to about 1900 there was a marked rise in the size of business enterprise and a growth in trusts and combines. This movement seems to have been checked, at least in the United States, partly as a result of its inability to command general political support. There has, however, been a great rise in the number and power of trade associations, which now number about 1,500.

5. Along with the rise in the power of private economic organizations, there has also been a great rise in the economic power of national governments. This movement is seen in its extreme form

in the rise of Communist states like Russia, where the nation becomes virtually the only economic organization, all other organizations being subordinate parts of the state organization. Even in capitalist countries, however, we have seen the national state assuming more and more economic responsibility, through the development of social security schemes, aids to depressed (or politically powerful) industries, protective tariffs, the regulation of industry and labor, and the expansion of nationalized industry.

Much of our basic economic thinking assumes an economic system which is not dominated by large economic organizations, but which is composed of many small units. Even today, of course, many areas of the economic system—e.g., retailing, the service trades, agriculture—are still in the hands of small-scale units and are not much affected, directly, by large economic organizations. Nevertheless the rise of the economic organizations mentioned above has profoundly changed the economic system, whether for better or worse is not always easy to say. A system which is dominated by economic organizations presents problems, both for economic policy on the part of government and for standards of economic morality on the part of individuals, which are very different from those of an unorganized society. It is doubtful whether our thinking in these matters has caught up with the changes that have taken place in the system, and we are in real danger of accepting principles and beliefs which were applicable to an earlier system but which do not really apply to the present.

1. CAUSES OF ECONOMIC ORGANIZATION

It is important to understand something of the causes underlying this broad historical movement toward economic organization if our attempt to understand the problems which it creates is to bear any fruit. It is no use preaching against the inevitable, and if moral principles are to be effective we must have some idea of the essential causative factors in social change. Unfortunately many of these factors are far from clear, and in the present state of knowledge any suggestions regarding these causes of social change must be regarded as tentative.

Nevertheless we are not wholly without light in this matter. Consider the problem first from the point of view of economics.

The rise of economic organizations can be regarded as the development of a new "commodity" or industry. New industries arise either because of changes in "demand," i.e., in what people think will satisfy their wants, or because of changes in "supply," new methods of production or new ways of doing things or changed willingness to do them. A new industry may arise, for instance, because of a change in tastes or fashion. A fashion for beaver hats may create a beaver industry; when they go out of fashion, the industry languishes. Similarly, it may arise because of a change in techniques—i.e., in ways of doing things. Thus the automobile industry arose not particularly because of a change in the desire for transportation (though that may have played some part), but mainly as a result of the invention of the automobile, and especially the invention of cheap methods of producing automobiles.

We may ask, therefore, whether the rise of economic organizations is a result of changes in "demand" for them or of changes in their "supply." That is, is the rise of economic organizations a result of a more deeply felt *need* for them, on the part of those who participate in them, or is it a result of an improvement in the techniques of organization which makes it easier to develop and then to supply whatever "need" these organizations satisfy? Both these elements undoubtedly played some part in the movement; there is some evidence, however, that the second—that is, improvements in the skills of organization—has been more important. Both sets of causes, however, need to be studied.

A. *The Factor of Need*

We must ask first what the "needs" are which economic organizations satisfy in their own members. This is not an easy question to answer. The obvious answer is that these organizations produce "results" in at least making their members *feel* better off as a result of participating in them. Higher wages, shorter hours, better prices, less work, less trouble, are by no means negligible in explaining the attraction of organization, whether labor, farm, professional, business, or national. Nevertheless this is not the whole story.

In the first place, there are a great many other aspects of the relation of individuals to the organizations to which they belong, and many other motives which lead people both to join and to support organizations. There is a need for "belonging" itself; a need for the identification of the individual with something which is larger and more significant than his own pleasures and pains, and which makes demands upon him, even for sacrifices. There is the desire for power—or at least a desire to find in the success of the group with which one is identified a substitute for personal power and prestige, or an escape from the feeling of impotence which comes over an individual when he faces the big, buzzing, impersonal universe of society. There is a desire also for *status*. The most powerful and successful organizations have been those drawing their membership from groups which have regarded themselves as "underdogs"—especially wageworkers and farmers. Much of the drive which leads people to join labor unions is the desire to be able to look the "boss" squarely in the eye as an equal; much of the drive which leads farmers into their organizations is the desire to show the rest of the people that they are not "hicks" and "rubes" but are as good as anybody else. By contrast trade associations, catering mainly to the business community, which in our society already has a high prestige, have been relatively weak and unstable and hardly represent anything that could be called a "movement." Nobody is ever going to die for the dear old Association of Widget Manufacturers, or even for the N.A.M!

We must now inquire whether there has been any intensification of these needs or demands for organization during the past seventy years. There are several reasons for supposing that there has been some rise in the intensity of these demands. First, the logic of democratic societies implies dissatisfaction with any kind of subordinate status. We have seen the continuing crumbling of societies based on class or caste. The aristocratic ideal of a society in which everyone knows and nobody questions his "place," and nobody aspires to a higher position in society than his birth allows, has continually given way before the ideal of a society of equal opportunity for all, in which anyone has not only the right, but almost the duty, to better his position if he can. Economic organizations, especially in the labor and farm movements, have been regarded as instruments for the rise of "lower" groups *as a whole.*

The phrase "as a whole" must be emphasized. For an individual there are two possible avenues of advancement. One is to rise *out of* his present class into a higher. The other is to rise *with* his class as it achieves higher status. On the whole the main roads between classes in our society have been in the business and professional communities. It has not been by staying either on the farm or at the bench that men have become rich, but by developing or managing enterprises. The general rise in levels of living and of education which we have experienced has made people in general less and less content to remain in their existing "station" in life, and where opportunities for rising out of one's present class have proved inadequate (as in general they must be) the forces of hope and discontent have moved men to join group organizations. "Solidarity forever, for the Union makes us strong," as the C.I.O. sings.

The hope—and consequent discontent—which a dynamic, mobile society creates also must have some effect in creating a more intense demand for income. Most of the scientific studies of the problem indicate that there is little evidence that organization, especially of a large group, has much effect in improving the average income of its members. Over the years, for instance, nonunion wages have increased just about as fast as union wages; all the efforts of the farm groups achieved little change in their income until industrial recovery and the war inflation came along. Nevertheless there exists a strong belief among the members of these organizations that the organization itself has in fact improved their condition. In certain cases, for instance in the case of some of the craft unions which have been able to establish effective monopolies, or in the case of the lemon growers who also have been able to establish something like monopoly power, organization has enabled the group to exploit a monopoly position and to improve its income at the expense of the rest of society. These cases, however, are few, and the number of people affected is not large. They are certainly insufficient to explain the general belief that organization improves the income of the organized. To some degree this belief arises because the organizations get (or take) credit for improvements which would have taken place without them. This happens partly because periods of rising income (e.g., of recovery from a depression) are also times which are favorable to the growth of organizations; people are sore because of the depression experience which they have gone through and are *able* to do something (organize) because of the economic recovery.

B. *The Factor of "Supply"*

These changes in the demand for organization do not seem to be sufficient, in themselves, to explain the enormous increase in

organization of the present century. There have also been significant changes on the "supply" side—i.e., in the skill of organizing
itself. Most organizations are not the result of a spontaneous coming together of their members; they are organized by organizers,
and the rise of organizations often goes hand in hand with the rise
of a special class of full-time paid organizers—whether the minister
of the church, the business agent or "walking delegate" of the
trade union, the county agent of the Farm Bureau, the managing
director of the corporation, or the secretary of the trade association.
These organizers often have created the organization which they
direct, and they are always of great importance in sustaining it—
in getting new members, in encouraging the old members, in
making the members feel that the organization "pays" them. Established organizations wishing to extend their geographical boundaries
employ full-time "missionaries" to create new units of the organization in other places. Thus the C.I.O. was organized to a considerable extent by organizers supplied by the United Mine
Workers; when the C.I.O. itself was established it set up "organizing committees" in many industries to organize new unions. If the
"missionary enterprise" is successful, of course, "the mission church"
eventually becomes self-supporting, or even develops missions of
its own.

The changes in communication brought about by the railroad,
the automobile, the telephone, and other inventions have also
affected the skills of organization, especially in regard to the possible
size of organizations. A single executive, whether of a corporation,
a union, a farm organization, or a state, can now keep in effective
contact with many more people than was possible two or three
generations ago. It is perhaps no accident that the Age of Organization is also the Age of the Telephone. Organizations as large as
General Motors, or the United Automobile Workers, or the Farm
Bureau, or the Department of Agriculture—even the present-day
United States itself—would have been almost unthinkable in 1850;
the sheer difficulties of handwritten communication would have
bogged them down. The development of business machines which
can control large volumes of information has also been important.
Where, for instance, would almost any large organization be today
without even such a simple thing as an addressograph? The

development of electronic "brains" makes the possibility for the growth of organization frighteningly great.

The conclusion is apparent: that large economic organizations are here to stay, and that, short of an almost inconceivable revolution in public opinion, there is no way of getting rid of them. They have arisen in response to certain profound human needs—not so much economic needs as deeper, one might almost say "spiritual," needs. They have arisen also because of an increased ability to organize, and this ability is not going to be lost. It is of the utmost importance, therefore, that we examine what problems such organized groups create in economic and political life and in individual conduct.

2. THE IMPACT UPON ECONOMIC LIFE

In regard to economic life, the main impact of the development of large economic organizations has been to make prices and money wages more "sticky" and less flexible than they would otherwise have been. It is commonly believed that labor and farm organizations, for instance, have had an important effect on the relative prosperity of these groups. It is supposed, for instance, that labor organizations have raised real wages at the expense of profits, and that farm organizations have raised farm income at the expense of nonfarm income. Some small effects in this direction there may have been; the chart in the Appendix, however, showing the distribution of income in the U.S.A. from 1929, suggests that these effects on distribution are small, and are quite overshadowed by the general effects of inflation and deflation. Special studies all point to the same conclusion.[1] This conclusion contradicts the "mythology" of many of these groups; nevertheless the evidence seems irrefutable.

Even if the organized economic groups do not succeed very well in bettering themselves at the expense of others, this does not mean that they have no impact on economic life. Their development means in general the replacement of simple person-to-person transactions and price setting by collective bargaining or by businesses with some degree of monopoly power. This means that the price-

[1] See especially Harold M. Levinson, *Unionism, Wage Trends, and Income Distribution*, 1914-1917, Ann Arbor, Michigan, University of Michigan Press, 1951.

setting process becomes "public" rather than "private"; it achieves much greater social visibility. Contrast, for instance, the way in which agricultural wages are set, by man-to-man agreement over the fence among millions of farmers and hired men without any fuss or feathers or publicity, with the determination of steel or automobile wages in months of bargaining between giant organizations and a great fanfare of excitement. Yet, during the war inflation, the wages of the unorganized agricultural workers rose much faster than trade-union wages. Similarly during depressions the wages of unorganized workers fall much faster than the wages of the organized workers. Before the days of agricultural organization agricultural prices were much more flexible than industrial prices; they fell in depression and rose in prosperity.

The development of inflexible prices and wages has important effects upon the economic system and economic policy. Still more significant perhaps is the fact that the inflexibility of prices is not universal. It applies only to part of the price system, so that in effect the price system is broken in two, one set of prices being rather inflexible and the other set being flexible. If there were no changes in the general level of prices or of money incomes, price inflexibility would not create serious problems, though it might prevent certain desirable shifts of resources between occupations, and it might result in certain injustices and exploitation of the unprotected and unorganized people by those protected by organized groups. When, however, various basic economic changes, such as changes in the quantity of money, in its velocity of circulation, in population, or in productivity, necessitate changes in the general price level or in the national money income, the presence in the system of "sticky" prices that are resistant to pressures for change may cause serious trouble.

The difficulty may be illustrated by supposing (what is approximately true in short periods) that, when the national income changes, the *value* of the output of various industries changes in approximately the same proportion. Now the value in dollars-worth of the output of any industry is equal to the physical quantity of commodity which it produces, multiplied by the price of that commodity. Thus if the wheat industry produces 100 million bushels of wheat and the price of wheat is $2 per bushel, the total dollar value of the wheat output, which is the same thing as the gross contribution of the wheat industry to the national income, is $200 million. Now let us suppose that for various reasons the national money income is halved. The total dollar value of the wheat output is likely to be about halved too—say, to $100 million. If the price is flexible, it will fall to about $1 per bushel, and the output will remain the same at 100 million bushels. If, however, the price were inflexible, and stayed up at $2 per bushel, the only way in which the total value of the output could be reduced would be by reducing the physical quantity of output—say, to 50 million bushels.

What this means is that if the national money income is permitted to decline in a system with inflexible prices, the decline will be taken out in the form of reductions in output and employment in these industries and occupations where prices are inflexible, as it cannot be taken out in the form of a decline in money prices and money wages. Where prices are flexible, however, a decline in the national money income can be achieved without any reduction in output and without the development of unemployment, if the price and money wage level falls in rough proportion to the decline in the national money income.

Statistical evidence strongly supports these propositions. In the course of the great depression, for instance, agricultural output and employment were approximately constant, but agricultural prices fell sufficiently to reduce the money value of agricultural output to about half what it had been before. We may have been acutely uncomfortable in many ways during the depression, but at least we had as much to eat—on the average—as before. Industrial prices and wages, however, fell less in proportion to the national income, and hence severe unemployment and reduction of industrial output took place. The above picture is complicated, of course, by the fact that the decline in investment (which was the main factor in the depression) shifted demand away from industrial goods, but in outline it is substantially true.

This does not mean, however, that we must advocate a policy of price flexibility at all costs—the cost being a ruthless policy of suppression of organizations of all kinds, trusts, labor unions, and farm organizations alike. Organization-busting is neither practicable nor desirable; and, unless organization of the market can be reconciled with price flexibility (a choice which does not seem to be open to us), the only alternative is to design over-all economic policy on the assumption that many prices will not be flexible. What this means in practice is that we cannot afford to have a monetary deflation; any substantial *reduction* of the price or money-wage level is simply out of the question. The national money income must be kept constantly rising, or at least must be kept from falling. If there are substantial areas of inflexible prices in the economy, we cannot afford even to keep money incomes per head constant and allow real incomes to rise through a fall in prices. The prices will simply not fall adequately, and incomes will adjust through a decline in output and in real income per head.

If population is increasing and if rising productivity brings rising real output per head, money income per capita must increase as fast as productivity, and total money income as fast as population, if a declining price level is to be avoided. There must be a continual increase in the quantity of money unless there is a constant increase in velocity of circulation, which, short of constantly increasing inflation, is unlikely. This increase in the quantity of money can most conveniently come in our society from deficits in the federal cash budget; if government pays out more money than it takes in, the result is an increase in the quantity of money in the hands of the public. The banking system also is a potential source of increased money holdings in the form of bank deposits, and has functioned as such over the decades. Its tendency to cumulative contraction or expansion, however, makes the banking system unreliable as an automatic governor of the money supply.

It is clear, then, that the development of strong economic organizations does not *necessarily* mean that we must have depressions and unemployment. The budgetary and monetary policies of government can be adjusted to prevent this kind of deflationary situation in which the price inflexibility attendant upon economic organization produces unemployment. Nevertheless the question remains whether in a highly organized society it is possible to prevent an almost constant rate of inflation. If deflation is impossible, inflation cannot be corrected. Even if the problem were not complicated by war, therefore, a full employment policy in a highly organized society would almost inevitably lead to a slow but steady increase in the general level of prices. It should be recalled that even an increase at 5 per cent per annum is a 32-fold increase during a lifetime; at 10 per cent per annum the price level will increase a thousand times during a lifetime!

With war becoming the normal relationship of states, much larger rates of inflation may be looked for, as it is virtually impossible to finance even a small war, starting from full employment, without inflation, as the Korean instance indicates. It must be confessed also, since the growth of economic organizations has made price and wage determination so much more publicly visible than it used to be, that a highly organized society is much easier to run in an inflationary period. The organizations can "bring home" to their members "bacon" which they would have got anyway, and hence can retain the support of their membership even in the absence of any real services performed. Thus unions get credit for higher money wages, but get no credit for higher real wages when these are due to falling prices. It is no accident that the lot of the union leader is much easier in inflation than in deflation.

It is not impossible, of course, for a society to adjust to a constant inflation, but we have certainly not faced the many problems involved. A great many of our economic institutions are based on the assumption that the price level may be expected to be reasonably constant in the long run—an assumption which over the past 150 years has been justified. The accounting system, the financial system, including the whole structure of borrowing and lending, provision for old age in the form of pensions, insurance, and money or bond savings, are all based on the assumption of a constant value of money. If the value of money is constantly going to decline, most of our pension and insurance plans will be worthless, and unless nominal rates of interest rise markedly the real rate of interest will become permanently negative, with consequent disorganization of the whole system of finance. If prices are rising at 5 per cent per annum, the nominal rate of interest would have to be 8 per cent in order to make the real rate of interest 3 per cent.

Another important aspect of the rise of organizations is the increase in conflict which may result. This is a problem which goes beyond the limits of economics, though it has important economic aspects. The improvement in organizing techniques has removed, or rather pushed back, some of the internal limitations on the growth of organizations. As organizations grow, however, we find the external limitations becoming of more and more importance.

Firms run into imperfect markets; an expansion of sales requires either a price cut or further selling cost. All organizations run into increasing difficulties in attracting new members as they grow in size beyond the point where the most easily organized come in. This principle is so universal that we have named it the Principle of Increasingly Unfavorable External Environment.

The external environment, moreover, involves direct conflict with other organizations, and the fewer the number of organizations in contact with each other, the more acute this conflict becomes. One organization among many can expand without affecting any single one of its rivals enough to provoke notice or retaliation. One organization among few, however, can expand only at the obvious expense of its rivals, and such expansion is likely to provoke counter-attacks. Thus we have price wars and advertising wars in business, jurisdictional disputes among labor organizations, and an immense intensification of the burden of international warfare. The very success of an organization may spell its doom. It grows to the point where it cannot live with its neighbors, and yet it cannot grow to the point where it absorbs its neighbors. This dilemma is particularly acute in international relations, and is threatening our whole civilization with destruction.

3. The Ethical Problems

Ethics—at least "practical" ethics—is concerned mainly with the standards or criteria by which conduct is judged, both the conduct of individuals in purely personal relationships and of individuals in their roles as responsible directors of organizations. By implication, therefore, it includes the standards by which the behavior of organizations is judged. There is not universal agreement as to what these standards should be. Nevertheless, ethical ideas are not arbitrary; a pattern of both form and development can be traced through their diversities. The difficulties of ethical thought arise mainly because we are faced with a number of different "goods" or ends which may compete. A thing which is good in itself may have to be sacrificed to obtain a greater good. The greatest ethical confusions have arisen because people have assumed that if something is good it should be pursued indefinitely, or that some particular good is to be identified with good-in-general or with bad-in-general. Thus statements such as "trade unions are bad (or good); cooperatives are good (or bad); cartels are bad (or good)" are almost meaningless. The truth is that *some* unions, co-ops, cartels, etc. are good and some are bad, or that some *aspects* of unions, co-ops, cartels, etc. are good and some are bad.

All conduct conforms to *some* kinds of standards. When, however, we are distinguishing between "ethical" and "unethical" conduct, we are thinking largely of the *objectivity* of the standards concerned. "Disapproved" conduct is that which conforms only to the standards of the individual concerned, and does not conform to the accepted standards of the society in which he lives. Not all conduct, however, which is disapproved is unethical. Indeed conduct may be disapproved for two reasons: either because it falls short of the standards of society or because it rises above them (the saints and prophets have nearly always got themselves into serious trouble!). From the side of motivation, therefore, it seems not unreasonable to regard ethical conduct as that which is motivated by the larger and more objective interest as against the smaller and more personal interest. This is one meaning of the injunction to love our neighbor as ourselves: that we should not act as if we were the center of interest of the universe, but that we should see ourselves as we really are, and should act in the interest of the "whole." Action in the general interest is the heart of ethical conduct.

Perhaps the two most difficult groups of ethical problems which arise out of the development of economic organization are, first, those connected with the conflict between the private and the general interest, and, second, those connected with the use of coercion.

A. *Conflicting Interests*

Difficulties arise, however, where general and particular interests conflict. The ability of men to act in the general interest depends first on the extent to which they identify themselves with the general interest (i.e., on where they draw the line between what concerns "them" and what does not). It depends secondly on the extent to which action in the general interest actually involves their personal survival. If action in the general interest leads to self-destruction, it demands a sense of identity with the whole greater than most people seem to possess. It is indeed the main object of social institutions of all kinds to create artificially a situation in which the conflict between the personal and the general interest is not so acute as to cause a breakdown of ethical conduct, so that within reason the individual in acting in his own interest is also acting in the general interest.

There are two broad devices through which individual interest is brought closer to the general interest. One is the economic device of competition and specialization; i.e., the "market," which creates a situation in which the welfare of an individual depends on his ability to satisfy the market demands of others more satisfactorily than his competitors. The other is the political device of *representation*, whereby an individual is made responsible for his action "to" others because of their power to elect other representatives to fill the role he is playing. This too is a form of competition. A representative if he is to stay in office has to "sell" himself to his constituents much as a manufacturer has to sell his products to his customers.

The development of economic groups has made the "market" somewhat less effective as a protector of the general interest, and has increased the importance of "representation"; it represents, that is to say, a shift from more strictly "economic" to more "political" institutions. In some directions this involves gain, and in other directions loss.

From the point of view of ethical *motivation* there is sometimes a real gain in this broadening of the individual's interest. Insofar as people are motivated by loyalty to a group and are prepared to make personal sacrifices for the group, their motives must be rated ethically superior to those of persons who are motivated only by personal interest. The danger, however, is that the motivation, by the very intensity of its association with a group which is less than the whole, comes to stop all the more sharply at the boundaries of the group; that there is no carryover beyond the organized group into society at large. The "good union man" identifies himself so completely with his fellow workers and makes such personal sacrifices for their cause that he becomes blind to the larger interests of society —or assumes unquestioningly that the interests of his group are identical with those of society at large. Similarly, the patriot identifies himself so completely with the national interest that he becomes blind to the interests of mankind at large; or he habitually identifies the good with the welfare of his own country. It must be emphasized that the national state is one economic group among many and that there is no ethical superiority of the national interest over, say, class interest.

The principal disadvantage of control by representation over control by the market is that representatives are usually responsible *to,* and are elected by, a much smaller group of people than their actions affect. Consequently the representative who acts deliberately in the widest possible public interest is all too liable to find himself out of a job—whether he is a director of a corporation elected by stockholders, a director of a cooperative or of a trade union elected by the members, or an executive or legislator of a nation elected by popular vote. There is a profound tendency for leaders of any group to "grow away" from the followers, and even to become "reasonable" to the point where their followers no longer support them. Representation cannot, it seems, in the present state of political skill and organization, be regarded as a complete substitute for the market as a check on arbitrary power, though it may be used to correct some of the defects and abuses of an unregulated market mechanism.

B. *The Use of Coercion*

Coercive power is the ability of an organization to defend and maintain itself by influencing the behavior of those within its sphere of influence by *fear* of possible injury which the organization has power to inflict. The opposite of coercive power is "attractive" power, i.e., the ability of organizations to attract voluntary allegiance and support. Virtually all organizations rely on a mixture of attraction and coercion to insure their continued existence. The national state, of course, relies principally on the coercive power, though there are great variations between the tyrannies which have so little attractive power that they must rely almost wholly on the coercive power and the democracies which can inspire the voluntary allegiance of most of their own citizens. Economic organizations on the whole have to rely mainly on attractive power for their defense. A business, for instance, survives mainly by being sufficiently productive of things for which there is a demand, so that it can attract workers and managers to it voluntarily.

There is a tendency, however, for economic organizations to attempt to capture the coercive power of the state for their own defense. Legal monopolies (e.g., in Elizabethan times) are a striking example. In our day the labor movement has also come to rely more and more on legal sanction to get and keep its membership rather than on "selling itself," as in an earlier day employers relied on legal sanctions such as the injunction to prevent unions from "selling themselves" to their potential members. The tariff is another good example of a successful attempt by minority economic groups (frequently in this case rather loosely organized and bound together by a community of interest rather than of organization) to channel the coercive power of the state in directions which they believe (often falsely) are in their own benefit. Agricultural policy is, by and large, another example.

The ethical evaluation of coerciveness is not easy. Unless one is a complete anarchist one must admit the historical necessity of certain coercive elements in social life. Nevertheless it should be possible to agree that coerciveness *in itself* is an evil, and that any development in society toward less coercive forms of social organization that have survival value is desirable. The problem is one of substituting competition in "love" for competition in "fear"; that is, of creating a moral and organizational environment in which those organizations which are not meeting the needs of man, and which are not serving to right wrongs, will not survive in competition with those organizations which are meeting the needs of man. This is the problem of ethical dynamics; that is, of how things in fact get better instead of worse. Organization of some kind is essential to this process, for only by an organization—that is, an information-communication-executive-effector chain—can knowledge be transformed into action. If things go from bad to worse, instead of from bad to better, the reason must be looked for in a failure of the organizational system. One of the principal reasons for such failure is the existence of coercion, for it is this which permits the survival of those organizations which are *not* making things better. The reduction of coercion, however, is itself a problem in organization, and many institutions—for example, schools, churches, clubs, families at the local level, and representative government and international organizations on the larger scale—have this end in view. We need to organize still more consciously, and more imaginatively, toward the great objective of a noncoercive society.

On the score of its contribution to ethical dynamics—that is, to the "rate of betterment"—the organizational revolution has, like most movements, a mixed record. There is a general presumption that improved techniques of organization will have a favorable impact on the rate of betterment, simply because betterment always comes about through organization of some kind, even if it is through the mental and physical bodily organization of a single individual. Nevertheless, the rise of *large* organizations has created certain important special problems. The rise in the technical proficiency of organizations has made the power of coercive organizations greater, and thereby increased the danger that coercion will undermine the forces of betterment. On the other hand the improved ability to organize has resulted in some cases in the substitution of conflict for coercion, where a coerced group has been able to organize and apply countercoercion to the coercer. Thus the labor movement has arisen largely in response to the feeling which the individual, unorganized worker has—in the absence of an active labor market—of being coerced by his employer. Its object up to a point has been to neutralize the coercive power of the employer by developing coercive power of its own.

The rise of nationalism has similar roots, as the essence of nationalism is the use of the coercive power against potential or actual foreign coercers of the national group. Zionism is an interesting example of this phenomenon: the Jew is hoping to get rid of his age-old oppression by organizing a military power in Israel. Unfortunately it seems to be almost impossible to get rid of oppression in this way without becoming an oppressor. There is still something to be said for Isaiah, and the Jew as the suffering servant may be remembered when the state of Israel is a forgotten footnote on the page of history. Two opposite coercions do not necessarily cancel out, and, indeed, frequently result in extremely destructive forms of competition, both economic and political. The appalling breakdown of national defense in our day is a sad tribute to the dead end into which the short cut of countercoercion leads.

C. *The Continuing Dilemma*

The only answer to the problem of coercion which does not seem to end in frustration and conflict is that of the *integration* of the coercer and the coerced through the spread of the ideal of responsibility and organs of control. What this means is that *the interaction of organizations must itself be organized*; otherwise this interaction is capable of producing intolerable ethical strains. Unorganized and ungoverned interaction produces too great a conflict between the individual and the general interest for the individual to bear.

An interesting example of this proposition is found in the ethical conflicts which are raised by inflation and deflation. Any individual who expects, with some degree of certainty, that there is going to be either an inflation or a deflation will, if he acts in his own interests, intensify the very thing which he anticipates. Thus a businessman who wants his business to survive an impending deflation may try to become "liquid" by turning as much of his assets as possible into cash or safe bonds, even at the cost of closing down much of his operations and creating unemployment. Such a course of action applied generally will accelerate the deflation, and if prices and money wages do not fall as fast as money incomes, unemployment and depression will result. Each individual in attempting to save himself only pushes the economy farther down. Similarly, in a time of inflation, the individual seeking to protect himself will get rid of as much of his cash and bonds as possible and rush to buy the things that he expects will rise in price or become short. This action will raise prices faster and make supplies still shorter.

The search for national security lands us in a rather similar dilemma. Every nation tries to make itself secure by increasing its armaments. The armaments of one nation, however, make other nations feel less secure. Hence the attempt on the part of each nation to establish its security by its own efforts results in greater insecurity for all.

Unfortunately exhortation has proved to be an ineffective instrument for resolving the conflict of the particular and the general interest. This is especially true where the conflict is one not of individuals but of organizations. The "ethical breaking point" at which the individual finds the conflict between the private and the general interest too great for him, and acts to defend himself rather than his society, comes at a low enough level for most individuals acting on their own account. But it is apt to come at much lower levels for individuals acting as representatives of a group. Individuals can sometimes be found who will sacrifice themselves for the group, especially for a small group. Indeed, the phenomenon is not at all rare—"Greater love hath no man than this."

I know of no instance in history, however, where a group or an organization has voluntarily laid down its life in the interest of humanity. In the defense of their nation, their church, their union, their business, their family, men have been known to lie, cheat, steal, and even murder with a single-mindedness of intent that an individual as such rarely achieves. A divergence of private and social interest is all the more serious, therefore, when the private interest concerns a group within society, even where that group is as large as a nation. It is a divergence of interest against which moral exhortation is singularly ineffective, because the fact that the individual is serving *some* group which is greater than himself blinds him to the fact that his group is only a part of the whole. There is no substitute, therefore, for government, in the literal sense of a governing mechanism, universally operative, which will act counterwise to the kind of movement which creates dangerous divergences of private from general interest.

The case of inflation and deflation is again a good example of the above principle. There is clearly need for a monetary governing mechanism—an agency which can act in an inflationary manner when the rest of the economy is being deflationary, and in a deflationary manner when the rest of the economy is being inflationary. Such machinery would not be too difficult to construct if people could be convinced that it can be done. In the case of national security the problem is more difficult. The more complex the variables, the less mechanical the apparatus for controlling them, the more difficult becomes the question of what to control and how to control the controller. The perfect world state would no doubt be able to prevent war. It might also degenerate into a world tyranny from which there would be no escape, a "brave new world" of technical skill and clever manipulation. It is a slightly nightmarish thought that social science may be even more damning to mankind than physical science. Physical science merely culminates in the pain and death of the body under the bomb; social science may culminate in the damnation of the soul in the manipulative society.

The final conclusion, therefore, is that though organizations are here to stay and though the only solution to many of the problems which they raise seems to be ever more and larger organizations, yet there is also no substitute for the Word of God—the sharp sword of truth in the prophetic individual, the penetrating moral insight that cuts through the shams and excuses of even the best-organized society. However clever we become and however far we move toward betterment through cleverness and skill, there is always a place for wonder, for humility, for reverence, for sensitivity to the still small voice of the Creator of all men and all morals.

PART III

The Discussion

Introduction to the Discussion

The present volume, like the others of the series, is conceived not as an authoritative pronouncement, but as a contribution to a discussion. It seems not inappropriate, therefore, to start the discussion within the framework of the volume itself. Accordingly, copies of the manuscript in its first draft were sent out to a number of individuals, and replies were received from some twenty-five of them. Many of the comments and criticisms have been incorporated into the final draft, especially those which corrected errors of fact or called attention to omissions. Many of the comments, however, reflect points of view differing basically from those of the author, and it has seemed wise to summarize these in the form of a discussion. This discussion also has been submitted to the various contributors to ensure that their views have not been misrepresented in the summary.

The commentators fall into several categories, and are grouped accordingly. By himself stands Professor Niebuhr, whose commentary essay entitled "Coercion, Self-Interest, and Love" is reproduced in full, together with the author's reply. Next comes a group of "academic" commentators: Professors Bowen, J. M. Clark, Giffen, Keene, Lombard, Lowe, Muelder, Riesman, Stigler, Tintner, Underwood, and Vickrey. Most of these comments were in the form of detailed criticisms, and many of the points raised have been incorporated into the document. Where, however, a point of principle seems involved, I have endeavored to summarize and reply. Then there is a group of mainly "agricultural" commentators: Davis, Fichter, Taylor, Voorhis, and Wieting, most of whom deal also with the cooperative movement. There are also three who would be considered representative of organized labor—Dudley, Harrison, and Meacham—and one representing the business-man-

agement point of view, Sargent. A list of the commentators is
appended.

[Editor's note: Several of the persons in the list have asked
for an emphasis on the fact that they are not sponsors of the book
and its ideas—that, as Professor Boulding points out and the discussion itself makes clear, some of the critics oppose strongly one
or more major points in the analysis.]

Ralph C. Abele, Pastor, Holy Ghost Evangelical and Reformed
Church, St. Louis, Missouri
Howard R. Bowen, Professor of Economics, Williams College
John M. Clark, John Bates Clark Professor of Political Economy,
Columbia University
John H. Davis, Executive Vice-President, National Wool Market-
ing Corporation, Boston
Tilford E. Dudley, Assistant Director, Political Action Committee,
C. I. O., Washington, D. C.
Joseph W. Fichter, Past Master and Member of the Executive
Committee of the Ohio State Grange, Oxford, Ohio
Roscoe R. Giffen, Professor of Sociology, Berea College, Berea,
Kentucky
George M. Harrison, Grand President, Brotherhood of Railway
and Steamship Clerks, Freight Handlers, Express and Station
Employes, Cincinnati, Ohio
J. Calvin Keene, Professor of Religion, Howard University, Wash-
ington, D. C.
George F. F. Lombard, Associate Professor of Human Relations,
Graduate School of Business Administration, Harvard University
Adolph Lowe, Professor of Economics, Graduate Faculty, New
School for Social Research, New York
Stewart Meacham, Methodist missionary, formerly Assistant to
the President, Amalgamated Clothing Workers of America
Walter G. Muelder, Dean and Professor of Social Ethics, Boston
University School of Theology
Reinhold Niebuhr, Dean of the Faculty and the William E. Dodge
Jr. Professor of Applied Christianity, Union Theological Semi-
nary, New York
David Riesman, Professor of Sociology, University of Chicago

Noel Sargent, Secretary, National Association of Manufacturers, New York

George J. Stigler, Professor of Economics, Columbia University

Carl C. Taylor, Head, Division of Farm Population and Rural Life, Bureau of Agricultural Economics, Department of Agriculture, Washington, D. C.

Gerhardt Tintner, Professor of Economics, Iowa State College, Ames, Iowa

Kenneth Underwood, Assistant Professor of Social Ethics, Yale University Divinity School

William Vickrey, Associate Professor of Economics, Columbia University

Jerry Voorhis, Executive Secretary, The Cooperative League of the U. S. A., Chicago, Illinois

A. Dudley Ward, Director of Studies, Department of the Church and Economic Life, National Council of Churches of Christ

C. Maurice Wieting, Vice President and Director of Organization, Ohio Farm Bureau Federation, Columbus, Ohio

12

Coercion, Self-Interest, and Love

by Reinhold Niebuhr

Professor Boulding's brilliant analysis of the growth of large-scale
political, economic, and social organizations in modern technical
society is governed, as all such analyses must be, by several basic
presuppositions. One of these belongs in the realm of social theory
and the other in the realm of ethical theory. Though the present
reviewer has more competence to deal critically with the latter than
with the former realm, it is nevertheless important to consider the
two in their relation.

In the realm of economic and social theory the analysis rests upon
the assumption that the growth of organization in modern society
is primarily due to the ability of modern technics, particularly the
arts of communication, to provide the instruments for large-scale
organization. He acknowledges some social "need" for this development; yet he believes that, on the whole, the growth is due to the
capacity to "supply," rather than to the pressure of "need" for, this
development. He is the more convinced that this is true because he
thinks "that there is little evidence that organization, especially of
a large group, has much to do in improving the income of its members."

In the realm of ethical theory the analysis rests upon the assumption that the uncoerced and unintended mutual and reciprocal
relations of a market economy more nearly approximate the
Christian ideals of justice, freedom, and love than the more conscious but usually also more coercive disciplines of large-scale
organization.

These two presuppositions must be considered together because
they are very closely related. It is quite possible in fact that the assumption in the realm of economics is derived from the assumption

in the realm of ethics. In any case both are determined by the attitude of the author toward the problems of power and interest in the achievement of social justice. In the realm of economic and social theory the emphasis lies more upon the perils to society which have arisen from modern large-scale social organization than upon the evils of an earlier state in modern liberal society which they were intended to correct. In the field of ethical theory, the unintended social harmonies of a market economy are regarded as approximating the Christian ideal of love more nearly than coercive forms of justice because it is assumed that coercion is in more absolute contradiction to love than is self-interest.

I

In considering his economic and social analysis one must recognize the validity of Professor Boulding's enumeration of the disadvantages which have resulted from what he defines as the "politicizing" of human life. Political organization is rightly distinguished from economic organization by defining the one as the "conscious planning through instruments of authority and subordination," and the other as the "unconscious and automatic coordination of human activity." The primary disadvantage arising from the growing "politicizing" of life is to make the economic structure inflexible because "prices and money wages become more 'sticky.'" The effect of this inflexibility is to subject modern society to the perils of a permanent inflation, since there is no possibility of shaking down inflationary prices through periodic deflationary movements. The political and economic power of the organized groups prevents the "automatic" forces of the market from being effective. I would not have the competence to challenge this conclusion; but I would not be inclined to challenge it, even if I had the competence. It seems to me irrefutable. The evidence which Professor Boulding marshals in support of the conclusion is convincing. So also is the evidence for the ancillary charge that political interference in the economic process, as for instance the political struggles around the concept of "parity" in farm prices, makes for some curious and capricious results.

The paramount question concerns not the fact of these disadvantages but whether they represent too high a price for the advantages gained by the more and more consistent organization of modern life. Professor Boulding regards the price too high because he believes that no real advantages have been gained. He is certain that all modern achievements in social justice would have been gained in any event by the operations of a free market in a dynamic economy. He thinks in fact that the prestige of modern labor and farm organizations is partly derived from mistakenly ascribing inevitable gains to their own intervention in the economic process. His judgment is based upon the presupposition that the increasing production of a dynamic and ever-expanding economy would have been equitably divided and distributed among the various claimants through the automatic competitive processes of a free economy. An expanding industry would have increased wages by competitive bids for the labor of the workers, just as the same competitive process would have prevented prices from becoming exorbitant. Professor Boulding does not of course propose a completely free market system, but he would like to limit state intervention to minimal terms and primarily for the purpose of arresting the downward spirals of deflation before they have run their course.

Such an analysis of the possible workings of a free market seems to obscure certain important factors in the situation. Among them the most important is the factor of power. Modern liberal society came into being by destroying the traditional political restraints upon the operations of the market. But a commercial society was quickly transmuted into an industrial society, with its inevitable centralization of power. The little craft unit gave way to the factory, and the little factory gave way to the larger one. Modern technical efficiency required production units of larger and larger dimension. These production units created dynamic inequalities of power much more disproportionate than any known in the traditional agrarian economy.

The prior condition for modern large-scale social organization must be found in this large-scale economic organization. The social organization does not develop as a kind of unnecessary by-product of modern technics, as Professor Boulding assumes. All of the socioeconomic organizations which he describes are created under the pressure of a "need" which he denies. The need is to balance the unbalanced disproportions of power introduced into modern life by large-scale production and distribution. This balance is necessary because disbalances of power prevent competitive bargaining from being as free and as equitable as classical economic theory assumes.

According to the classical theory, which Professor Boulding accepts in modified form, a worker does not require collective power to set against the collective power of the factory which employs him. He will be saved from exploitation by the possibility of accepting a higher bid for his services from some other industry. Unfortunately, however, the worker is much more bound than the theory assumes. He cannot pick up his family and shop around from city to city. Furthermore, his economic weakness, compared with the strength of the company's financial reserves, makes it difficult for him to bargain at all. For he cannot hold out in the hope of securing a better bid from the bargainer. He can hope only that competing companies may bargain against each other for his services rather than that they may bargain with him. Professor Boulding admits the "psychological" advantages which workers derive from the ability to bargain collectively. But he obscures the economic advantages which they have in fact derived, because he believes that the bargaining process overleaps all disproportions of power. The actual history of modern industrial society, particularly its dismal early chapters, hardly supports this optimism.

An example from the agrarian side of the economy will reinforce the conclusion. The dairy farmer cannot deliver his milk to the big city or in most areas start his own milk route. Milk processing and distribution, as nearly everything else in the modern economy, require large-scale units. There may even be some good reasons why milk distribution in a given city ought to be a regulated monopoly. But, in any event, the dairy farmer has little possibility of getting out of his particular "milk shed" and bargaining with a processor of another city for higher prices than the processor of the city nearest his farm is willing to pay. How can he possibly secure bargaining power, except by acting collectively? He may go farther and use his political power to secure political intervention as well. He may, in fact, become politically so powerful that he will achieve certain unjustified advantages over the milk consumers of the city. But this proves merely that unequal power is always a threat to justice. It does not refute the necessity of individuals' organizing for the sake of gaining collective power. Justice in a technical society requires that the centralization of power inherent in the industrial process be matched by collective social power.

One further power factor must be taken into consideration in dealing with the operations of a market economy. A productive unit in this economy must compete not only for labor but also for markets. It gains its market by underselling competitors or by advertising pressure. The consumer has a much greater freedom in accepting or rejecting the offered product than has the laborer in accepting or rejecting the offered wage. The consumer's greater freedom is derived from the immediacy of alternative options at his command. It is much easier to "shop around" for the lowest-priced dress or suit of clothes than it is to shop around for a job.

In consequence the power of the consumer determines economic policy much more than the power of the individual laborer. That is why in some industries of America (as for instance the clothing industry) its more socially minded employers have secretly, and even openly, connived in the organization of the labor force of the industry. They welcomed the standardization of wage rates, so that they might escape the necessity of debasing the wages of their own workers for the sake of meeting the price competition of less scrupulous producers. They felt themselves capable of carrying on a competitive undertaking with others on the basis of efficiency in production but were anxious to eliminate competition in wages. More recently employers in this industry have demanded of the unions that they organize those industries which sought escape from high wage rates by moving to states in which labor was unorganized.

While there have been industries which thus welcomed stabilization and universalization of wage rates, other industries have achieved stabilization of wages on a low level by covert agreement. Thus they prevented a genuine bargaining procedure for higher wages. A highly localized industry, requiring particular skills which are not quickly transferable to other industries (as furniture for instance), can thus debase wages indefinitely. The organization of labor for collective bargaining in such industries is therefore a special case of the general necessity of organizing collective labor power for the sake of equalizing the advantages gained by previously organized collective industrial power. Undoubtedly modern technical society has consistently increased the mobility of workers, but no development along this line can quite overcome the difference between the freedom of the consumer in choosing his product and the freedom of the worker in choosing his job.

Neither the original nor the subsequent organizations of collective power are free of economic motive or bereft of economic consequences. The simple fact is that a technical civilization produces large-scale organizations, not primarily because people enjoy exploiting what has become technically possible, but because every interest of life, including the economic interest, tends toward collective expression in any event. But the development of the modern machine also makes the collectivization of power in industrial management a technical necessity and the subsequent organizations of labor power a necessity of justice.

Large-scale social organizations are so built into the pattern of a modern community that it is of course difficult to isolate particular motives for them, or consequences of their activities. They are undoubtedly institutions of social power, and this social power includes political and moral prestige. This prestige may have economic consequences in increasing the share of the worker in the total product even when this is not directly apparent. These matters cannot be either proved or disproved. What is important to recognize is that they belong to the social equilibria of a technical society.

II

In analyzing the political power of the modern state Professor Boulding recognizes the increasing tendency to bring economic forces under political control. The most consistent form of this process ends in the omnicompetent state of communism. But Professor Boulding recognizes the partial validity of a more moderate form of this tendency in the "social-democratic" state. In this category he includes not merely the European democracies in which socialist principles are explicitly followed, but also the variants in which there is no nationalization of private property but in which "a great proportion of the national income" is absorbed by the central government. This absorption may be partly because of the expanded activities of government in "social insurance, health, education, regulation of business, etc." and partly because of "the ever-increasing cost of national defense."

He does not completely reject this development as undesirable, but he would regard it as a more ideal solution if the government would limit its responsibilities primarily to stabilizing the economy according to Keynesian principles. This he regards as necessary because, if the economic process has no other than automatic controls, both inflationary and deflationary spirals take too much time in running their course and create too much misery. The intervention of the state beyond this minimal function seems to him politically inevitable, however, because "it is generally felt that the distribution of income which results from an unfettered market economy is too unequal." But he is not altogether happy about the tendency to correct this inequality, because it is difficult to determine "what should be the minimum standard" of welfare for the establishment of which the state intervenes, and "what degree of inequality should be regarded as satisfactory." He also believes that the sense of responsibility of "all for all" within the national community is primarily the fruit of the "universal rise of nationalism."

If one questions these judgments about either the motives for or the consequences of the social equalization undertaken by the modern state, one immediately lays bare the "subjective" character of all judgments of such issues. They are obviously beyond anything that could be called "scientific." Some of us would be inclined to give a higher ethical meaning to the "all for all" development and regard the purely "nationalistic" motive as less potent than he does. Our evidence for such a judgment could be found in the fact that a nation such as Britain, for instance, does not stand under greater external peril than either France or Germany; yet it has a much higher sense of community responsibility than either of these two nations. Its ideal of "fair shares for all" is primarily a moral achievement. It is the fruit of a sense of community within the nation which is older than present international tensions and conflicts and has deeper roots than any modern socialistic tendencies. This sense of community can hardly be defined as "nationalistic" because national self-interest is not involved.

With reference to the feeling of Professor Boulding that interference with the inequalities of a market economy proceeds capriciously without any defined standard of equality or inequality, one might observe that there are naturally no possibilities of arriving at explicit agreements in any society about the degree of inequality which is necessary for the proper performance of different functions or for maintenance of social incentives, or how much equality is necessary to meet the requirements of justice. But it is significant that any unregulated enterprise or relationship in human life will tend to produce more inequality than is morally justified or scarcely acceptable. This tendency is due to a simple fact. If there are no restraints upon human desires, any center of power in human society will be inclined to appropriate more privilege to itself than its social function requires. Therefore, no matter how inexact are the equalities and inequalities which emerge from a political interference with a market economy, they are probably closer to the requirements of justice than those of a completely unregulated economy. They have been established, not by nice calculations of "natural law," but by tensions and contests of power which are a legitimate part of a democratic society. They serve the general ends of justice because the equality of political power (inherent in the rights of universal suffrage) has been used to level undue inequalities in the economic sphere.

Professor Boulding pays tribute to the salutary nature of this general process of equalization by observing that "in no Western nation is the state threatened by an internal group who feel so little a part of it that they wish to destroy it. This is far from true in other parts of the world, and it must be counted one of the most remarkable achievements of social-democratic states."

This admission by Professor Boulding is highly significant. It comprehends a great deal of Western social history. The Marxist rebellion arose in Western civilization in the early days of modern industrialism precisely because the justice which was promised as a by-product of a free economy failed to materialize. In fact the new freedom created so much misery, and the inflationary and deflationary fluctuations of the market had such serious human consequences, that the industrial workers were driven into a mood of desperation. This mood was given a creed and a program by Marxism. Subsequently the healthiest modern industrial nations saved themselves from the prospective civil war, implied in orthodox Marxist politics, precisely because they used various political devices to mitigate the inequalities of privilege and power which were inherent in economic society as such. They also prevented disastrous fluctuations which are admittedly inevitable in a pure market economy. It might be added in passing that it is not quite true to say that "no Western nation" is threatened by an internal group which feels itself so little a part of the nation that it wishes to destroy it. In France and Italy, for instance, revolutionary communism still claims the allegiance of roughly one third of the population. These are the nations in which an old feudal injustice (as in Italy) or the injustices of a free economy (as in France) drive either the agrarian or the industrial poor, or both, to desperation.

It would be idle to deny that many new hazards to justice and stability have emerged from the general "politicizing" of life, particularly the hazard of continued inflation in the sphere of economics and the hazards of bureaucratic caprice and corruption in the field of politics. Yet a just estimate of these perils is possible only if we weigh them against the perils and evils from which we have been delivered by the general tendency in modern democratic societies to bring economic life under moral and political control.

III

Professor Boulding's value judgments in the field of economic and social theory are, as he himself suggests, ultimately rooted in specifically ethical presuppositions. These ethical presuppositions are much more explicit and more explicitly Christian than one usually finds in social and economic theory. In the course of his fifth chapter he offers a fully rounded theory of the relation of ethical and religious ideals to the complexities of social organization. According to this theory, it is necessary for social ideals to become embodied in social organizations; but at the same time the organization corrupts the ideal which it ostensibly embodies. "We know," he declares, that "the spirit giveth life," but why is it "that the letter killeth"? He answers this question by making "the letter" and "the flesh" into the very bearers of evil. "The trouble lies of course," he declares, "in the 'flesh'—that is, in organization. All bodies are corruptible whether the body of the literal flesh or the body of the state, the corporation, the trade union, the philanthropic organization, or the church."

His theory represents no simple body-mind dualism; for he insists that " 'bodies' are necessary if the 'word' [ethical insight] is to be made 'flesh.' " Yet the theory does come close to a fairly unmodified dualism in which the body as Plato conceived it, rather than "flesh" as St. Paul conceives it, is the source of evil. For Plato, evil is in the body because it is corruptible in contrast to the incorruptible soul. For St. Paul, the "flesh" is evil in the sense that he uses this term to designate the sinful; that is, the selfish self in contrast to "spiritual self which knows that the law of love is the final law of human existence."

Before enlarging upon this difference between the Platonic and the Pauline conception, it is necessary to summarize Professor Boulding's indictment of the organization as the evil "body" or "flesh." The first weakness of organization is the difficulty of communication. This grows with the size of organization since the "social distance" between the members of the executive and the humblest receptors at the end of the line of organization makes it difficult for the organization to fulfill the function for which it was intended. The second weakness in organization is that the larger it grows, the more hierarchical becomes the structure and therefore the greater the inequality in the organism. But the primary difficulty with organization is the necessity of coercion. Coercion is defined as "any device which involves the fear of injury rather than the hope of benefit as the motive in attracting support for an organization." Professor Boulding's basic ethical presuppositions are fully revealed in his analysis of the evils of coercion. His preference for a "market economy" is due to its "noncoercive" nature. If economic units fail to function properly, they die through bankruptcy. This is a way of eliminating organizations which have lost their usefulness preferable to those used in the political realm. For in the political realm the coercive power of the organization prevents the collapse of outmoded institutions. "One of the greatest obstacles to progress," declares the author, "is the coercive nature of political organizations."

Here lies the heart of the ethical issue. Voluntary economic organizations are believed to be closer to the Christian ideal of love than political organizations because the latter contain the final contradiction to the Christian love commandment: coercion. What is left out of account in such a formulation is another factor which also contradicts the law of love. This is the factor of self-interest, whether in its individual or in its collective form. The most ideal social organization is obviously one in which men work harmoniously together without coercion. This requires that each seeks the good of the other. But this ideal is not easily achieved. The family, among all human communities, comes closest to this ideal; but even in the family some coercion is used to preserve order and harmony against recalcitrant tendencies. The more complex the human community becomes, the more it is subject to the perils of chaos arising from conflicting interests.

A market economy is one in which there is a certain tolerable chaos, or a harmony distilled from the chaos of conflicting interests. But the harmony is tolerable only insofar as the conflicting interests are fairly evenly matched. When they are not, the contest of power results in injustice. It may even result in tyranny. Individual industrial units may have freedom for their operations in the larger economic realm, but they will be tyrannically organized as to their internal structure if the social situation is such that powerless men are delivered into the hands of the powerful without recourse. A harmony of a market economy is, in any event, not a harmony created by mutual forbearance and consideration. It is a harmony of special interests held in equilibrium. It is tolerable if the interests are armed with fairly equal power; but the situation can become intolerable if the disproportions of power are too great.

But an uncoerced equilibrium is something short of a real society, not only because any *ad hoc* balance of power is inadequate for the attainment of justice, but also because there is an incipient chaos in an uncoerced equilibrium. A tension of competing interests may quickly degenerate into an anarchy of conflicting interests. That is why a community must avail itself of coercion to establish a minimal order.

The distinction between a noncoercive economic society and a coercive political society is therefore somewhat misleading. The political society has not been created by a factitious element of coercion. Political society is an inclusive nonvoluntary society which cannot afford to deal with recalcitrance by the slow method of allowing it to destroy itself. It must suppress all harmful expressions of self-interest or particular interest which threaten the order of the community; furthermore it must provide various coercive and quasi-coercive forms and structures for the proper functioning of the total social organism. The state is not analogous to a corporation which can drop a member for inefficiency. The citizen of a state, whether guilty of criminal recalcitrance or merely of inefficiency or of mild forms of antisocial conduct, cannot be "eliminated" by any natural process of competition. The criminal recalcitrant is jailed. The inefficient member of the community may be "eliminated" in the economic process, but the political community finds itself responsible for the effects of that elimination upon his family. Furthermore it must provide for the greatest degree of order and harmony for all of its "average" citizens who cooperate with each other partly from motives of mutual concern, partly from motives of prudent regard for their several interests, and partly because they are "coerced" by the mores, the laws, and the police power of the community.

If the various forms of coercion which enter into the proper functioning of a well-ordered society are fully analyzed, it will become apparent that no simple line can be drawn between "devices" which involve "the fear of injury" and those which involve "the hope of benefit," the former being coercive and the latter non-coercive.

A conscription law in a democracy, for instance, which Professor Boulding attributes purely to the rise of nationalism and regards with great disfavor, may represent, not so much the unjust claims of a national community upon the individual, as the recognition by many individuals that it is fairer for an impartial judge to determine what order of preference family duties and specific skills ought to have in relation to the duty to defend the nation and the skill of the potential soldier. In the individual instance the effect of the law may be "coercive" upon a given young soldier. He might, nevertheless, upon reflection vote for such a law rather than for a system of free enlistment, on the ground that, all things considered, the quasi-coercive scheme will be more just than a purely voluntary one. He will be the more likely to express such a preference if he considers that there is no protection in a system of free enlistment against the "slacker" who has no good reasons for evading his contribution to a common task.

Taxation schedules are another case in point. Any system of taxation is coercive as it impinges upon the individual taxpayer. But the same taxpayer who feels the coercion when he pays the tax may vote for it as the most equitable way of distributing the common burdens of a community. In a democratic society there are many policies in which consent and coercion are compounded in varying proportions. The consent to the coercive measure may be freely given, not only because the citizen regards the coercive measure as the best method of achieving common standards of sacrifice, but also as a method of supporting his own long-range sense of duty toward the community as against a short-range disinclination to do so.

If the force of particular interest of individuals or groups is fully measured as a factor to be considered in the achievement of justice and order, the attitude toward coercion must inevitably be less negative and critical than it is in Professor Boulding's treatment. It will become apparent why some of the traditional organic societies of the past in which order and community were maintained by a multitude of covert and overt forms of coercion have seemed to many secular and Christian historians as preferable to a modern "free" society in its unmodified form. For the modern society seemed to be merely a cockpit of warring interests. And purely contractual relations, as contrasted with more organic and historically determined relations, seemed to embody not the Christian ideal of love but the very secular ideal of a self-sufficient individual who acknowledges no claims upon him except those which he may freely accept, from time to time, so long as he is also free to renounce what he has accepted, if the contractual relation no longer suits his purpose.

In building and preserving any kind of community, we must give due weight to the following factors:

1. The inclination of the individual to consider other than his own needs. Without this capacity for justice, the harmony and order of communities would depend purely upon coercion. In social philosophies such as that of Thomas Hobbes, the presupposition that men are consistently egoistic naturally leads to political conclusions in which freedom is sacrificed to the supposed necessities of order and no guarantees of justice are given.

2. Despite the capacity of men to consider the needs and interests of others, they also have an inclination to follow their own interests with little regard for the larger interests. This inclination must be defined not merely as "self-interest" but as "particular" interest in contrast to a more universal system of interests. The particular interest may be that of the family or of an economic group, in contrast to that of the community; that of a parochial community in contrast to that of the national community; or the

interest of the national community in contrast to that of the community of nations.

3. Traditional, historical, organic, and natural forces of communal cohesion such as common language, ethnic kinship, geographic factors, common experiences, and common perils. All of these factors operate below the level of conscious decision and bind men together in ways which are not explicitly coercive on the one hand but are on the other hand not the contractual relations of the business community. These are the factors which distinguish a political community from a purely economic one and which prevent the classical economic theory from fully covering or explaining all the facts and problems of the human community. They create large areas of habitual rather than voluntary association, but their cohesive force is implicit rather than explicit and covert rather than overt.

4. The conscious contrivances of statecraft which seek to prevent partial and parochial interests from clashing in chaotic competition or conflict, which provide channels for the maximum degree of cooperation, which suppress undue recalcitrance against minimal standards of justice and order, which equalize fortuitous inequalities in the interest of justice, and which create a larger community than is possible upon the basis of the "natural" limits of human sympathy and concern for the neighbor.

This fourth factor, in which there are large elements of "coercion," does not stand in simple contradiction to the ideals of justice and love. It is just as near and just as far from the ideal of justice and brotherhood as is individual liberty. For individual liberty offers the possibilities both of exploiting the neighbor and of entering into just relations with him on a voluntary basis. The quasi-coercive contrivances of statecraft, on the one hand, offer the possibilities of community and justice beyond the natural limits of the primitive kinship society; and, on the other hand, they contain the perils of injustice and tyranny.

Such justice as the best communities of human history have achieved has been attained between the Scylla of anarchy and the Charybdis of tyranny. It is instructive that, if anarchy is feared too much, a society may easily be delivered into tyranny; but, if it fears tyranny too much, it may also fall into anarchy. Power and coercion are not, in short, the simple devils of the drama of man's age-old struggle to gain community. Coercion is pregnant with both good and evil possibilities—exactly as is freedom.

One of the dangers of government is, as Abraham Lincoln observed, that a government strong enough to preserve order may be so strong as to threaten the liberties of the people. Furthermore, centralization of political power is as fruitful of injustice as undue power in any realm of life. But we cannot solve this threat of inequality by Professor Boulding's proposal. He declares: "We cannot achieve equality by establishing large integrated organizations. The only hope for an equalitarian world is a world of small organizations held together by contractual relations." Such a system might indeed avoid the perils of tyranny and inequality; but would it escape anarchy?

It is obviously impossible to build either an international or any other community upon pure power. There must be other forces of cohesion than the threat of explicit coercive power. But if many small organizations are held together purely by "contractual" relations, this means that too much freedom of action is reserved and the fateful necessity of holding together is obscured. On the basis of such a principle Abraham Lincoln's dictum, "My purpose is to save the union," was dead wrong. The Southern states should have been permitted to renounce their contract. A war would have been avoided. But we might have had many subsequent wars between the two confederations of states. In other words, a too strong emphasis upon freedom and contract means that the peril of injustice and tyranny has driven the social philosopher too close to the edge of the Scylla of anarchy.

The interests of justice require, it is true, that no perils in the application of coercive power be obscured. Obviously an organization which is preserved from disintegration primarily through the application of coercion is not worth preserving. Furthermore it destroys the very human potential which a human community is intended to serve. That is why power must be "weighed out ounce by ounce," in the words of Sam Rutherford, a seventeenth-century Calvinist. A healthy society must seek to achieve the greatest possible equilibrium of power, the greatest possible number of centers of power, the greatest possible social check upon the administration of power, and the most effective use of forms of coercion in which consent and coercion are compounded. But all of these reservations

still do not make "coercion" the villain of the piece. Coercion is seen
in that light only if it is supposed that modern economic society has
given a completely new turn to the age-old problem of human to-
getherness.

The modern liberal society has indeed given a creative thrust to
the emancipation of business enterprise. But it has frequently obscured, as much as it has illumined, the perennial problems of
community. The confusion has taken place because the contractual
relations of business enterprise have been regarded as too simply
normative for all human relations. Actually most human relations,
from those of the family to those of the inchoate world community,
have a greater degree of "destiny" and a smaller degree of revocable
choice in them than those of the business community. In these
relations human beings and communities are bound together in
such a way that it may be neither possible nor desirable to contract
out of the relation if it proves vexatious, or to eliminate an inefficient
member if he proves recalcitrant. Therefore more attention must
be given to various strategies for preserving the good order and a
tolerable harmony between the various forces in such a community
by whatever stratagems prove most effective and least injurious to
freedom.

If "coerciveness" is not so simply the "villain of the piece," it must
follow also that organization, or "the letter" of the law, is not so
simply the source of evil. The church of Christ does not produce
the "Grand Inquisitor" by any force inherent in organization *per se.*
Nor does communism's original ideal become corrupted merely
because the idea becomes "enshrined in a vast instrument of exploitation." A church of Christ produces a Grand Inquisitor if it
loses the modest awareness of the fragmentariness of all human wisdom and virtue and pretends that a historic community perfectly
embodies absolute values. The tension is not between the true ideal
and the organization which embodies it. The tension or contradiction is between the true ideal, according to which men achieve a
loving relation with each other because none of them pretends to
be the absolute center of truth and justice, and the false idea,
according to which men or churches make themselves into false
divinities.

Communism is not a true ideal which becomes corrupted because
it is embodied, though it may well be that Lenin was personally

more disinterested than Stalin. Communism has generated corruption because it is essentially a false ideal. It pretends that a certain class in society—the proletariat and its nursemaids, the party—have a monopoly of all virtue and wisdom by the authority of which they rule the whole of society. Naturally such a monstrous pretension creates tyranny.

To put this matter in Biblical-theological terms, it is not the "body" which is the adversary of the "spirit." It is, as St. Augustine said, "not the bad body which causes the good soul to sin but the bad soul which causes the good body to sin." This is to say that the contest in life is not between a discarnate spirit and the body. The contest is between the spirit of love and the spirit of self-love. It was this spirit of self-love which St. Paul designated with the term "flesh." But this meant something quite different from Greek philosophy's discovery of the source of evil in the "body." This important distinction is relevant to our consideration of the problem of justice, freedom, and order in the community.

It means that, from the Christian standpoint at least, we cannot regard as evil the structures, systems, laws, and conventions by which partly selfish and partly unselfish men are held together in large-scale cooperation. The order and justice which they achieve must be regarded as an approximation of a loving community. It is of course not *the* loving and just community. It is merely an approximation under the conditions of sin. So long as men are selfish these hard shells of community must be preserved.

Naturally the purest forms of love always transcend these structures. The purest forms of love are, as Professor Boulding rightly observes, in the realm of pure spirit. But if we discount the structures in the name of love we may easily achieve anarchy and injustice. The "letter of the law" does indeed kill, if it is made into the final good. The finest forms of human goodness are in the realm of grace which is beyond the law. But this realm of grace does not abolish the law. It expresses itself beyond the limits of the law. Every human community would degenerate into pure anarchy or tyranny if there were not forces in it which draw human goodness beyond the limits of the law. But insofar as the law achieves a tolerable justice and prevents men from taking advantage of each other, it is a vestibule to the realm of brotherhood, rather than its polar opposite.

13

In Reply to Professor Niebuhr

by KENNETH BOULDING

Professor Niebuhr's provocative essay makes it clear, I think, that there are profound differences between us. These differences arise mainly, I suspect, out of a difference in our theological positions, a difference which further may arise out of differences in religious experience. One suspects sometimes that there are only two rational sciences, theology and mathematics, and that all differences arise from the first and agreements from the second.

I might deal first with some points where I suspect we are basically in agreement. I do not, of course, advocate a completely nonpolitical, laissez-faire economy. I have cast some doubt, it is true, on the view that organized economic groups have been able to shift the distribution of income markedly in their favor. This does not mean, however, that I regard their relative impotence in this direction as anything in their disfavor. Indeed, I would regard it as extremely dangerous to society if economic groups in fact had the power which their advocates sometimes claim. On the whole, I regard the rise of the labor and farm organizations as a necessary and desirable step in the development of our society, not because it has made a great deal of difference to the *economic* power relationships as expressed in the price-wage system, but because it has made a substantial difference to the configurations of status and to the political power structures of our society. In particular, the great achievement of the farm and labor movements, in America at least, has been the virtual abolition of the proletariat and the setting up of organizations which make the mass of the people feel that they "belong" to the whole society.

I

On the question of the causes and economic consequences of the rise of organized economic groups, however, I feel I must stick to my main thesis, while recognizing the need for much more empirical and historical research before the thesis can be regarded as definitely established. In the first place, I cannot accept the view that "the real root of modern large-scale social organization must be found in this large-scale economic organization." This seems to me to embody all that is naïve and unrealistic in the economic interpretation of history. My view is that changes in the scale of *both* economic and social organizations arise from the same principal source, which is the progressive improvement in the skills of organization itself. We do not have big organizations of business and of labor because we have big machines dropped from heaven; we have big machines because we have learned how to unite large bodies of men in a cooperative effort. Modern technology cannot develop until the social skills permit it.

We are, of course, faced with a hen-and-egg problem here: social and technical skills are all part of a complex culture pattern and act and react on each other in an endless process of ecological succession. The view which I cannot accept, however, is that a series of fortuitous inventions gave rise to the "factory" and somehow the "factory" created the labor movement because it created a demand for it. It was not, as a matter of fact, in large-scale industry and in factories that the historical roots of the labor movement are to be found, but in trades like construction, mining, printing, and the metal trades, which are characterized by small-scale enterprise and scattered jobs. The organization of the great factories—steel and automobiles—came much later, and came largely as a result of "missionary" effort on the part of the existing organizations, almost all of which were in fields where small-scale enterprise was dominant. There is a myth here which must be exploded.

The view that there is an inherent weakness in the bargaining position of labor implicit in any "free market" economy also, on the whole, strikes me as a myth. Professor Niebuhr immensely underestimates the mobility of labor, especially in an automotive age. It was true, of course, in feudal and early capitalist times that, as Adam Smith remarked, "man is of all kinds of baggage the most difficult to transport," and that ignorance and repressive laws kept most people tied to the places of their birth. It has been one of the happiest results of the technical revolution, however, to diminish this immobility, even to the point where it is no longer possible to maintain any substantial differential between urban and rural wage rates, in time of full employment.

The rub here, of course, is in the words "full employment." Most of the dismal pictures of the weak bargaining position of the unorganized worker are drawn, quite understandably, from conditions of large-scale unemployment. A depression is precisely a time when the market is not functioning; when the alternative to one's present position is not a job with somebody else, but unemployment. Under these circumstances it is true that unorganized workers, like unorganized farmers, are unable to resist the deflationary pressures of the times. Even this, however, does not truly represent a weak bargaining position in regard to the over-all distribution of income. Indeed, one of the striking empirical facts of our society is that it is precisely in depression, when the individual worker is presumably in the weakest bargaining position, that the *proportion* of national income going to labor rises. In the depression of 1929-32, for instance, it rose from 63 to 74 per cent. This is, it should be pointed out, a larger piece of a smaller pie, so that the absolute income going to labor may decline in a depression; but there is nothing to support the "weak bargaining power" theory.

A similar argument applies to the supposedly weak bargaining position of the farmer. If the price of milk is not adequate to attract farmers into milk production, milk will not be produced in adequate volume and the price will rise. The establishment of milk marketing boards and marketing agreements has much to recommend it in the way of preventing unnecessary fluctuations in the price of milk; but we shall be deluding ourselves if we think that the establishment of these organizations has much effect on the "bargaining position" of the farmer, unless the power of the organizations is exercised to prevent new milk producers from entering the industry.

I am aware that in stating this thesis I may seem in the minds of many people to be undermining the economic foundation on which they have based the ethical justification for organized economic groups. I write, however, as that most disagreeeable of all people, the candid friend. Ethical houses cannot be built on economic sand, and the economic myths must be exposed if an adequate ethical structure is to be raised. I want to make it clear that I do not deny that many important cases can be found in which, for instance, labor organization has materially increased the real incomes of the organized. What I am saying is that in the over-all picture there is not much evidence that particular bargains, or even the particular bargaining process, have much ultimate effect on the distribution of income as between the big shares of labor, agriculture, business, etc., as a whole.

The wage bargain, for instance, is not a simple division of a fixed total revenue between employer and employed; it is merely one element, and not perhaps even a very important element, in the multitude of factors and decisions which go to determine the over-all distribution. Under some circumstances, for instance, an "improvement in the bargaining position of labor," creating a rise in money wages, will enable employers to pass on even more than the wage increase in higher prices, so that real wages may actually fall. Under other circumstances this is not the case. It is this manifoldness of causal relations in the economic system which makes ethical judgments in economic life so difficult.

II

To come now to the second section of Professor Niebuhr's paper, again I suspect that our disagreement is an economic rather than an ethical one. I believe I am as much of an equalitarian as he is, and I am not at all unhappy about the tendency to correct inequalities. I still think that the rise of the welfare state is closely correlated with the rise of nationalism, and that this admixture may ultimately destroy the welfare aspects of the state because of the dynamic instability of national defense. But the connection between the "all for all" aspects of the welfare state and nationalism is a good mark for nationalism rather than a bad mark for the welfare state. Indeed, I would go even farther and argue that the future of the national state depends on which of these elements—welfare or defense— dominates its policy in regard to other nations. Either the welfare attitude of concern for all will overcome the defense attitude of fear of all or defense will overcome welfare. In my more optimistic moments, therefore, I look to the redemption of the national state by an extension of its welfare aspects to all people everywhere, rather than the destruction of the national state in an all-embracing world empire.

Where I think we differ is that I would lay a great deal more stress on economic development rather than on equality itself as an ideal to be striven for in the economic system. I cannot escape the feeling that Professor Niebuhr thinks of "justice" in economic life as the problem of how to divide up a *fixed* pie, whereas I am much more interested in how to increase the size of the pie. It is not inequality as such that troubles me but poverty, and the problems of poverty and of equality are by no means the same. Indeed, "redistribution" is not an important weapon in the abolition of poverty; where poverty has been reduced it has been mainly because of the rise in per capita incomes due to an over-all rise in the productivity of the society.

The interactions between progress and equality are extremely complex, and not well understood; but the possibility that within certain limits these objectives may compete with one another cannot be cast aside. The experience of Russia suggests that equality may have to be sacrificed ruthlessly in the interests of rapid economic development, even by a society which has strong equalitarian prejudices. It is clear that the ethical problem here is one of a delicate balance between possibly conflicting ideals. Unfortunately, the economic problem is also difficult. We do not know much about the degree to which political forces, especially in the long run, are *able* to affect the structure of distribution. I am extremely doubtful that there is much latitude in this direction. My attitude to this question, therefore, is governed somewhat by the suspicion that it is difficult, even by the direct organization of political and economic interest groups, to affect distribution greatly, whereas it is disastrously easy by politicizing the society to suppress economic progress.

It is true, of course, that "any center of power in human society will be inclined to appropriate more privilege to itself than its social function requires." This, however, looks to me like an argument *for* the market as a regulator of society, and against the planned economy. It is precisely the *political* centers of power, because of their command of the means of violence and coercion, that are most able to appropriate to themselves these inappropriate privileges. What Professor Niebuhr does not seem to understand about the market is that it is a destroyer—i.e., a diffuser—of power, not a concentrator. Positions of power which are based in mere market advantage (monopoly) are highly insecure; they are constantly threatened by technical change, by the development of substitute products, by shifts of population, by the inescapable sand blast of the long run. Positions of power which are based on the control of the instruments of coercion are much more difficult to dislodge, and are much more likely to "appropriate more privilege than their social function requires."

It is true, of course, that democratic institutions operate as an important check on positions of political power. The vote, in fact, is the political substitute for the market. It is, however, an increasingly inadequate substitute in an age of complex technology. The utter helplessness of the citizen, for example, when faced with the problems of atomic power is an example of the breakdown of the political process. The atomic energy question is shrouded in military secrecy and technical difficulty to the point where the ordinary citizen is quite incapable of forming an adequate judgment and has precious little opportunity to express such a judgment if he could form it. Increasingly, therefore, the state becomes an entity separate from its citizens even in democratic societies, making decisions of which they are not aware, maneuvering them into positions from which they cannot retreat, itself creating the public opinion on which its power ultimately rests, until the state is now in danger of becoming the greatest enemy of man instead of his wisest friend.

Like Professor Niebuhr, however, I should count myself as a social democrat. I do not believe that the market can do everything, and have said so many times. I also regard the moral achievement of the British people as a remarkable one and as an expression of the concern of all for all which is not merely confined to the national group. Nevertheless there are the "iron laws," malleable as some of them may be, and moral insights will be frustrated unless they are embodied in appropriate institutions. Because of the ethical and economic implications of unlimited national defense I think it extremely probable that the welfare aspects of the national state will be eaten up by the defense aspects, and that therefore the national state itself may not in the long run prove an adequate defense against the concentration of economic or any other kind of power.

III

Now we come to the more directly ethical and theological sources of our differences. In regard to the "body" and the "flesh" I think there is some misunderstanding, and the view of St. Paul which Professor Niebuhr describes is exactly what I think I hold. I do not think that I have fallen into whatever heresy it is that identifies "spirit" with goodness and "flesh" with evil. The division between good and evil cuts right across the division between spiritual and material. This indeed seems to me one of the points where Christianity carries a unique and precious insight; it is the splendid materialism of the Word made flesh that saves it from being a purely spiritual religion. There are good spirits and bad; there are good bodies and bad. Having said this, however, the problem of how the good is encouraged and the bad discouraged in both bodies and spirits is still with us, and the problem of how to make corruptibility put on incorruption. I have never argued for disembodied spirits, but I am arguing that the problem of how to prevent the corruption of the spirit by the weaknesses of the body is an immensely real one.

I cannot help feeling that Professor Niebuhr has rather missed the point of my attack on coercion. I am not, of course, an anarchist, though I must confess that anarchism strikes me as being a much more appealing ideal than socialism, and the anarchists as much more agreeable people than the socialists. One must recognize that there are elements of coercion in any human relationship and in any society, and that it is extremely unlikely that a purely non-coercive society can be established among men. Nevertheless, I regard the lessening of coercion as one of the most fundamental long-run objectives of human organization and one of the most profound moral tests by which any social movement is to be judged. No doubt I am prejudiced in this direction by my Quaker principles; but it seems to me also that this is a conclusion which necessarily follows from the theory of organization and the ecological view of society, and that in this regard the insights of social science and of radical Christianity are in remarkable accord.

The great case against coercion is that it permits institutions and organizations to survive which are not serviceable, for in the absence of coercion only those organizations and species will survive which serve the needs of others. If—as I think in Christian thought we must—we place a high value on the ideal of service, we must recognize also that this implies placing a high value on defenselessness. It is the productive and defenseless lamb that is the symbol of Christ, not the predatory, unproductive, and armed eagles, lions, and suchlike beasts that are the symbols of the national state. And if the lion and the eagle are to survive, they must learn to lie down with the lamb, to become loved rather than feared, meek rather than proud, productive rather than predatory. The proposition that the meek (that is, the adaptable and serviceable) inherit the earth is not merely a wishful sentiment of religion, but an iron law of evolution.

Professor Niebuhr's argument seems to me to depend upon an identification of noncoerciveness with self-interest, which seems to me like the identification of two completely unrelated concepts. This identification profoundly affects his ethical judgment of the market as an institution; for he somehow seems to assume that a market economy must be one in which everyone is actuated by self-interest, and that a thorough spanking by the coercive power of the mother-state will make everybody love one another. In fact, there is nothing inherent in the institution to prevent everyone in a market economy from being actuated by the loftiest altruism. It may be true that the institutions of the market economy do not by themselves generate altruism, and it is probable that altruism is generated in the home, church, and school rather than in the bank or the counting-house. It is also true that prisons are poor generators of altruism!

The problem of the generation of ideals by institutions is acutely difficult, and imperfectly understood. It may well be that a certain optimum degree of temptation is necessary in order to develop moral character, and that the ultimate test of institutions is their ability to provide just the right amount of temptation. On the whole, however, I think we shall not go far wrong if we assume that temptation is normally too great, and that a reduction of temptation is desirable. On this score the market as a generalized type of institution makes a good record; its impact is to diminish the power of one person over another, if only because it tends constantly to substitute many masters for one. The difference between the status of the serf and that of the modern workman is largely the achievement of the institution of the labor market, which has liberated the worker from his dependence on a single master.

I believe I have dealt adequately in the body of this work with the technical weaknesses and imperfections in the market institution, which are grave. Nevertheless my interest is in the cure of these weaknesses rather than in the death of the market; for I believe the market, when it works well, is a true instrument of redemption, though a humble one, not only for individuals but for society. It gives the individual a sense of being wanted and gives him an opportunity of serving without servility. It gives society the opportunity of coordinating immensely diverse activities without coercion. The "hidden hand" of Adam Smith is not a fiction.

There are forces operating in society, as there are within the human organism, which make for health. The doctor is merely the cooperator with these great forces in the body. The doctor of society—who is equally necessary—must also be a humble cooperator with the great forces of ecological interaction, which often restore a society to health in spite of his medications. It is precisely this "anarchy" which Professor Niebuhr deplores which saves us, in both the human and the social organism. If we really established conscious control over the heartbeat and the white blood cells, how long would we last? Health is achieved by the cooperation of consciousness with a largely unconscious physiological process. Self-consciousness is not always an aid to health, either in the individual or in society.

The difference in our basic ethical views, as well as the grounds for this difference in our differing theologies and religious experience, is brought out with dramatic clarity in our attitudes toward conscription. I must confess that I was even a little shocked by Professor Niebuhr's attitude on this point. My attitude toward conscription is determined sharply by my belief in the immediate experience of the Holy Spirit, or Inward Light, available to every man to teach, guide, reprove, and draw him up toward goodness. Conscription utterly violates this concept of Christian vocation based on sensitivity toward the light of Christ. The idea that one should blithely hand the determination of one's duty over to an "impartial judge" (even if the draft board is qualified for this exalted status) seems to me a denial of the very heart of the Christian experience of guidance and the leadings of the spirit.

It is true, of course, that the guide can be blind and the light dark, and that self-indulgence and cowardice may masquerade as a self-imposed sense of duty. This is always the cost of freedom. But unless there is freedom to follow the Inward Teacher, how can man ever develop a sensitivity to His voice? The abdication of the moral freedom of the individual which is involved in conscription seems to me to lead to the ultimate corruption of the whole moral fiber of society. France and Germany are dreadful examples of this corruption. In the smaller European countries like Switzerland it has not gone so far, because the moral defenses of the society are stronger. Even there, however, the cancer is at work.

Conscription is to my mind a form of slavery, and an evil even more repugnant than slavery; for whereas the slave is generally compelled to do humble and productive tasks, the conscript may be compelled to become a killer of God's children and a destroyer of His creatures. It seems to me but a step from Professor Niebuhr's position to a wholesale defense of slavery—why not, after all, put the whole burden of a man's duty on an "impartial judge"? The condemnation of slavery—that it corrupts both the judge and the judged, and puts a power into the hands of Man which is only appropriate to the spirit of the Living God—applies with equal force to conscription. Draft boards are for the most part composed of fallible and untrained individuals, however well-meaning they may be. It imposes an impossible moral burden on them to allot to each young man his "duty," a burden which will be corrupting to them and also to the young men who are in their power. This is a priestcraft of the state more dangerous than any priestcraft of the church. It seems to me utterly repugnant to the message of the burning and immediate reality of the living God which Christ lived and died to bring us.

I may perhaps sum up the difference a little ruthlessly by saying that Professor Niebuhr is afraid of freedom, seeing always behind it the specter of anarchy; whereas I am afraid of justice, seeing always behind it the specter of tyranny. The difference between us is perhaps the difference between the Lutheran vision of God as a Mighty Fortress and the Quaker vision of God as the Living Seed. That both these visions describe a vital religious experience can hardly be doubted. The former I appreciate intellectually; the latter I claim as my own. For that very reason, however, I am profoundly grateful to Professor Niebuhr for raising so clearly and so forcefully the issues between us; he is an enemy that I delight to love. Perhaps we shall yet reconcile freedom and justice, and make the lion lie down with the lamb.

14

General Discussion

It seems ungracious to the other discussants, many of whom wrote detailed and helpful comments, to lump them all together in a single chapter. Where the points they raise are matters of detail, however, I have tried to take care of them in the revised text, and it seems wise to confine this discussion to matters of principle where there seems to be some basic disagreement.

CAUSES OF THE "ORGANIZATIONAL REVOLUTION"

Some commentators expressed doubt about the basic thesis that the rise in organization has been a result of changes in techniques of organization, rather than a result of a rise in "demand" for them. Thus I quote Professor Howard R. Bowen:

I have some serious question about your thesis that the growth of organization is a result mainly of changes in supply rather than demand. It seems to me that the demand for organization has increased tremendously as a result of the development of our large and complex society, the increase in social and geographic mobility, and the secularization of society. I would argue that we are in the process of evolving new types of groups which tend to take the place and assume the functions of the local community and the family of an earlier day. The community and the family no longer have the same functions or the same self-sufficient status that they once had, and our points of common interest do not always center in one geographic locality. Hence, we are in the process of building new communities in which the points of common interest are professional, occupational, and political.

I am also somewhat dubious about your theory that there has been a great increase in supply or in the means of organization. My reading of history indicates that both the propensity and the means to organize have existed in many diverse times and places. I think immediately of the Roman Empire, the Catholic Church, the Greek city-states, even the British Empire of the nineteenth century. Even primitive tribes are able to organize themselves into nations, and sometimes differentiated organizations are found within primitive groups; for example, the secret societies which correspond somewhat to our lodges.

You refer to the invention of the professional specialized organizer. It seems to me that you would find plenty of these people in connection with the early development of business from the twelfth century on. At least a book like Miriam Beard's the *History of the Business Man* is full of such allusions.

To sum up, I feel a little dubious about your theory of the growth of organization, although I do not have constructive alternative suggestions to offer. I suppose my main point is that I feel that the modern movement is really a substitute of one kind of organization for another. The church, the family, and the local community have probably diminished in importance as organizations, or at least in range of functions, and we are in the process of developing other kinds of organizations to take over the functions once carried on by these simple and less specialized organizations.

In so far as Professor Bowen is protesting against a certain over-enthusiasm on my part in stressing the "supply" side of the organizational movement rather than the demand side, he may be right; Professor Niebuhr, it will be recalled, makes the same point. I am still convinced, however, (1) that there has been a remarkable growth in the *size* and complexity of organizations, and (2) that this has been on the whole a result of increasing skill in organizing rather than any great change in the need for organization—a need which has always been strong, and which is as strong as it ever was. That is to say, I believe the main *changes* have been in the opportunity to organize rather than in the inherent desire for organization or for what organization yields. It is true of course that man has always lived in organizations, and it is true also that the rise of large organizations involves a certain diminution in the functions of the small. But it is precisely this change in the *scale* of organization which is the phenomenon to be explained, and which constituted the "organizational revolution." Whether there is "more organization" now than there was in the middle ages is an almost meaningless question. What is certain is that the size of organizations, in terms of the number of people involved and the territories covered, is much greater. This is true even of the Catholic Church.

It is nice to be able to throw one commentator at another, and

I can hardly resist the temptation to quote Professor Riesman, who writes:

I think you are entirely right concerning the growth of skills of organization. As I think you know, my own belief is that without the communications revolution, modern operations, including war, would be quite impossible. The army marches on the punched card—indeed, the University of Chicago could not run without it! I think perhaps more could be said than you do say, about the growth of social competence as a factor in the growth of organizations. The whole development of schools as teachers of teamplay might be stressed. You are entirely right, I think, about the "invention" of the organizer . . . I'm inclined to think that people may also be seen as "movements," some with stable and some with growing identities.

BIOLOGICAL AND MECHANICAL ANALOGIES

Now perhaps I can leave Professors Bowen and Riesman to fight it out, and pass on to another rather fundamental criticism, of a methodological kind, from Dr. Carl C. Taylor of the U. S. Department of Agriculture, who objects strongly to the biological and mechanical analogies. Unfortunately I am not clear from his letter as to the grounds for his objection. He says:

I think his mechanical parallelism is almost as bad as his biological parallelism. Neither the neuroglandular system of the individual human organism nor the communication system of a complex social organism is completely mechanical. Each can be described in terms of its own mechanism rather than in terms of thermometers or other mechanical controls. Maybe this is another way of saying that the two best approaches to an analysis of social organizations are through an understanding of the psycho-physical mechanism of the human organism and an inductive study of social organizations themselves. . . .

Every time the author comes back to an attempt to force social situations, which are compounded of much more than economic behavior, into purely economic terms such as marketing, selling, etc., he weakens rather than strengthens his exposition.

It is clear that there is a basic methodological difference between Dr. Taylor and myself. What it seems to me Dr. Taylor is saying is that everything is unlike everything else, whereas I am convinced that everything is rather like everything else. I believe firmly that reality is continuous, and that between the simplest particle of matter or the most elementary idea and the most complex of organisms or philosophies there are ladders of many steps. Hence we should always look to see the similarities among things as well as the differences. The process of understanding is the process of working up from the simple to the complex; the more we can see the similarities among apparently diverse objects, therefore, the better our understanding will be, for we shall be able to climb the ladder of complexity rung by rung.

I do not suppose for a moment, of course, that the concept of a thermostatic control, or "servo-mechanism," is *adequate* to explain the complexities of behavior of either physiological or social organism; nor is the relatively simple concept of a biological ecosystem adequate to deal with the immense complexities of the social system. Nevertheless there *is* machinery in the body, and there are both life and machinery in an organization; so we can learn things about complex organizations by studying simple ones. There is a danger, of course, that enthusiasm for the simple may cause us to overlook peculiarities in the complex; oversimplification is a danger of all analysis. Nevertheless, without simplification there can be no analysis at all. Unless Dr. Taylor can point to some specific case where the theory of organization has led me astray, I shall still have to confess that I have found these similarities among the different levels of science remarkably stimulating and instructive. I am sorry that he does not find himself similarly stimulated and instructed.

However, I find that what seems like a purely biological and mechanical approach to the problem has disturbed more than one reader. Thus Professor Keene writes:

I wonder if you have not made organizations appear too impersonal and automatic? They seem to become what they *must* become, and the individual, personal factor, which is so often really determinative, seems swallowed up in the automatic growth of the organization, analogous to the automatic growth of a plant, given its surroundings. Even our large organizations are dependent upon the insights and acumen of their individual directors to a very marked degree.

Professor Keene's point is good. It is true that when we look for the reasons for the success of any particular organization we shall almost always find some outstanding personality at its center. It is the unavoidable weakness of the analytical method, however, that it abstracts from reality in order to gain perspective, and that it looks for the similarities which are the bare bones of things, rather than the differences which are their flesh and blood. The reader is warned, therefore, against thinking that the theory of organization, as I have described it, is anything more than a diagram or map of reality. Nevertheless we can often find our way around more easily on a map than on the ground itself.

Many of my readers find the analysis of the theory of organization pretty heavy going. To make things a little easier I have segregated the more difficult part of the analysis into the Preface, so that the reader who finds abstraction difficult may be able to pass quickly to the more concrete discussions. Nevertheless I must ask the reader's patience. This is not a work of journalism or of popular exposition, but an attempt to think certain difficult and fundamental problems through to their foundations. It seems inevitable that parts of such a work should be both abstract and difficult.

ECONOMICS OF THE LABOR MOVEMENT

I must now pass to some of the special comments regarding the chapters of Part II. If one attempts to survey vast fields of human activity, such as labor, agriculture, business, and government, one can hardly expect to achieve complete accuracy or agreement, and the weaknesses of one's preparation and knowledge are apt to be shown up. The reader will not be surprised, therefore, to find that many of my comments in these special fields arouse considerable controversy; but I must insist again that these chapters especially are to be regarded as contributions to a discussion, not as authoritative pronouncements. What I have written is how things look to me—a professor of economics, a little insulated from the hurly-burly of the world, and not too well acquainted at first hand with many of the matters on which I touch. I survey the world, as it were, from the academic mountain and must resist the temptation to claim it as my own. Nevertheless, while I am sure that in innumerable details the picture which I have given is faulty and will be perceived as such by those who actually work in the land-scapes which I merely spy out from afar, I feel some confidence in claiming that the broad outline which is all that my peculiar vantage point permits me to see is not too far from the truth.

The three commentators from the labor unions—George M. Harrison, Tilford E. Dudley, and Stuart Meacham—all are critical of many of my comments and conclusions. Economists have a not wholly undeserved reputation of being unfriendly to the labor movement, and my commentators all feel that I am somewhat tarred by that brush, though not, as Mr. Harrison puts it, to the point of viciousness. It is true that the economist, because the core of his analysis is the market and the price system, is apt to feel a certain irritation at forces—like the labor movement—which interfere with the operation of his ideal abstraction. The market, as I have remarked elsewhere, is our baby, and we cannot help loving it a little.

For this reason perhaps I have leaned over backward in emphasizing the sociological and political aspects of the labor movement at the expense of the economic. Mr. Dudley especially feels that I have underemphasized the importance that wages play in industrial relations, and that in emphasizing the noneconomic aspects of status, political maneuvering, social ritual, and so on, I have led my readers too much away from the hard economic realities of wages and hours. It may be that I have been assuming that my readers tend to think too much of the purely economic aspects of the labor movement, and that by assuming that these are familiar I have given a picture that is too one-sided in the other direction.

The core of my disagreement with my union friends, however, is my contention that unions have not, in fact, made much contribution to changing the proportion of national income going to labor. Mr. Meacham has expressed this most eloquently as follows:

My deepest question goes to the recurring theme that unions have not won any economic advantages for their members that would not have been provided by the economy anyway. In support of this claim it is said (1) that the rise of unionism has not had any large effect on the distribution of national income, and (2) that unions make it impossible for society to correct inflationary dangers by deflationary devices. . . . Now if these two propositions are true, they represent the sharpest attack that could be launched against the labor movement as it exists in America. Nevertheless, *if they are true*, it would be immoral for the church to refuse to accept responsibility for them. But if they are not true, if indeed they represent at best a complete mis-understanding of the facts of our economic life, and at worst a fatal marriage to the illusions of a "free market economy," it would be nothing short of disastrous for the church to associate itself with such notions.

My first objection, then, is that these vastly significant assertions are presented as a mere line of argument in an almost casual way. If they are to be presented at all, it must be with a completeness, conviction, and awareness of the total implication that will do honor to the church's responsibilities. . . . For what is involved is a platform from which the entire labor movement can be attacked in a most devastating way.

It is my strong conviction that these assertions are not accurate, are based on only a part of the significant facts, and indeed, tend to contradict themselves if closely examined. Take, for instance, the claim that during an inflationary period unorganized workers receive wage increases much more frequently and quietly than do organized workers, and, by the same token, have their wages reduced more quietly and rapidly during a deflationary period. Could there be a flatter admission that the union organization *does* result in higher wages than the free market, except during times of such heavy in-flationary pressure that the labor market becomes a natural seller's market?

It tells us very little merely to point to long-term trends in the distribution of national income. Of far greater importance is the *size* of national income. It seems quite obvious to me that the vast productive powers of our economy could never have been developed if labor had been left to the tender mercies of the so-called free market. In the first place, it would not have stayed free very long, but would have been strongly influenced by overt and tacit collusive arrangements among employers to resist "natural" pressures tending to increase the price of labor. In the second place, to the extent that the market did remain free it would be evident in the most disgraceful competitive drives toward the increase of every sweatshop device and starvation-wage technique. The wiser or more decent employer who could think in terms of long-term benefits and higher ultimate profits from a more enlightened personnel and wage policy would be at the mercy today and tomorrow of the cut-rate chiseler who was out to drive all competition to the wall.

An expanded economy capable of providing food and clothes and housing and all sorts of luxuries for the population did not just happen. It took more than the competitive zeal of capitalists. It took more than their hunger for larger and larger profits. It took a population capable of buying back what they produced. This means that it took precisely the opposite of what Professor Boulding seems to regard so highly—i.e., a free market. Indeed it took the removal of labor costs from the area of the free market. To the extent that organized labor has been able to remove wages from the free market, wages have been maintained at a level that at least would lend some hope that workers could also be active consumers and thus maintain the kind of demand that provides jobs and production incentives. Where wages are left to the determination of those who pay them it is only natural that they would combine to keep them from rising and compete to drive them lower faster. This of course would be suicidal, but that would not keep it from happening.

It may be true that profits continue to run as high percentagewise as ever despite union organization. Maybe so. This is an important and even an alarming fact if true. But it isn't the crucial fact. The crucial fact is that these are profits made off the expanded demand of worker-consumers who are able to buy more stuff rather than less in the market place precisely because they have collectively asserted a power in the market place that they could never assert individually.

Contrary to Kenneth Boulding, jobs are not "provided" by employers. Jobs are created by a very complex process, and an employer without a market can no more "provide" jobs than can a consumer without a purse, a banker without accounts, or a worker without tools. And the building blocks of unions are not, as he says, jobs, but people.

I cannot for the life of me conceive of so poorly aimed a piece being done on labor by so able an observer, were it not for the fact that the depression is so far in the past and the artificialities of a war-stimulated market are so accepted as normal in the present that it is easy to lose contact with flesh-and-blood realities of economic need. If these were closer to mind, I do not believe that the place of unions in a democratic economy would be dealt with so casually. Surely there is a wider dimension for assessing the value of unions than the narrow issue of how much has or has not been taken away from employers. Certainly unions do not attempt to justify themselves on this ground. Why then should this be made the main issue?

I have quoted Mr. Meacham at some length not only because of the eloquence and forcefulness of his remarks, but also because the position which he represents is typical of many people who have given their lives to the labor movement with a sincerity and devotion that can command only respect and admiration. It is clear, I think, that Mr. Meacham somehow feels threatened by my analysis, and the same is true in a somewhat lesser degree of my other labor correspondents. In part I think this is a misunderstanding because I have not made myself clear. I have perhaps taken it too much for granted that I regard the labor movement as an enormously important and necessary force in Western society, one which has performed the almost miraculous achievement of virtually abolishing the proletariat and giving the worker a voice in the society which he serves. In no way do I regard the justification of the labor movement as dependent on its ability to shift the distribution of income. Indeed, if I thought it had much power in that direction through collective bargaining, I would be much less favorably disposed toward it; for it is most dangerous when any section of society can redistribute income toward itself by its own acts, rather than through the general framework of government in which it has to justify politically its own claims against the claims of others.

In fairness to my critics I must point out that they did not have before them the Appendix, in which I elaborate in more detail the evidence for the relative unimportance of organized labor and agriculture in effecting changes in the distribution of income. The evidence strikes me as impressive, though it is not, of course, conclusive. If one points out that the great rise in the power of labor and agriculture after 1933 has been accompanied by little change in the proportion of national income going to these two sectors, the critic is always at liberty to say that if it had not been for the power of these organizations their share in national income would have fallen, or would have fallen more than it has. Nevertheless, not only the empirical evidence but also analytical reasoning point to the immense importance of general movements of deflation and inflation in determining the changes in the distribution of income. Here the evidence is unmistakably clear. In the case of the effect of collective bargaining or of agricultural policy, the evidence is doubtful and uncertain.

When we turn to the problem of the impact of the labor movement on the rate of growth of real national income, the evidence is still more doubtful and the result still more uncertain. There are two problems here: one is the effect of the labor movement on the amount of unemployment, that is, on the extent to which the system operates below capacity. The other is the effect of the labor movement on the rate of growth of capacity of the system, i.e., on the rise in productivity. Unfortunately there is little evidence to support the view that the impact of the labor movement as such is great either on the degree of unemployment or on the rate of economic progress. The view that high money wages create purchasing power and so increase consumption, and therefore employment, is at worst a crude fallacy based on the assumption that wages and prices are unrelated; and at best it must be hedged about with so many conditions which may or may not be realized that it cannot safely be used as a general principle. If a union-induced rise in money wages comes at a time of general deflation and pessimism, it may easily increase unemployment; at a time of inflation and optimism it may decrease unemployment.

Similarly there is not much evidence to show that the labor movement as such has had much impact, one way or the other, on the rate of economic progress (i.e., on the rise in per capita national income). Unpalatable as the fact is to the friends of labor, economic progress is mainly the work of businessmen and adventurous capitalists—or of their socialist equivalents, the bureaucratic planners. This is not to deny the part played in stimulating economic progress by the "gadfly" aspects of unionism, which prevent businessmen from taking what seem to be easier ways out of their difficulties, such as reducing money wages, and force them, especially in depression, to concentrate their energies on cost reduction. Nor is it to deny the many instances of fruitful labor-management cooperation in the introduction of technical change. All these things, however, are small beer compared with the enormous impact of the unaided capitalist constantly seeking improved ways of using his capital.

I cannot help being impressed by the extent to which the conventional economic justifications for labor unions are dominated by the experience of deflation and depression. This is not surprising, in view of the sad experiences of depression to which American society especially has been subject. Nevertheless, it results in a misapprehension of the nature of the competitive process and a great underestimation of the power of the market to distribute income to labor. The fall in money wages which is characteristic of a period of deflation is mistaken for "competitive pressure" on real wages, whereas frequently it is nothing of the sort. Indeed, it is precisely in depression, when money wages sag, that the real wages of those employed tend to rise and the proportionate share of labor increases. This is not to say that labor is better off in a depression. It is no fun to get a larger share of the pie that is so much smaller that the absolute size of the piece probably falls even when the proportionate share rises. Thus while labor's slice of the pie was 74 per cent in 1933 as against 58 per cent in 1929, the pie itself was only 70 per cent as big as the 1929 pie, in real terms, so that the absolute income going to labor in 1933 was about 90 per cent of its 1929 income.

I must emphasize again that I regard the weakness of the conventional economic argument for unions, as expressed by Mr. Meacham, as strengthening rather than weakening the *moral* position of the labor movement. Indeed, Mr. Dudley, while he disagrees with my analysis quite as strongly as Mr. Meacham, sees that it may have some value in softening the opposition of employers to the labor movement. Indeed, if my analysis is correct, the leaders of labor may find themselves in the position of finding it easier to justify the movement to the rest of society, and harder to justify it to their own members.

My labor commentators take me to task also on one or two other points connected with the sociology rather than with the economics of the labor movement. Thus they all feel that my remarks on seniority, racketeering, featherbedding, the union shop, and so forth are too severe. Mr. Dudley complains that I lay too much stress on grievance procedure. They all feel that I lay too much stress on the noneconomic aspects of unionism, and find my comparisons rather high-flown. The labor movement is so large and varied that many people with much more intimate personal acquaintance with it than myself will find that my attempt at summarization of so vast a field does not correspond to their experience. I can answer only that I have written how it looks to an outside, but I hope not unsympathetic, observer.

NEED AND IMPACT OF VOLUNTARY ORGANIZATIONS

The comments of Jerry Voorhis cover labor, agriculture, and cooperatives, and involve so many important matters of principle that I take the liberty of quoting them at some length:

Mr. Boulding has written a powerful and penetrating document. It contains passages which present new vistas of analysis and evaluation of economic organizations which will, it is hoped, enable many individuals and organizations to see more clearly their Christian obligations. Mr. Boulding's concluding paragraph is a sermon in itself, whose truth and eloquence make one hesitate to add comment.

On some points, however, such comment seems needed.

First, I would like to make a general comment as follows: I believe the general tone of the manuscript is too negative with respect to voluntary organizations of the people and their general place in a democracy. It seems to me that the point should be made quite strongly that one of the essential differences between a democratic society and a totalitarian one is the opportunity which a democratic society presents for the formation of voluntary organizations among the people. Basically, it appears to me this is a very good thing and a very desirable one from a Christian point of view; for while, as Mr. Boulding so forcefully points out, many such organizations fall far short of the development of Christian relationships among their members as the primary goal of their activities, nonetheless most of them offer the opportunity at least of development of such relationships, and should, I think, be viewed in that light at least as one of their aspects.

Mr. Boulding shows a good deal more wonderment over the coming of what he terms the "organizational revolution" than appears to me logical. A number of very powerful causes have brought into being these organizations among the people. In part they represent a counteraction to the concentration of control over capital and economic resources which came about in the later stages of the Industrial Revolution. They are in part the fruit of mass education, which is not much older than the date Mr. Boulding fixes for the beginning of this trend. They are in part the natural fruit of a maturing economy.

This joining together in groups is an expression of what is probably the most basic social urge of man—the urge to "belong," to be a part of something bigger than oneself.

And finally, in most cases these organizations came into being as soon as it was legally possible for them to do so. Labor unions were illegal, and those who joined them were subject to prosecution, for many decades after there was clear need for them among the workers. The right of farmers to join together in cooperatives without having that very act regarded as violation of the law was not clearly established until 1922.

So it would appear that it would have been strange indeed had this "organizational revolution" *not* taken place at the time it did.

Second, it appears to me that in Mr. Boulding's altogether proper concern over some of the problems connected with economic organizations he fails to stress nearly enough one of their most important features for our time. For voluntary organizations of the people are the one most dependable bulwark against a drift toward totalitarian power in the state. This is evidenced by the promptness with which dictators, on coming to power, proceed either to destroy or to "take over" every such organization. And the basic antidote for dependence upon the state is clearly the success of voluntary action of groups of citizens in solving their insistent problems by reliance on their own efforts.

From this point of view it would seem important that much more stress be laid on the difference between *voluntary* economic organizations on the one hand and compulsory ones on the other. Mr. Boulding's attempt to liken the state itself to purely voluntary organizations in society hardly seems valid.

In the state, membership is compulsory on all citizens, and this makes a very basic difference in the situation. Furthermore, as the power of the state increases, one of the most important counterbalances to that power is the formation of voluntary organizations among the people of one sort or another. If this did not take place, individuals would indeed be helpless before the growing power of the state, and the situation would be aggravated far beyond what it is today.

His own case for showing the inherent dangers in overpowerful self-centered organizations would have been strengthened, too, had more emphasis been given to the loss of precious values which takes place when membership in an organization becomes practically compulsory even if nominally voluntary. Mr. Boulding is correct, indeed, when he points out what dangerous ground organizations embark upon when they begin to rely upon any type of coercion, especially legal coercion for their membership. The old American Federation of Labor leadership saw this much more clearly than does some of the labor leadership of today.

There is another distinction which I consider to be fundamental. On the one hand there are organizations whose membership is necessarily confined to special and relatively small groups of people, having particular economic interests and seeking primarily to advance those economic interests of this particular group, even though this is done at the expense of society as a whole. Organizations of this sort, I feel, ought to be contrasted with those organizations whose membership could be indefinitely extended throughout all groups in the population, limited only by the desire of people to become members rather than by any fixed boundaries to the group which is eligible. In this second group of organizations, furthermore, are included some at least whose economic purposes are closely identical with those of society as a whole. It appears to me that this point ought not to be missed. We are so much concerned with attempting to resolve conflicts between groups where conflict of interest is evident that I feel we frequently lose sight of what is at least an equally pressing duty, namely, that of emphasizing in every possible way the common interests of the members of our society and attempting to advance those relationships among them which center about these common interests.

Mr. Boulding assumes too much, I think, in making so great a point of his contention that in periods of inflation the wages of unorganized workers tend to rise more than those of organized workers. He seems to believe that this is evidence of futility in labor organization. Quite the opposite would seem to me to be true. For one thing, as Mr. Boulding himself mentions, wages of unorganized workers certainly fall faster in times of depression than do those of organized workers. But even if Mr. Boulding is correct in his general contention, the more important point is that almost certainly the fact that many workers *are* organized, and that employers are not particularly anxious for more of them to be organized, is the main reason for the rise in unorganized workers' wages. Were it not for the existence of strong labor unions it is doubtful, indeed, that *any* wages would rise in proportion to increases in living costs. And I cannot agree with Mr. Boulding's assumption that the marked improvement in the relative economic position of the mass of workers "would have happened anyway" even if no labor unions had been in existence.

Repeatedly Mr. Boulding speaks of "labor unions and farm organizations" as if they occupied comparable positions and performed comparable functions in industry and agriculture respectively. This is not the case. Labor unions are economic agents, directly and primarily. Farm membership organizations are not. It is true that farm organizations do attempt to influence legislation that is economic in character. But this function is a different one from the direct economic action which is the primary business of labor unions. Political and educational associations of union members, such as are frequently formed, are more nearly like the farm membership organizations in their economic impact. And the organizations in the agricultural field which correspond much more closely to labor unions than do the farmers' membership organizations are the agricultural marketing cooperatives.

Mr. Boulding says that the "market" is one of the devices through which individual interest is brought closer to the general interest. Often, of course, this is the case. But not always. It is at least a question, for example, whether the general interest is served when the "market" so operates as to depress the incomes and living standards of large numbers of people—workers and farmers, for example—below the point of decency. The "market" sometimes does precisely this—particularly in the absence of effective voluntary organization on the part of groups of producers or consumers who are many in number, hence individually unimportant from an economic standpoint and possessed of little or no economic bargaining power. And it is hard to see how the "general interest" can be separated from the circumstances of life of great numbers of the general population.

Mr. Boulding is everlastingly right when he says that no group can be greater than the sum of all the groups, that is, the whole of society. He is right that there is danger in intense pursuit of group interests which sets those interests over against the whole of society. He is right in extending this same principle to the relationship of nation-states to the whole of humanity in the world. But there are times and circumstances when the improvement of the status of a large and individually weak (from an economic viewpoint) group of people is decidedly in the general public interest. This is a "plus" point with respect to economic organizations which Mr. Boulding seems almost to overlook.

I am particularly grateful for Mr. Voorhis's comments because I find myself in such substantial agreement with them. In a work which is focused mainly on the economic impact of organizations it is difficult to create just the right atmosphere of emphasis on the other aspects of the problem. I am entirely in sympathy with what Mr. Voorhis says about the "educational" value of voluntary organizations in a democratic society, and on the dangers of coercion. Indeed, certain others of my critics felt that I had rather overstressed this point.

The point which he raises regarding the improvement of "weak" groups in a society is a very important one, and one to which I think I have perhaps given inadequate attention. My diffidence in tackling it is due mainly to a certain feeling of professional inadequacy; the problem is essentially not in economics, but in cultural anthropology, a field in which I cannot pretend to any special competence.

The economic "weakness" of a group is related intimately to weaknesses in its culture, relative to those with which it is surrounded. Poverty, that is to say, is a culture product, intimately related to the educational and family patterns of the society. This is particularly true of geographical differences, but it is true also of the different culture strata in a given community. "Shantytowns" and "suburbias" both tend to reproduce themselves and represent different, but internally consistent, cultures. In the shift from one type of culture to another the development of organizational skills is of enormous importance. In particular, the development of organization in weak cultures may set them on the road to strength. This, to my mind, is the essential secret of the successes of the labor movement in raising the status and standards of its members, and of the success of the cooperative movement in a place like Nova Scotia, rather than any direct impact on the market environment. These considerations, however, would almost require a separate study, and I can do little more than to suggest possibilities at this point.

FARM ORGANIZATIONS

Among my other commentators, Mr. Davis also felt that I had overstressed the economic aspects, especially of farm organizations; thus he writes:

It seems to me that the almost total emphasis on price supports and "revolt against the market" as the function of farm organizations is unreal. Actually this is relatively a small part of the functions of national farm organizations. One important phase is cultural and educational activities as reflected in the strong emphasis of farm organizations on youth programs, women's programs, fairs, and their great interest in research and education. Another strong interest of the farm organizations has been international affairs. Reflection of this has been their activities promoting FAO and the Point Four program, and their participation in the International Federation of Agricultural Producers. In general, the national farm organizations have supported reciprocal trade treaties and a liberal trade policy.

He goes on to point out that farm organizations should not be blamed for all the economic foolishness of Congress, and that Congress has actually forced higher support prices on the farmers than the farm organizations wanted.

My discussion of cooperatives not unnaturally aroused a good deal of criticism. My good friend Jerry Voorhis believes the section to be prejudiced and distorted. His point of view seems to be shared by the other critics representing the cooperative movement. Many of the criticisms were well founded, and I have incorporated them in the revised version of the text. There are still some points, however, where I am unable to agree with my critics. I must confess that nowhere do I find it harder to be an economist than in dealing with cooperatives. I have so much admiration for the devotion and self-sacrifice which has gone into the building of the cooperative movement that I hate to subject it to the seemingly unfriendly blast of economic criticism.

The main question at issue turns on whether the cooperative form of business organization, as such, makes any substantial contribution to the solution of our most pressing economic problems. I have argued that while the contribution it makes is almost certainly in the right direction, it is very small. All my commentators point to the substantial achievements of the agricultural marketing and distributing cooperatives, while admitting that urban consumers' cooperation, in the United States at least, is a small-scale operation. However, I am afraid I remain unconvinced. If all the co-ops in the United States were to be transformed into conventional businesses overnight, the effect on the distribution of income, on economic stability, on the rate of economic progress, or on any other significant *economic* variable would be almost imperceptible. It is equally true that if, say, 5 per cent of conventional businesses were replaced by cooperatives, the result would also be economically imperceptible. And in so far as the cooperative movement draws the attention of its members away from the really great economic problems, it may even be a positive hindrance to their solution. I can hardly forbear quoting another of my critics on this point. Dean Walter G. Muelder writes of the last section of Chapter 8:

A much needed treatment of cooperatives. The preachers who have ritualized co-ops won't like it, but the issues must be recognized. There is more recognition of social factors here than elsewhere. Social costs and values should be stressed even more, however.

ETHICAL vs. ECONOMIC APPRAISAL?

My two critics from the business world made mostly comments in detail, many of which were incorporated into the revision of the manuscript. Mr. Noel Sargent, however, makes some points of principle. Thus he writes:

My first general observation is really a question of whether an appraisal of the ethics of economic organization, either necessarily or logically, incorporates an economic appraisal of such organizations. If economic appraisal is intended—as distinct from an ethical appraisal—I have some question as to whether the Church and Economic Life Department is the proper body to make such an appraisal. It would have been much better to have constituted an entirely separate group of economic experts to make the appraisal. I have the feeling further that if an economic appraisal is to be attempted, it may arouse wide disagreement and controversy.

As a number of my correspondents seem to be under a certain misapprehension as to the relation of the study to the Department of the Church and Economic Life of the National Council of the Churches of Christ in the U.S.A., it may be well to state again that the present document is not to be regarded as an official pronouncement—not even of the author—but is essentially an individual contribution to a continuing discussion. The views expressed in the study are those of the author, not of the National Council of Churches. Nevertheless, the point which Mr. Sargent makes is an interesting and important one: is it possible to make an "economic" appraisal which is in some sense distinct from an "ethical" appraisal? This is a question which has exercised economists a great deal in the past two or three decades, and the answer at present seems to be "No." Welfare economics, which is essentially the study of "economic" as distinct from "ethical" appraisals, has turned out to be largely a blind alley (though one which it was necessary to explore). It now seems clear that the sense in which it may be possible to say that something is "economically" good, independent of whether it is "ethically" good, is extremely limited, and that in fact all appraisal is at bottom ethical.

Mr. Sargent goes on:

Secondly, I really thought that the term "economic organization" was intended to include business associations, labor associations, and others, but I had not realized that it was to include the individual corporations in the same sense as the others. If it is intended to include private business organizations, I believe the treatment in the manuscript is inadequate, and that it should cover the relative advantages and disadvantages of the corporation as distinct from other forms of business enterprise, the special factors and problems involved in corporate organization, the role of the directors and stockholders, etc.

With this criticism I have a good deal of sympathy, for when I started the study I intended to confine it to "associations" in the narrower sense of the word. It became evident as I proceeded, however, that there was no hard and fast line between an association and an organization, and that what I was in fact studying was a great and rather unified movement in history, of which the corporation and the national state—even the Communist state—were as much a part as the labor union and the farm organization. I chose, therefore, to follow the broad sweep of history which had opened out before me, rather than confine myself to the narrow limits of the original problem, and there is an inevitable cost in terms of sketchiness of treatment.

The chapter on business organization particularly suffered from this change in viewpoint, the more so as I do not have the special knowledge of business organizations which I can claim to some degree for the labor and farm movements. The reader should bear in mind that this chapter especially is to be read as an interim report. Mr. Sargent remarks later in his letter that he feels I have not given an adequate account of the work of the National Association of Manufacturers and the U.S. Chamber of Commerce, and I am fully conscious myself for the need of further research into their nature and functions, especially as there is astonishing little published material on this subject that is not emotionally biased. However, I must excuse myself by the limits of time, for a study of the magnitude which the subject requires could not be carried out in the short time allotted for the present inquiry.

This about brings to an end my "commentary on the comments." I am conscious of having done less than justice to many of my critics, especially as so many of their most valuable comments are invisibly embodied in the revision of the manuscript. Thanks to them, however, the discussion is now launched.

Appendix

*Factors Affecting the Proportion of National Income
Distributed to Various Groups in Society*

The problem of what determines the proportion of national income
distributed to various groups in society—e.g., labor, agriculture, bondholders, shareholders, and so on—is one of the most difficult and
unsettled questions in economics, and even the immense growth of
statistical information since 1929 is not sufficient to settle it. I have
argued in this work that in regard to changes in distribution the
impact of organization is slight, that it is not always clear even in what
direction the impact is made, and that the major determinants of
changes in the distribution of national income are the great movements
of inflation and deflation which are not particularly under the control of
the organized groups.

The problem that has received the most attention is that of the impact
of unionism on wages. The pioneering study in this field was that of
Paul Douglas.[1] Important recent studies have been those of Arthur
Ross[2] and Harold M. Levinson.[3] The significant thing about all these
detailed studies is their inconclusiveness. There is evidence that in
some periods—particularly in periods of much new organization—
unionization causes a rise, sometimes a sharp rise, in the wages of the
newly organized. Over the long pull, however, the effect is much less
noticeable. Thus Douglas found that between 1890 and 1914 unionists
were able to get appreciably shorter hours and higher wages than the
mass of the workers, but that from 1914 to 1926 nonunion wages rose
at least as rapidly as union wages. Ross finds a little more advantage
to union wages. Levinson finds that "the major changes in distribution
of income from 1919 to 1929 cannot be attributed to union bargaining
power." From 1929 to 1947 he finds that the slight shift in favor of labor
cannot be accounted for by the changes in unionization, but that
there is good evidence for a shift *within* the working population toward
the unionized at the expense of the nonunionized.

[1] P. H. Douglas, *Real Wages in the United States*, 1890-1926, Boston,
Houghton, Mifflin Co., 1930.
[2] A. M. Ross, *Trade Union Wage Policy*, Berkeley, California, University
of California Press, 1948.
[3] H. M. Levinson, *Unionism, Wage Trends, and Income Distribution*,
1914-1917, Ann Arbor, Michigan, University of Michigan Press, 1951.

Since 1929 the United States Department of Commerce has published a computation of the distribution of national income by functional shares, which is illustrated in the figure and table. This is the first time that we have had a comprehensive view of the distribution of national income over a period of a complete cycle, and the results are most instructive. We see how in the great depression the "Compensation of Employees" rises, as does interest, to squeeze corporate profits out altogether and turn them into losses in 1932 and 1933. We see interest almost squeezed out of existence by the inflation and the low-interest policies of the government. We see likewise a declining trend in the "Rental Income of Persons" (a hodgepodge of house and farm rents). We see that there seems to be little long-run trend in the proportion of income going to farm proprietors, which was 6.52 per cent in 1929 and 5.73 per cent in 1950, in spite of the enormous efforts of government on their behalf. We see little trend also in the income of unincorporated enterprises. Corporate profits, on the other hand, are highly subject to the movements of the business cycle. We see also that the great growth of the labor movement from 1933 to 1950 has gone hand in hand with rapidly rising proportion of profits and slowly declining proportion of wages. Indeed, the years of most rapid organization (1933-1940) show the strongest declining trend in the proportion going to wages, which recovers somewhat after 1940, in a period of relative stagnation of growth in the numbers of trade unionists.

I am not supposing that these facts are conclusive in regard to the effect of organization, as it can always be argued that had it not been for the unions the proportion of national income going to labor would have fallen still farther. That the facts are suggestive can hardly be denied.

Certain warnings regarding the interpretation of the table and figure should be given. The corporate profits and the incomes of unincorporated enterprises have an inventory adjustment which diminishes the effect of inventory profits or losses due to changing price levels. That is, they represent "real" rather than "accounting" profits. Without this adjustment the rise in corporate profits is even more startling. The income of farm proprietors does not include that of farm laborers, so should not be regarded as an adequate measure of the share of "agriculture"; it does, however, represent roughly the share of that sector of the agricultural population which is most concerned with the farm organizations. The "Compensation of Employees" also includes salaries, so that it is not to be regarded as quite equivalent to "wages" of workers. According to Levinson, however, the percentage changes in the share

APPENDIX 277

of salaries has been small, and most of the changes in this item are due to wages.

The most difficult matter to interpret is that of taxes. In the figure as shown the national income and the shares are calculated *before* deduction of taxes. It can be argued that income *after* taxes is what is really significant. Unfortunately it does not seem to be possible to allocate taxes among the various shares, except as between corporate profits and the rest of the shares. The upper dotted line shows the division of corporate profits into the corporate tax liability and profits after taxes. The lower dotted line shows net government transfers from persons, i.e., personal taxes less government transfer payments (pensions, relief, and so on), which can be regarded as a kind of "negative taxes." It will be seen that taking account of taxes would not substantially modify the conclusions. The rise in corporate profits after taxes is of course less than the rise of corporate profits before taxes. Incidentally, the relative stability of profits after taxes in the face of enormous increase in corporate taxes is evidence that the corporation profits tax is in fact almost entirely shifted; the government simply uses the corporation as a tax collector. The sharp rise in net government transfers from persons after 1942 suggests that the apparent rise in the proportion of national income going to employees after 1942 is largely illusory and would not show up nearly so plainly if we could get detailed "after taxes" figures.

Neither income before nor income after taxes is a satisfactory measure of distributional shares. Income before taxes would be an accurate measure of distributional shares if we could assume that the benefits received by each sector from government were in direct proportion to the taxes paid. Income after taxes would be an accurate measure if we could assume that individuals received no benefit from government whatever. Neither of these assumptions seems particularly realistic, and the best one can do is to study both distributions as far as possible. It is pretty clear that the same general conclusions emerge from both: that the distribution of income by sectors depends much more on the general movements of depression, deflation, and inflation than on all other factors taken together. Roughly speaking, depression, because it is highly destructive to profits, raises the proportionate share of labor. Deflation raises, and inflation lowers, the proportionate share of interest. Depression lowers, and full employment raises, the proportionate share of farmers. Beside these immense movements the changes due to the organization of the market, to collective bargaining, and even to government agricultural policy are seen to be relatively minor.

In the upper part of the diagram, for the sake of comparison, I have

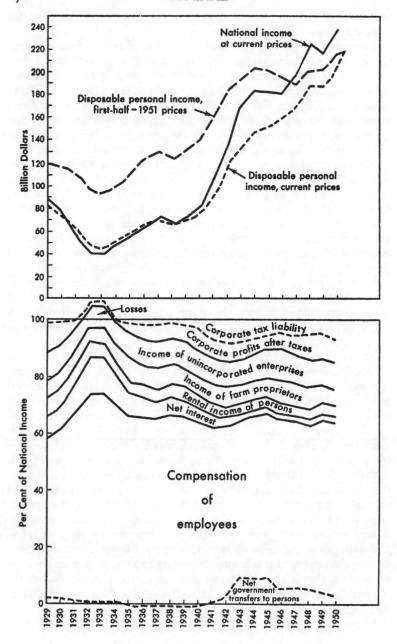

graphed three series: the national income itself at current prices, disposable personal income at current prices, and disposable personal income at first-half-1951 prices. The gap between national income and disposable income which develops after 1941 is, of course, a reflection of the increasing proportion of the national income absorbed by government, mostly in war and war preparations. The gap between the disposable personal income at 1951 prices (which measures "real" income) and disposable personal income at current prices is a reflection of the degree of price rise up to 1951. It will be observed that the rising national income since 1942 has been largely swallowed up by war expenditures. This is particularly noticeable if we look at per capita disposable personal income, which has not risen since 1944 (see table).

DISTRIBUTION OF UNITED STATES NATIONAL INCOME AND RELATED ITEMS, EXPRESSED AS A PERCENTAGE OF THE NATIONAL INCOME

Note: National Income does not include columns 9 and 10. Columns 7 and 8 are a breakdown of column 6. Columns 1 to 6 exhaust the national income, but the figures may not add up to exactly 100 per cent because of rounding. The source (and the definition of national income) is from the U.S. Department of Commerce.

	Percentage of National Income										Billion Dollars			
Year	Compensation of Employees	Net Interest	Rental Income of Persons	Income of Farm Proprietors	Income of Unincorporated Enterprises	Corporate Profits Before Taxes	Corporate Tax Liability	Corporate Profits After Taxes	Net Government Transfers to Persons	Government Net Interest Payments	National Income (Current Dollars)	Total Disposable Personal Income (Current Dollars)	Total Disposable Personal Income (1951 Dollars)	Per Capita Total Disposable Personal Income (1951 Dollars)
	1	2	3	4	5	6	7	8	9	10	11	12	13	14
1929	58.1	7.4	6.6	6.5	9.5	11.8	1.6	10.2	1.9	1.2	87.4	82.5	123.9	1017
1930	62.0	8.2	6.4	5.2	9.3	8.8	1.1	7.7	2.0	1.3	75.0	73.7	115.9	942
1931	67.1	10.0	6.1	4.9	9.0	2.7	0.9	1.8	0.2	1.9	58.9	63.0	110.7	892
1932	73.9	12.9	6.0	4.1	7.7	−4.8	0.9	−5.7	0.2	2.6	41.7	47.8	95.6	766
1933	74.0	12.6	5.0	5.8	7.3	−5.1	1.3	−6.4	0.0	3.0	39.6	45.2	94.8	755
1934	70.2	9.9	4.3	4.7	8.6	2.3	1.4	0.9	0.0	2.5	48.6	51.6	102.0	807
1935	65.3	7.9	4.0	8.6	8.6	5.3	1.7	3.6	0.2	1.9	56.8	58.0	112.0	880
1936	66.0	7.0	4.1	6.0	9.4	7.6	2.2	5.4	−0.9	1.7	64.7	66.1	126.1	985
1937	64.8	6.0	4.2	7.6	9.0	8.4	2.0	6.4	−1.4	1.6	73.6	71.1	130.7	1015
1938	66.3	6.4	4.9	6.5	9.4	6.4	1.5	4.9	0.7	1.8	67.4	65.5	123.1	948
1939	65.9	5.8	4.8	6.2	9.4	8.0	2.1	5.9	−0.1	1.6	72.5	70.2	133.2	1018
1940	63.7	5.0	4.4	6.0	9.5	11.3	3.6	7.7	−0.1	1.6	81.3	75.7	142.0	1075
1941	61.9	3.9	4.1	6.6	9.2	14.1	7.5	6.6	0.6	1.2	103.8	92.0	162.5	1218
1942	61.9	2.8	3.9	7.7	9.2	14.5	8.5	6.0	2.4	1.1	137.1	116.7	184.1	1365
1943	64.3	2.0	3.6	6.9	8.8	14.3	8.5	5.8	8.9	1.2	169.7	132.4	191.6	1401
1944	65.9	1.7	3.5	6.4	9.4	13.1	7.3	5.8	8.6	1.5	183.8	147.0	203.0	1467
1945	67.3	1.6	3.4	6.8	10.2	10.5	6.1	4.4	8.4	2.0	182.7	151.1	201.2	1438
1946	64.9	1.6	3.7	8.2	11.4	10.2	5.3	4.9	4.4	2.4	180.3	158.9	196.4	1389
1947	64.4	1.8	3.6	7.8	10.0	12.4	6.0	6.4	5.2	2.3	198.7	169.5	191.1	1326
1948	62.7	1.9	3.4	7.9	9.9	14.2	5.8	8.4	4.7	2.0	223.5	188.4	201.5	1374
1949	64.6	2.3	3.5	6.0	9.6	14.1	5.1	9.0	3.2	2.1	216.7	186.4	202.0	1354
1950	64.1	2.3	3.4	5.7	9.3	15.1	7.8	7.3	2.6	2.0	239.0	204.3	217.8	1436

Index of Names

Abele, Ralph C., 226
Adventists, 13, 164, 167
Alderson, Wroe, cited, xvii
Aluminum Company of America, 40
Amalgamated Clothing Workers, 54, 95
American Association of University Professors, 51
American Farm Bureau Federation, see Farm Bureau
American Federation of Labor, 92, 95, 267
American Legion, 3
American Medical Association, 5, 202
American Telephone & Telegraph Co., 63, 136
Anabaptists, 85
Anglo-Catholics, 28
Augustine, Saint, 85, 244

Barnard, Chester I., cited, 18
Beard, Miriam, cited, 256
Becket, Thomas à, 80
Bishop, Claire H., cited, 151
Blake, William, 12
Bowen, Howard R., quoted, 255-6

Cambridge University, 52
Canada, 28, 126, 270
Catholicism, Roman, xxv, xxvii, 24, 28, 63, 78, 255, 256; Franciscans, 85
Chamber of Commerce, U. S., 142, 273
China, xxvii, 159, 171, 198, 199
Church of England, 28
Clark, J. M., 225-6
Committee for Economic Development, 150
Congress of Industrial Organizations (C. I. O.), 41, 92, 95, 206, 207
Coolidge, Calvin, 118
Cox, Reavis, cited, xvii

Davis, John H., quoted, 270
Douglas, Paul H., cited, 275

Dudley, Tilford E., cited, 260
du Pont Company, xxxiv, 131, 136

East India Company, 26
Egypt, ancient, 62
Eliot, T. S., quoted, 195
Engels, Friedrich, 161
Europe, Western, 20, 159, 233; Denmark, 159, 199; France, 62, 151, 200, 234, 236, 254; Germany, xxxiii, 30, 62, 147, 149, 172, 179, 187, 198, 254; Great Britain, 21, 51-2, 62, 64, 147, 153, 159, 171, 179, 199, 200, 234, 256; Ireland, 75; Italy, 149, 236; Luxembourg, 75; Norway, 151, 159, 179; Poland, 75; Sweden, 151, 159; Switzerland, 254

Fanfani, Amintore, xxvii
Farm Bureau, The, 17, 116-7, 124, 207
Farmers Union, 116
Federal Council of Churches, vii, viii
Federation of British Industries, 149
Fichter, Joseph W., 225-6
Formosa, 39
Freud, Sigmund, xiii

General Electric Company, 136
General Motors Corporation, xxxiv, 17, 35, 102, 136, 173, 207
George, Henry, xiv, 169
Giffen, R. R., 225-6
Graham, Benjamin, cited, 188
Grange, National, 116
Greece, ancient, xxvii, 62, 74, 255

Harrison, George M., cited, 260
Hegel, G. W. F., 162, 163
Hobbes, Thomas, 240
Hoffman, Paul, 150
Hudson's Bay Company, 26
Huxley, Aldous, cited, 67, 84

Index of Subjects

Accounting, 134, 135-6, 212
Advertising, 17, 27, 58, 232
Agriculture, xxiv, 5, 19 f., 36, 41 ff.,
    48, 89, 109-130, 144, 149, 155-6,
    170, 192, 202, 203, 209, 210, 231,
    247, 266 ff., 270-1, 275-9; income
    from, 113 ff., 206 ff., 275 ff.; migra-
    tion from, 113, 121, 128; subsidized,
    111, 120 ff., 192
Analysis, organizational, xvii-xviii
Antitrust laws, 39, 40, 136-7, 146-7,
    174
Associations, economic, 4-7, 267, 272-3;
    professional, 202, 267; trade, 3-4,
    131, 137, 145-150, 202, 205, 267.
    See also Farm organizations, Labor
    unions, etc.
Atomic energy, 62, 76, 190, 250
Authority, in organizations, xxxii ff.,
    39, 53, 99, 101, 105, 134 f., 207,
    216 ff., 238, 244

Bargaining, collective, xxx, 47, 52, 92,
    98-103, 105, 110, 126, 208-9, 248,
    262-3, 275
Biology, parallels with social science,
    xv-xxvi, xxvii-xxxii, 16, 18, 22-3, 26,
    34, 55-8, 62, 68 ff., 90, 257-9
Brannan Plan, 127

Capital, element of growth, 133-4;
    farm, 110; produced, xix, xxiii; sup-
    ply of, 153
Capitalism, adjustment to democracy,
    230, 233, 235-6, 241 ff., 244; effi-
    ciency of, 34-6, 73-4, 81, 138, 144,
    168, 169; ethics of, 131, 138, 139-
    144, 200-1; European, 147, 149
Cartels, 5, 60, 98, 110, 145, 147, 155
Catastrophe, stimulating evolution, xxv-
    xxvi
Christianity, xiv, xxxiii, 10, 11 ff., 27,

84-6, 107-9, 150, 163, 168, 170, 177,
    195, 196, 229, 236-7, 240, 243-4,
    250 ff., 266. See also Religion,
    Ethics, and Index of Names
Churches, 3, 5; as economic organiza-
    tions, 4; influence of, see Christianity,
    Religion; missionary activity of, 27-
    28; responsibilities of, 11-12, 67, 69,
    243, 260-1; two-sidedness of, 10
Clayton Act, 91
Coercion, 35, 39, 58, 61, 75, 84, 176 ff.,
    196, 216 ff., 228 ff., 237 ff., 251-2,
    267; as factor of production, xxxi,
    74 ff., 164, 166, 176; cumulative, 76,
    167, 178, 196; necessity of, 230 ff.,
    238 ff.
Commandments, The, 9
Communication, development, 25 ff.,
    60, 207, 257; mechanically regulated,
    xxviii; organizational, xxix ff., 24 ff.,
    65, 68 ff., 134 ff., 175 f.; problems,
    24, 56, 57, 68 ff., 73, 132, 134 ff.,
    149-150, 175-6, 237; social effects,
    111, 122, 207, 228
Communism, viii, 13, 30, 62-5, 66,
    72 ff., 78, 80, 89, 93, 95, 103, 159-
    178, 203, 236; in early America, 170;
    weaknesses of, 30, 63, 164 ff., 175,
    244
Community, sense of, 11, 12, 18, 97-8,
    117, 180, 234, 237 ff., 240 ff., 255
Competition, 110, 127, 153, 230 ff.,
    250, 261; biological, xx, 22; by sub-
    stitution, 17, 39, 40, 41, 143, 250;
    constructive, 82, 215; "cutthroat,"
    37, 82, 146-7; encouraging innova-
    tion, 39, 74; "imperfect," 37 ff., 44,
    100, 126; of states, 7, 38, 173; "per-
    fect," 36, 79; under oligopoly, 38,
    39, 238
Conservatism, 29, 63, 65, 132, 190